KU-195-942

Opportunity-Centred Entrepreneurship

DAVID RAE

2nd edition

macmillan
education
palgrave

© David Rae 2007, 2015

All rights reserved. No reproduction, copy or transmission of this publication may be made without written permission.

No portion of this publication may be reproduced, copied or transmitted save with written permission or in accordance with the provisions of the Copyright, Designs and Patents Act 1988, or under the terms of any licence permitting limited copying issued by the Copyright Licensing Agency, Saffron House, 6–10 Kirby Street, London EC1N 8TS.

Any person who does any unauthorized act in relation to this publication may be liable to criminal prosecution and civil claims for damages.

The author has asserted his right to be identified as the author of this work in accordance with the Copyright, Designs and Patents Act 1988.

First edition 2007
Second edition 2015

Published by
PALGRAVE

Palgrave in the UK is an imprint of Macmillan Publishers Limited, registered in England, company number 785998, 4 Crinan Street, London N1 9XW

Palgrave Macmillan in the US is a division of St Martin's Press LLC, 175 Fifth Avenue, New York, NY 10010.

Palgrave is a global imprint of the above companies and is represented throughout the world.

Palgrave® and Macmillan® are registered trademarks in the United States, the United Kingdom, Europe and other countries.

ISBN: 978–0–230–27518–8

This book is printed on paper suitable for recycling and made from fully managed and sustained forest sources. Logging, pulping and manufacturing processes are expected to conform to the environmental regulations of the country of origin.

A catalogue record for this book is available from the British Library.

A catalog record for this book is available from the Library of Congress.

Printed in China

Contents

List of Figures

List of Tables

Preface

■ What Does This Book Do?

Creating, recognising and exploiting opportunities are at the very heart of entrepreneurship. This book aims to help you to develop the entrepreneurial skills, awareness and mindset to find, create and develop opportunities. Taking 'opportunity for life' as its central idea, it proposes that entrepreneurship is a skill-set which can be learned, so that everyone can learn and develop enterprising skills and behaviours, if they wish to.

Whilst not everyone wishes to become an entrepreneur, the book does propose that enterprising skills are valuable for everyone, whether their life goals are concerned with business venturing, building a career in employment or in other areas. We all need to be able to find, select and work on opportunities, whether at work or in other aspects of our lives. The book provides ways of seeing the world which generate opportunities, ways of developing a wide range of enterprising skills which can be applied in many different environments and tools and techniques which can be used to create, select, plan and make opportunities happen. It also includes stories and examples of entrepreneurial people and organisations which show what can be achieved.

■ What Is Opportunity-Centred Entrepreneurship?

Opportunity-Centred Entrepreneurship describes the human activities which we use in thinking, learning, decision-making, working and managing in entrepreneurial ways. Thinking and acting as an entrepreneur are real-world learning processes through which people can develop the skills and confidence to recognise, create and act effectively on opportunities.

Opportunity-Centred Entrepreneurship is an active learning process which is stimulated by such fundamental motivations as curiosity, desire and the intentions to find out and achieve results. People may use this approach intuitively, without being aware of it, yet it can be learned consciously and the abilities enhanced. Opportunity-Centred Entrepreneurship enables people to identify, discover and explore opportunities, to select and make decisions on them, to relate them to their personal and social goals and to plan and work with others to act on and accomplish them. This is active learning through discovery, achieved through working with other people.

Opportunity-Centred Entrepreneurship is an integrative approach which connects entrepreneurship with creativity and innovation, and through which people can recognise their world as an opportunity-rich environment. In this world we all face the constant challenges of investigating, making sense of, responding creatively to, selecting and acting on opportunities. Opportunity-Centred Entrepreneurship helps people create new reality by doing new things and acting as innovators: to create new ventures, experiences, products, services and multiple forms of value.

This approach to entrepreneurship is innovative in several ways. The book makes a distinctive contribution by focusing on people at the centre of entrepreneurial action. It concentrates on the human interaction in generating ideas, opportunities and business ventures. It is not dominated by academic subjects such as business studies, economics or psychology, although these are used as important resources to help explore and act upon opportunities and business ventures.

■ Who Is the Book for?

The book is written for you, if you wish to enhance your knowledge and skills in entrepreneurial thinking and working, either from an academic or practitioner perspective. It is especially intended for use in entrepreneurship and enterprise teaching, at undergraduate (especially final year) and postgraduate levels. It is designed to be useful in courses and modules including, for example, enterprise, entrepreneurship, new venture creation, creativity and innovation, small business management, social enterprise and corporate entrepreneurship. It also aims to help practitioners such as managers in business ventures or larger organisations to develop their entrepreneurial skills.

Students from non-business subjects such as sciences, creative and applied arts, design, technology, tourism and sports are increasingly opting to study an enterprise, entrepreneurship or small business management course or module, and the book is intended to appeal to their interests too. It does not require prior knowledge of other business subjects. So if you are in one of the groups described here, the book is intended for you:

- students, especially on final-year undergraduate entrepreneurship courses
- students on postgraduate and post-experience courses in entrepreneurship
- start-up entrepreneurs in university and other business incubators
- people changing career or in mid-career (roughly mid-30s to mid-50s) who are considering self-employment
- managers and personnel within organisations (including corporate and public sector organisations) focusing on innovation, new opportunity and business development

- social entrepreneurs and community activists developing new forms of economic and social activity
- readers with a general interest in opportunity creation and exploitation.

The book is specifically intended to appeal to an international readership, both to students who are studying in the United Kingdom and those studying in other countries.

■ What Can You Get from Reading the Book?

You may wish to read this book for your personal direction, interest and motivation. In addition to its role as an academic course text, these are the aims of the book.

Firstly, to enable you as the reader to consider yourself as an entrepreneurial person, and to enhance your skills, confidence and capacity to act in entrepreneurial ways. It aims to build skills, confidence and entrepreneurial ambition in your career. Enterprising skills can be applied in employment as well as in creating new business ventures, so you can definitely benefit from the book if your aim is to enhance your career development and employability. The book can help you to challenge and go beyond your normal boundaries, by exploring new frontiers of skills, confidence, culture, types of venture, technology, resources or geography.

Secondly, by taking a 'practical theory' approach, the book aims to connect the theory and practice of entrepreneurship in useful ways which can be applied in the real world. So you are encouraged in the practical activities to try out and explore 'what works' for you, how and why.

Thirdly, to use the concept of Opportunity-Centred Entrepreneurship as an approach which enables you to accomplish the first two aims, and to access and use a range of ideas, tools and techniques, skills and insights in a structured yet flexible way.

Fourthly (probably the most important) to enable you, the reader, to achieve your personal objectives, which may be concerned with passing a course module successfully, planning an entrepreneurial project and making it happen or gaining a new career direction. Hopefully you will take away from the book more than you anticipated.

■ Note for Enterprise Tutors

Your role is vital in helping readers to gain the maximum benefit from the book. It is designed to help you as a teaching resource and can be used very flexibly to support your course or module. The revised tutor website provides guidance on using Opportunity-Centred Entrepreneurship as an educational approach, with reference to the related methods of teaching and learning. This emphasises an active and discovery-based approach to learning, in which students 'feel the enterprise experience' to learn collaboratively through practical activities, supported by tools and techniques, concepts, frameworks, examples and case studies. This is broadly similar to such approaches as problem-based, inquiry-based and action learning, with which you may well be familiar. The website includes a range of learning, teaching and support resources and materials, including a set of presentations for a full course on entrepreneurship.

Acknowledgements

Thanks are due to the many entrepreneurial people and learners who have contributed to this book, and who often unknowingly provided inspiration.

To the educators, scholars, experts, and colleagues who adopted the first edition and who provided intellectual foundations and ideas to expand the international scope of the book.

To Roz, for her encouragement and dedication.

Part I
Personal Enterprise

Opportunity-Centred Entrepreneurship

Chapter Contents

- Introduction to the book
- What you will find in the book
- Definitions: what do we mean?
- Entrepreneurship in the new era
- Why do we need to get better at creating and working on opportunities in the new era?
- Connecting learning with opportunities
- An outline of Opportunity-Centred Entrepreneurship
- How can the book increase your understanding of entrepreneurship?
- Critical questions to consider from this chapter
- How to use this book

■ Introduction to the book

Welcome. This chapter introduces you, the reader, to the approach taken in this book. It explains why entrepreneurship matters and shows how it connects with related subject areas. It also provides a plan of the book and a 'routemap' of how to get the best from reading it or using it as a resource as you work on opportunities. By reading the chapter, you should be able to accomplish these learning goals:

- to become familiar with the basic terms, concepts and definitions used in the book
- to recognise the critical role of entrepreneurship in our changing world
- to become familiar with the structure of the book, and how to use it to achieve your goals

● to reflect on and identify learning goals for what you want, and can expect, to learn from the book.

The first edition of this book was published in 2007, and since then there have been far-reaching and continuing changes in the world economy and society, which have major implications for entrepreneurship at an international level. These are summarised in a section titled 'Entrepreneurship in the New Era' in this chapter. The entire book has been revised and updated to take account of this new era and to introduce approaches to help the reader to succeed in it.

■ What you will find in the book

This book is about opportunities and their central role in entrepreneurial learning. It is designed to help and encourage you to find, explore, develop and try out ideas, opportunities and techniques for working on them. You will be able to select and make decisions on opportunities, to plan and act on them and accomplish your aims. You will be able to relate them to your own goals, interests and motivations, and by doing this to enhance your thinking, skills, confidence and experience as an entrepreneurial person.

Each chapter of the book starts with learning goals which suggest what you can expect to learn from the chapter and help you decide how relevant this is to your learning needs and goals, such as the course you may be following. Each chapter includes activities, such as short questions and practical exercises. These are designed to stimulate entrepreneurial thinking and learning, and to help you accomplish the learning goals for the chapter. They aim to help you to 'feel the enterprise experience' and to develop your enterprising skills and thinking patterns, or 'entrepreneurial mindset'. It is easier to skip past the activities and just read on – but this will not develop your skills and awareness, because enterprise requires *learning by doing* and practice, not just reading. The activities can be done by self-study, by working on your own opportunities, or as small group activities in a class. Ideally, you will identify one or more opportunities to work on and develop as a project to give your learning experience a focus and meaning as you read the book. Even if these seem small, that does not matter – you can gain experience and confidence by working on a personal project which interests you as a 'micro-enterprise'.

At the end of each chapter there are critical questions to help you reflect, review and consolidate what you have learned and think about how you could apply it, so that you really own your learning and are able to use it.

Wealth warning

Some of the activities will ask you to do things which may be new and unfamiliar. Being enterprising is about 'going into the unknown', experimenting and trying out new ideas.

Some activities ask you to work on real-life opportunities which you will choose. So there is a risk that you may enjoy and have fun with some of these activities! You may even make some money or possibly lose a little money! Sometimes, being enterprising means trying out new approaches which take you outside your 'comfort zone'. The biggest investment you will make is in your time and effort, and the return on this should be in developing your experience, confidence and capability as an enterprising person. None of the activities should place you at any personal risk to your safety, and all should be carried out entirely within the law.

■ Definitions: what do we mean?

It is important to understand the key ideas and concepts used in this book, so that we know what we are talking about when we use them. For this reason, here are short definitions to introduce and explain the main concepts in the book.

- *Enterprise*: is the application of creative ideas to practical situations. Everyone is capable of being enterprising. So when people show enterprise, it means they are using the skills, knowledge and personal attributes needed to apply ideas and innovations to practical problems and situations. These are generic capabilities which include taking the initiative, independence, creativity, problem solving, identifying and working on opportunities, leadership and acting resourcefully to effect change. These are explored more fully in Chapter 2. The term 'enterprise' is also often used to describe a small or new business venture.
- *Entrepreneur*: a person who acts in an enterprising way, and who identifies or creates and acts on an opportunity. This can be in any situation, an example being by starting a new business venture or a social enterprise.
- *Entrepreneurship*: the ability to turn ideas into action; the subject of enterprise and entrepreneurs, encompassing both practical and conceptual knowledge, skills and techniques used in being an entrepreneur.
- *Entrepreneurial learning*: learning to work in entrepreneurial ways, through recognising and acting on opportunities, as a natural process which can be applied within both everyday practice and formal education.
- *Entrepreneurial management*: applying entrepreneurial practices to the organisational environment, including self-employment, new venture creation and small business management, and managing in enterprising ways in corporate, public and social organisations of all types and sizes. Entrepreneurial management is the application of enterprising capabilities in different organisational settings and at differing levels.
- *Opportunity*: an opportunity is 'the potential for change, improvement or advantage arising from our action in the circumstances'. An opportunity is a situation in which *new value* can be created. There are multiple forms of value. These include not only financial and economic, but also social, environmental, creative and technological. The entrepreneur's role is to create value through working on opportunities.

Casson (2003) defined entrepreneurial opportunities as 'those situations in which new goods, services, raw materials and organising methods can be introduced and sold at greater than their cost of production'. Shane (2003) defined them as 'a situation in which a person can create a new means–end framework for recombining resources that the entrepreneur believes will yield a profit'. Both of these are only definitions of profit opportunities. This book takes a broader definition, in that the pursuit of profit is an important factor in but not the sole determinant of entrepreneurial opportunity. Entrepreneurship is about the creation of new value, which takes multiple forms, financial value being only one. Improvements in social, cultural, health and environmental arenas are also important, especially for social entrepreneurs and entrepreneurial managers in public sector organisations, as well as 'mainstream' entrepreneurs. Social enterprise features in the book as becoming an integral aspect of entrepreneurial activity, in which the returns are reinvested for social benefit.

The opportunity may be a situation which already exists, or one which we create and which would not otherwise have occurred. So it may be an opportunity, one which we can actually recognise now, or one which can be created or will arise in the future. Types of opportunity for creating value may include, for example,

- a 'gap in the market' for a product or service;
- a mismatch between supply and demand;
- a future possibility which can be recognised or created;
- a problem that can be solved, for example, by finding and applying a solution to a need;
- a more effective or efficient business process, system or model;
- a new or existing technology or approach which has not yet been applied;
- the potential to introduce something that works in one situation, such as a product, process or business concept, into another market or to make it generally available;
- a commodity or experience people would desire or find useful if they knew about it.

These types of opportunity will be explained in Chapter 4.

Enterprise involves using creative thinking, behaviours and skills to come up with new ideas and concepts. To innovate is to translate those ideas into practical solutions such as products or business models and to implement them, thus acting on the opportunity and causing change. Entrepreneurs recognise problems and unsatisfactory situations, then find ways of changing them, by seeing the potential of 'what could be' and acting to make it happen. Every person has this innate capacity for thinking and acting creatively, and as they grow up this may be encouraged and developed, or it may be stifled and constrained. Creative skills are explored further in Chapter 2.

The first activity asks you to think about your approach to enterprise. Everyone can be enterprising and can enhance both your own life and the lives of others through developing enterprising capabilities. Being enterprising is a way of thinking and being in the world as part of everyday life. The aim of this activity is to relate examples from your own experience to the key ideas in the book.

Activity

1. Are you an enterprising person? Can you think of examples from any situation when you have applied a creative idea to a practical situation, or acted in an enterprising way?
2. Can you think of an occasion when have you used your creative skills to invent or do new things?
3. Have you ever 'spotted an opportunity'? What did you do about it? Did you act on it? If not, what stopped you?

You may come up with quite 'small' examples from your experience or major ones; the scale does not matter, but the realisation that you are an enterprising person, in your own way, is important.

■ Entrepreneurship in the new era

In late 2008 the Western world economies were hit by banking and financial crises which almost caused a systemic collapse of major banks. It led to an economic downturn of major proportions which had worldwide effects and continued well into the next decade. It affected the context for entrepreneurship and the lives of almost everyone reading this book, so some awareness is needed of its implications for entrepreneurship. Firstly, entrepreneurship was one of the causes of the financial crisis. Secondly, the nature of entrepreneurship and its role in economy and society is changing as a result of the crisis. Both these assertions are debatable, and may not be accepted by all experts, but they are important.

Misplaced entrepreneurship, in the form of short-term mis-selling of financial products such as mortgages and complex derivatives, an obsession with short-term profit-seeking to the exclusion of other factors and inadequate regulation, characterised important parts of the financial, banking, property and other markets in the United States and other major economies, such as the United Kingdom, in the period of economic growth which ended with the first collapse of confidence in these markets during 2007. This 'irresponsible entrepreneurship' was funded by debt (borrowed money) and as the value of the assets plunged, it destroyed rather than created value. The resulting 'bad debts' became a major problem not just for banks but for entire countries and financial systems, such as the Eurozone in particular. These issues have been ably explored by writers such as Krugman (2008) and Kaletsky (2010). The wider effects, accompanied by other economic, social and technological shifts, have produced what we can term the 'new era' for the entrepreneurial economy (Table 1.1).

These effects, as well as causing a major recession which affected all businesses, made finding finance and lending to entrepreneurs much more difficult. Also, they led to cultural changes in the way people view certain types of entrepreneurship. It became apparent that many major banks were not operating in the interests of society, national governments, shareholders or customers, but simply for the self-enrichment of entrepreneurial senior managers and deal-makers. An example was the case of the hugely rewarded Bob Diamond, chief executive of Barclays Bank, who was forced to resign after his complicity in Barclays in 'rigging' the inter-bank lending rate (LIBOR) during the 2008 crisis was exposed.

Table 1.1   The new economic era (Rae, 2010)

Economic uncertainty and volatility in international markets
Lack of confidence in financial institutions, economic recovery and growth
High levels of personal, public and national debt
Constrained public spending limits state intervention and investment
Faster-growing Asian nations outstrip growth in Western-developed economies
Rising energy, commodity and food costs
Few jobs created by public and corporate organisations
High levels of youth and general unemployment
Entrepreneurship has a dynamic role in creating new activities

Table 1.2   Characteristics of old and new era entrepreneurship (Rae, 2010)

'Old era' entrepreneurship	'New era' entrepreneurship
Individual self-interest	Individual-team leadership
Free-market capitalism	Networked and collectivist
Opportunity pursuit regardless of resources, ethics or consequences	Socially connected and inclusive
	Ethically responsible
Business driven by short-term financial profit-ability and growth	Opportunities create multiple forms of value: financial, creative, social, ecological
Value creation solely financial	Sensitive to resource stewardship, conservation and re-use
Exploits and wastes resources	
Exclusive role models of 'the entrepreneur'	Economically and environmentally sustainable growth
Founded on masculine attributes of aggression, power, competition	Feminine values: relational, collaborative, intuitive working complement masculine attributes of competition
Fuelled by debt	Grassroots enterprise and resourcing

The excesses of such irresponsible, value-destroying entrepreneurship may be inescapable within the capitalist economic system, but they raised the issue of ethical behaviour and wider social responsibility of entrepreneurs within it. There have been many calls from politicians for 'responsible capitalism' in the United Kingdom. Also, where parts of this system do not work effectively, such as where there is 'market failure', an example being the supply of finance for smaller firms and first-time homebuyers, then there is a need for entrepreneurial innovation to address it. But the pursuit of profit alone is increasingly not the sole driver.

Prior to 2007, the development of social enterprise and entrepreneurship was growing rapidly; it is now firmly in the mainstream. Increasingly, entrepreneurs are expected (and expect) to work in socially responsible and also environmentally sustainable ways; to create social as well as financial value; and not simply to pursue individual self-enrichment. So alongside the new era, there is the emergence of new kinds of entrepreneurial behaviour. Table 1.2 intentionally simplifies this as the development of more diverse patterns of inclusive entrepreneurship for the new era alongside the individualistic model of 'free enterprise' which characterised the old era. There continues to be a tension between the individualistic, free-enterprise model and the socially accountable approaches which characterise the new era.

Example: Innocent

Innocent started as 'three friends with one idea' selling pure fruit smoothies in 1998 and became 'Europe's favourite little juice company'. Working to change industry norms, the company develops innovative new recipes and sustainable packaging with a distinctive style.

Its strategic framework includes 'wonderful drinks, robust supply, a great team, a trusted brand and customer growth'. Launching new product ranges helped to boost sales 92% a year from £10.6m in 2003 to £113m in 2008. Innocent aimed to be the world's first sustainable food business and has won many business awards.

Innocent has strong values of environmental sustainability, ethical trading and producing fresh fruit drinks with no additives. They recognised growing customer concerns about food additives, preservatives and artificial ingredients added by corporate producers, especially in food and drink for children. The norm in the industry was to increase shelf-life through additives and Innocent acted against this trend by producing short-life drinks without additives.

Innocent involves the customer, the consumer, fruit growers and others as partners in creating, producing and distributing their drinks. Exotic fruits such as acai berries are sourced through fair trade agreements with growers and they work with the Rainforest Alliance. As a permeable organisation it is open and attractive to customers, interest groups and children contacting them and interacting, both through their website and in other ways. Its products are distributed and sold by major cost-driven retailers including Asda and McDonalds, and across 13 European countries, enabling it to reach the mass market.

Innocent maintain a consistent approach to their image and to the purity and quality of their drinks. Combined with this integrity is a culture of creativity, in which people have fun, are empowered to turn ideas into products and work effectively in teams. They work informally but very effectively to address opportunities, solve problems, create and launch successful new products which outpace competitors. They employ 268 people, staffing having increased by 900% over 5 years. 10% of their profits are donated to charity, mainly via the Innocent Foundation, which supports projects primarily in countries from where Innocent sources its fruit.

In 2009 Coca-Cola invested to buy up to 20% of Innocent, a move which brought controversy and scepticism that the founders had abandoned their principles. The corporate backing enabled further expansion in European markets, doubling in size and increasing their charitable work. Coca-Cola steadily increased their shareholding to 58% in 2010 and in 2013 to over 90%, enabling the business to grow whilst the founders retained minority stakes and stepped down from running the business.

> Founder Richard Reed commented:
>
> Innocent has flourished since our deal with Coca-Cola, they have been hugely supportive of our mission of getting natural, healthy foods to more people and have been 100% committed to protecting our brand and the values it stands for. Importantly for us, the business will be run by a home-grown innocent team in the same unique innocent way, with the founders remaining involved to support the business in the years ahead. (www.innocentdrinks.co.uk)

Questions to think about:

- Do you think Innocent can maintain its principles after selling 90% of the business to Coca-Cola?
- Does the ownership of the business affect your perceptions of its values?

■ Why do we need to get better at creating and working on opportunities in the new era?

Being aware of opportunities is central to developing and learning entrepreneurial behaviours. This focus on opportunity at the heart of entrepreneurship is important, because opportunity recognition has been the subject of increasing academic study in recent years (e.g., Shane, 2003). Entrepreneurship literature increasingly views the subject as being connected closely with the concept of opportunity. McMullen et al. (2007) commented that 'a fog of uncertainty still remains around the topic of entrepreneurial opportunity', but whilst they recognised the centrality of opportunities to entrepreneurship, they failed to note that the human capacity for learning is an essential dimension in creating and acting on opportunities.

The recognition, creation and exploration of opportunities in practical ways will be explored in part II of the book. People need to become skilled in selecting, assessing and working on opportunities for these vital reasons.

- At a worldwide, macro level, there is a growing list of social, health, economic and environmental problems, including increasing shortages of water, food, energy, materials and other resources as the world population increases. Opportunity-oriented thinking and innovation are required to generate and implement new, workable and environmentally sustainable approaches which can help to address the challenges of population growth and their expectations when faced with limited resources. These can create economic growth and more efficient means of production and resource management to increase wealth and employment, such as moving from subsistence farming to commercial production. The alternatives are resource grabbing, conflict, poverty and famine.

- There is a need to re-energise societies to recover from economic depression and to overcome disadvantages, at national government and international levels, as well as at regional, local and community levels. It is significant that multinational organisations such as the United Nations, European Union (EU), Organisation for Economic Co-operation and Development (OECD) and the World Bank all emphasise the development of enterprise education, entrepreneurial societies and culture as a means of creating economic growth, change and social renewal. However there is often a gap between their policy rhetoric and taking effective action to achieve change.

- Regional and community economic development in both urban and rural areas is a priority in many countries, where major challenges such as de-industrialisation, the closure of old or uncompetitive industries, agricultural decline and poverty result in the need to grow economic activity and employment from new businesses and social enterprises. This is a major factor in Europe and in de-industrialised regions of North America, for example.

- The rate at which new knowledge is translated into business innovations and practical solutions is both lower and slower than it could be, because there is a lag between the creation of new knowledge and the rate at which it is adopted. Europe has lower and slower rates of productivity of its science and knowledge base and conversion of research into commercial technology and innovation than the United States, whilst India and China are accelerating their abilities to do this.

- The failure and closure rates of small business ventures within three years of starting remain consistently high, for example, within the United Kingdom. This suggests that entrepreneurs often do not develop the skills to identify the optimal business opportunities, cannot obtain investment or are unable to manage their response to business problems and opportunities, which are all required to enable the venture to survive and grow.

- The continuing decline in employment and career opportunities within big organisations, including state-owned firms, increasingly requires people to achieve their social and career aspirations through self-employment, entrepreneurship or working in small firms. The growing number of graduates looking for 'corporate' career opportunities need to develop skills of personal enterprise to get started, increasingly in smaller companies or through self-employment.

- Demographic changes and the reducing role of the state create the need for people to extend their working lives, to establish new careers and to find ways of caring for the increasing ageing populations in many developed countries.

- Many groups of people in all societies experience inequality of opportunity, disadvantage and discrimination, resulting from such factors as ethnicity, disability, geographical location, gender and family responsibility, including motherhood and age. This represents an underused resource of 'human capital'.

- In contrast, there is an increasing global concentration of wealth within an elite group of 'super-rich' individuals and families. Some are successful entrepreneurs and wealthy business owners; there are media and sports superstars; others have acquired wealth through oil revenues or in more questionable ways. A global priority is to find ways to attract the owners of this wealth to invest in value-creating projects which address some of the challenges identified in this summary.

Example: The Bill & Melinda Gates Foundation

The Bill & Melinda Gates Foundation was set up by Microsoft founder Bill Gates and his partner Melinda as 'impatient optimists' in 1994 to help all people lead healthy, productive lives. In developing countries, it focuses on improving people's health and giving them the chance to lift themselves out of hunger and extreme poverty. It takes on the toughest challenges in global development and health programmes, such as the elimination of malaria in sub-Saharan Africa, and the extension of educational opportunities to children in deprived communities in both the United States and other countries. It has invested over $26 billion in its first 17 years and is an outstanding example of how applying entrepreneurial innovation principles and investing the returns from business success back into grassroots development can achieve huge gains:

> The relatively small amount of money invested in development has changed the future prospects of billions of people—and it can do the same for billions more if we make the choice to continue investing in innovation. (Bill Gates, January 2012; http://www.gatesfoundation.org)

These are examples of the reasons why identifying, creating and developing opportunities is a concern of strategic importance in economic and social development. They are 'macro' issues, but they affect all of us, and are worth exploring in more detail than has often been the case in entrepreneurship literature. All of these challenging issues present major opportunities for change, because they show gaps between the current reality and future potential. They open up great potential for innovation and entrepreneurial action to provide solutions to the problems. First they require definition of the problems or unsatisfactory current situations and creative thinking to develop new initiatives and solutions. These solutions can create employment, reduce waste or conserve resources, improve the quality of lifestyles and generate financial income.

Activity

1. Choose an aspect of one of the following global macro issues that interests or concerns you most – you may have a direct personal experience.

   – shortages of food owing to changing climate, agriculture and price increases
   – increasing costs of carbon-based energy
   – growing populations with poor access to health care
   – loss of old industries and the jobs they provided

2. Define one small or specific aspect of the problem as you see it. Try using the following questions to do this:

   ● What is the problem? What is the difference between the current situation and what you think the situation should be?

- What results or effects does this have on the people concerned?
- What factors cause the problem? How does it occur, what events take place?
- What is the scale or measure, e.g., how many people are affected?
- Who is causing, and who is affected by, the problem? How do those causing the problem benefit from it?

Just defining the problem in this way is a useful first step in order to identify its scope and scale and parameters for solving it. It is too simplistic to claim that such macro problems are capable of being solved easily, permanently or by one initiative. Rather than attempting to devise a solution yourself, the next step is to find out what is already being done to solve or cope with the effects of the problem. For this you will require Internet access to gather information on the problem.

3. Carry out an Internet search on the problem. Aim to find examples of innovative actions, projects or initiatives which are taking place to act on it. These might be by government, business, research or community organisations, for example. Start by using search tools such as Google or Wikipedia. You may also find the social and 'not-for-profit' entrepreneurship websites shown here and in the further reading section useful.
   www.socialinnovationexchange.org/ (Social Innovation Exchange)
   www.ashoka.org (Ashoka social enterprise network)
   www.changemakers.com (Changemakers community for social innovators)
   www.drucker.org (Peter Drucker Foundation for Non-profit Management)
   www.globalideasbank.org (Global Ideas Bank)

4. Read and review the information you have gathered. What are the strengths and limitations of the initiatives you have discovered?
5. What opportunities can you see for initiatives to address and help to solve the problem you have identified? This may include learning from, replicating or expanding small-scale initiatives which already exist.
6. What benefits could one of these initiatives provide? How would these counteract the negative effects of the problem?

This activity has asked you to define one aspect of a problem and to research what is currently being done to address it. This investigation shows you can learn about the problem and also about current solutions. There is almost certainly more activity out there than you imagined. Once you know what is already being done, you can be more creative in extending, transferring or improving on these.

Example: Rising fuel costs

During 2011, the world price for crude oil rose past $100 per barrel driven by demand, fears of supply interruption and anticipation that future resources would be insufficient. The price fluctuated but it became apparent that $100 had become a benchmark value, with no sign that prices would fall significantly. Demand from Western and developing countries remained strong, with political instability in the Middle East and oil-producing countries accompanying a realisation that 'peak oil' production would deplete known oil reserves over the next 50 years.

Potential opportunities

- stop using oil for unnecessary transport and activities such as power generation where alternatives exist
- more economic oil use, for example, through smaller engine sizes and lean-burn technology
- extract oil and gas from shale as an alternative energy source
- improved energy conservation, lower emissions and better building insulation
- develop and use alternative energy sources, for example, solar, wind and wave power
- increased nuclear power generation
- hydrogen fuel cells
- bio-diesel production
- increased taxes such as road pricing and fuel duty to contain demand
- advanced logistics systems to gain greater efficiency and productivity from road, sea and air transportation by 'filling empty spaces'.

All of these are practical steps, although clearly none on its own is sufficient to resolve the problem. All involve innovation, by combining technology, resources and public policy in new ways to reduce energy use. Some have negative consequences, such as bio-diesel production affecting cereals for food consumption. Entrepreneurship is required to apply the innovation to the real-world problem, to produce both economic and other benefits.

■ Connecting learning with opportunities

How do we connect learning with opportunities?

The normal way of learning about subjects at school or college is curriculum-based. You may have had little choice about the way it was taught, the curriculum itself, the books, coursework or assessment method: it was imposed learning.

Now think of something you are interested in. Remember how you passionately learned all about it, by practical experience, reading, friends, TV and radio, the Internet and so on. People can become self-taught experts in subjects and skills such as sport, music, fashion, computers, gaming, technology applications or almost anything. This kind of self-motivated, self-directed informal activity we can think of as curiosity-inspired learning.

If we connect the ideas of opportunities and of learning about them, we can create this kind of inspired learning. This is a natural and social process which is stimulated by motivations of curiosity and desire to find out and accomplish things. This type of learning centres on recognising an opportunity, finding out about it, immersing ourselves in it, relating it to our personal and social being, planning intentionally to act on and accomplish it. We may do this much of the time, without realising it.

Recognising an opportunity is an act of learning. We may not be aware of this at the time, yet it creates new meaning at the moment of discovery. This is sometimes called the 'ah-ha' factor or 'lightbulb moment', and it will be explored further in Chapter 3. People tend to be curious about opportunities because they are novel, they may involve creative or unusual activity, they are future-oriented and positive and they offer the possibility of personal advantage, gain or growth. Learning about opportunities is similar to the instrumental learning people do to accomplish a desired goal or state. It recognises that achievement is an important motivation to learn, often more so than the desire to 'learn for its own sake'.

Example: Innovative CRT recycling

The shortage of basic resources, coupled with the need to improve recycling of manufactured materials to reduce waste disposal, is providing increasing opportunities for environmentally oriented businesses. In the United Kingdom and Europe, strict regulations to restrict the dumping of electrical and electronic equipment have been introduced to prevent land and water pollution. However, as old-style cathode ray tube (CRT) televisions and computer monitors come to the end of their lives and are replaced by flat-screen technology, there is a need for environmentally sound methods of disposing of millions of glass screens, which contain heavy metals. Most of these methods are labour intensive and costly.

However an entrepreneur realised that a government-funded CRT manufacturing plant had closed, and that this had included an automated recycling facility for defective screens produced during the manufacturing process. Local authorities were keen to find a cost-effective means of disposing of life-expired screens without the additional costs of transporting them to mainland Europe.

Restructa Ltd created a new business to meet the demand for CRT recycling and opened a plant in Southern Scotland. This produces sand from the recycling process which can be used in golf bunkers and other applications. The business added IT equipment disposal and recycling or re-use and LCD panel repair and recycling into its services. These have reduced the dumping of toxic products, extracted value from recycling them and extended the lifecycle of the business as well as creating and safeguarding jobs in an unemployment black spot.

By using opportunity-centred learning, we can recognise the world as an opportunity-rich environment, in which we face the constant challenge of investigating, making sense of, selecting and acting on opportunities. We can both become more aware of existing opportunities and learn how to create new ones. We can also learn to be more effective in selecting which opportunities to work on, and in developing these into real ventures or projects. Opportunity creation and selection is at the heart of entrepreneurship and of developing enterprising skills. It means working in conditions of speed, uncertainty and competition, so learning to be effective in managing or adapting to these is vital. It means learning to think as an entrepreneur.

■ An outline of Opportunity-Centred Entrepreneurship

Opportunity-Centred Entrepreneurship is a learning process which developed from teaching students entrepreneurship, working with owner-managers of small firms to enhance their venture management skills and researching how entrepreneurs learn. After being developed during the 2000s, the approach has been shared with, adopted and adapted by many educators and learners at different educational levels and in many countries. It focuses on four interconnected themes, which are shown in Figure 1.1. These are essential to exploring and understanding an opportunity by relating it to personal (individual and group) interests and goals, planning to realise it and acting to make the opportunity happen. The book takes an action-based approach to these themes, introducing tools for thinking, planning and learning, and using case studies and connections with related conceptual material. The action-based approach means that the book will encourage you to identify a range of opportunities and apply decision-making skills and techniques to select and work on developing the most promising opportunities.

The reason for taking an action-based approach is that other texts inform people and help them to learn about entrepreneurship, enterprise and small business management. Allan Gibb, who pioneered new thinking in enterprise education in the United Kingdom, distinguished between learning *for* and learning *about* enterprise. To learn *for* enterprise it is necessary to learn through direct, practical, hands-on experience of doing it. This book will encourage you to find, explore, develop and try out ideas, opportunities and techniques for working on them, and by doing this to enhance your skills, confidence and experience as an entrepreneurial person. In doing this you will also understand and become more knowledgeable about enterprise. An important aim of the book is to enable the reader to relate theory

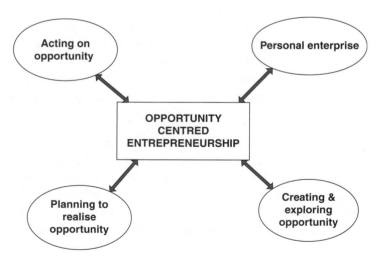

Figure 1.1 Opportunity-Centred Entrepreneurship

to practice, using principles which work in real situations. This is accomplished partly by encouraging activity, or practice, and partly by prompting you to reflect on 'what works', how and why, in given situations; this approach is called *practical theory*.

Developing and managing opportunities requires skills of creative thinking, planning, managing human relationships, marketing and selling, and project and resource management. These management skills must be deployed and in many cases learned through experience. We can term these the skills of *entrepreneurial management*. Opportunity-Centred Entrepreneurship is an integrative approach which connects with the broader subjects of business and organisational management, creativity, innovation and learning.

The learning process of Opportunity-Centred Entrepreneurship focuses on the identification, development, planning and implementation of an opportunity, from idea to realisation. In developing the opportunity, we work and learn through four interconnected processes. Each of these forms one section of the book. These are developed in the map in Figure 1.2 which shows four learning modes. This is the starting point for you in using the book, which will guide you to focus on each of the four arms, or quadrants, in turn:

- Personal enterprise – Reflecting & relating the opportunity to your personal goals (Section 1)
- Creating and exploring opportunity – Generative curiosity (Section 2)
- Planning to realise opportunity – Prospective imagination (Section 3)
- Acting to make the opportunity happen – Active & social engagement (Section 4).

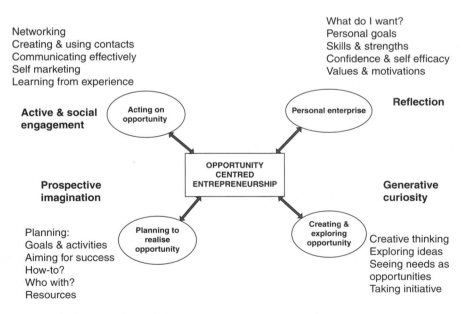

Figure 1.2 Opportunity-Centred Entrepreneurship – learning modes

This provides the structure for the book, which is designed to be used as a learning guide for developing opportunities by using entrepreneurial approaches. This can be accomplished within an academic or a work-based learning process, or as an independent personal project. However it is essential that the reader does identify and work on one or more real opportunities, to engage with the action-based learning approach and to gain full value from the book, rather than reading it simply to learn 'about entrepreneurship'. This opportunity can be of any type and any scale. Suggestions of how to identify opportunities are given in part II. The fully detailed activity map of Opportunity-Centred Entrepreneurship is shown at Figure 1.3 which closes this chapter.

■ How can the book increase your understanding of entrepreneurship?

This book provides a new perspective on the subject, by concentrating on opportunity as the defining concept at the heart of entrepreneurship. This moves away from considering entrepreneurship as being aligned only with starting and managing new or small enterprises, because Opportunity-Centred Entrepreneurship can be applied in a wide range of different contexts, including large, corporate organisations and the social and 'not-for-profit' sectors. Entrepreneurship is not limited to those people who start and run their own businesses: increasingly, students and graduates, former employees, managers, technologists and professionals from many backgrounds must learn to think of themselves as, and to act as, entrepreneurs.

The book is not intended to be an 'all-purpose' textbook on entrepreneurship; there are other excellent alternatives which do this, but they are becoming large and heavy with comprehensive information. Instead, this book has a clear and distinctive focus on developing opportunities as an entrepreneurial learning process.

Example: Opportunity-centred entrepreneurship in action

William Chase: Tyrrell's potato chips

Personal enterprise

William Chase grew up in rural Herefordshire in a potato-farming family. His mother died while he was young, and William raised the money to buy the family farm from his father. He was keen to be a farmer, but struggled to meet the debt repayments on the farm and the 1992 recession led to his own bankruptcy. As a result of this he evaluated his life, 'grew up' and subsequently bought back the farm a second time from the receiver.

He grew potatoes successfully for a few more years, but realised that the major super-markets were constantly forcing down farmers' prices and profit margins. He concluded that there was no future in growing potatoes as a commodity: 'I had to change direction or go out of business.'

Creating and exploring the opportunity

William needed to consider other options to use the farm and the high-quality potatoes he could grow. He sold potatoes to a crisp manufacturer and realised that the profit margin was around 35%, far higher than on potatoes, with crisps being sold for thousands of pounds per ton. Visiting the United States, he found sales of gourmet hand-produced chips were growing by 15% each year, and discovered that farm-based production was feasible.

Assessing the UK snack food market, he concluded that whilst there were potato crisp brands which were perceived as 'premium', there was an opportunity in the market for a genuine top-quality brand of potato chips aimed at premium customers. He decided that making hand-produced chips from potatoes grown on his own farm, aimed at the gourmet end of the market, would be unique and this was where he wanted to be. He knew nothing about making chips but realised from his experience with the super-markets that 'you have to find a niche.'

Planning to act on the opportunity

Initially he produced and successfully test-marketed batches of crisps using an adapted chip-shop fryer. This, together with market research, proved that demand existed. On the strength of this, William prepared a business plan to invest £1m of a bank loan, a small grant and personal equity in buying chip-manufacturing equipment from the United States, converting a potato storage shed into a production plant and training the farm staff to become chip makers, 'starting off as you mean to go on, with good people and equipment'.

Chase also invested in creating the Tyrrell's brand, named after the farm. The identity, packaging and marketing materials are carefully produced to 'sell the story' and convey the 'magic' of the farm-grown, hand-produced chips with a distinctive range of 'natural' flavours, and even root vegetable and apple chips. Having experienced downward price pressure from supermarkets, he refused to supply these and instead targeted the product at up-market retailers, independent stores and gastro-pubs, which enabled Tyrrell's to offer a premium-priced product with a good profit margin and avoid the pressure to discount: 'I decided to be the little guy who took the supermarkets on.'

Acting to make the opportunity happen

After starting full production in 2002, Tyrrell's grew rapidly through successful marketing, product innovation and distribution to achieve over £7m turnover by the end of the fourth year. The brand involved customers and retailers closely from the beginning, continually gaining customer feedback and giving excellent support and service to retailers with independent distribution.

However, William felt that 'there are no rules, no limit to keeping the magic going' and aimed to grow to be a £50m turnover brand, growing 100% per year and becoming the country's foremost innovative producer and supplier of excellent-quality, farm-produced artisan delicacies for the discerning customer. Chase saw his role as 'doing the thinking, moving the business forward, anticipating issues and responding to potential cracks before they appear'.

By visiting trade shows, talking to retailers and observing customers, he predicts international market trends, and has a growing export business: 'I'm learning all the time, gaining ideas from the United States and Spain.' Based on the successful first few years, Chase invested a further £2m to build a new factory on the farm, doubling the production area and potato planting acreage, whilst aiming to move into cereal-based healthy and organic products, but this had limited success and the core of the business remained the potato chip, later supplemented by other snacks such as popcorn, tortilla, rice crackers and coated nuts. Chase credited much of the success to the staff: 'a successful business attracts people – you find and develop the best people, who come to work with passion.' The business success was recognised in 2005 when William Chase won National Business Awards for Entrepreneur of the Year and Small-Medium Sized Business of the Year.

In April 2008 Tyrrell's was sold to Langham Capital, a venture capital fund, for £40m, valuing Will Chase's stake at £30m. Tyrrell's sales soared 64% to £9.6m in the year to February 2008. 'The headline price of £40m for Tyrrell's is an amazing amount for a company with a turnover of £10m', said one private equity source.

William Chase Vodka

Chase retained a stake in the business, but as early as 2004 he had been planning to create vodka distillery on the farm after seeing a distillery making potato vodka in the United States. Again, he saw an opportunity for a high-quality product using farm-grown potatoes with 'provenance and pedigree'. It took until 2008 and the commissioning of a bespoke still to produce the first batch of vodka, 16 tonnes of potatoes producing just 1,000 litres of vodka, and justifying the premium priced product. Chase Gin and other premium drinks are also produced (www.chasedistillery.co.uk).

Everyone working, teaching or researching in the field of entrepreneurship must take an international and multicultural perspective. Many of the 'classic' texts on entrepreneurship were written from the economic and cultural context of the United States of America, and were rooted in the assumptions of the US internal market. Today, the entrepreneurial person may be acting in any economy, worldwide. Nations which once had state-controlled economies, including China, Russia, Poland and other East and Central European states, now have flourishing enterprise economies. Increasingly, these are interdependent, with the domestic markets of each country opening up to global trade and competition. The entrepreneurs of today are more likely to be Indian, Chinese, African or Arab than they are to be either white or American. They are increasingly likely to be female, and to come from any occupational background, including the rural economy, food production, tourism, creative arts, health care and many others. And they will come from a broad age spectrum: young people and students, early career entrepreneurs, and increasing numbers of mid-career and 'third-age' entrepreneurs.

Although, when considering any entrepreneurial opportunity, the obvious first place to look may be the immediate, accessible local market, the challenge must also be to think of the wider international markets, both the opportunities and competitors, and the international and multicultural networks and potential alliances and partnerships which are possible. The Global Entrepreneurship Monitor (GEM website www.gemconsortium.org) is an international research resource which is recommended because it allows international comparisons of entrepreneurial performance.

Entrepreneurship is not a 'pure' subject to be studied in isolation. It is an area of applied knowledge and practice which is continually changing and evolving, and which connects with related subjects and draws on skills, expert knowledge and contextual application from them. You may already have studied some of these subjects, and if so you should be able to apply them in entrepreneurial working. Equally, you may need to develop your skills and knowledge further in some of these areas. Entrepreneurship is an evolving subject which is expanding to create new and related areas of knowledge, and is an applied subject which connects other areas of knowledge and implements them in practical ways.

■ Critical questions to consider from this chapter

This activity aims to help you to identify goals for what you would like, and can expect, to learn from the book.

1. What does entrepreneurship mean to you?
2. What aspects interest you? What aspects do you find less easy to understand?
3. What skills and knowledge do you think it would be useful to learn?
4. What would you like to be able to do as a result of reading the book?
5. Write these questions and goals down.
6. Then read through the rest of this chapter, including Tables 1.3 and 1.4, to understand the structure of the book and to see if you can find the chapters where your questions will be covered, and note these against your questions.

■ How to use this book

The book is structured in four sections, which follow the four themes of the opportunity-centred approach. Each of these includes two chapters, and these are introduced here.

Part I: Personal Enterprise

Chapter 1. Opportunity-Centred Entrepreneurship

This sets out the wider context for the book, introduces the key concepts and outlines the approach and structure.

Chapter 2. Personal Enterprise: Connecting Opportunities and Personal Goals

This chapter explores the human aspects of the entrepreneurial process, especially in exploring how you can learn to work in entrepreneurial ways, why people select the opportunities they do and the connections between learning and selecting opportunities. It covers the first quadrant of Opportunity-Centred Entrepreneurship.

Using recent research on entrepreneurial learning and education, it introduces a model of entrepreneurial effectiveness, based on awareness, mindset and capabilities which you can apply to help your own development. The role of values and self-confidence in entrepreneurial working are explained. Methods for assessing the 'fit' between ideas and personal goals are evaluated, together with personal orientation to risk and uncertainty. Personal skills and readiness for entrepreneurial working, including personality, learning and working style, expertise and capabilities, are explored. It covers the role of social processes such as leadership in forming and leading entrepreneurial teams, and your own preferred role and development. The skills required to seed opportunities through networking, influencing and selling are explored. Finally, a self-assessment of personal confidence, self-belief and essential capabilities for entrepreneurship is undertaken. The outcome of the chapter is a reflection on personal entrepreneurial learning and an understanding of your approach to selecting and working on opportunities, either individually or acting with others.

Part II: Creating and Exploring Opportunities

Chapter 3. Creating and Recognising Opportunities

This chapter provide an introduction to opportunity recognition and exploration. It demonstrates how entrepreneurial opportunities can be created and identified. The two chapters together provide a detailed exposition of the second quadrant of Opportunity-Centred Entrepreneurship, creating and exploring opportunities.

Chapter 3 takes a creative approach to opportunity generation. It introduces the recognition and generation of opportunities in the external environment, and explores the role of 'critical moments', serendipity and time perspectives in recognising opportunities in opportunity recognition, and especially the use of future scenarios. It addresses the roles of creativity and innovation in the entrepreneurial process. Creative thinking tools are used to generate ideas and build on them to form opportunities, through association. Opportunity and problem mapping are introduced as core techniques. Finally the role of intellectual property rights and their importance in the entrepreneurial process are summarised.

Chapter 4. Opportunity Exploration and Assessment

This chapter takes a practical and analytical approach in relation to selecting, assessing and evaluating opportunities, building on the creative foundations of Chapter 3, showing how these approaches can be combined. It shows how gaps, needs and problems can be identified and matched with resources and capabilities. Skills and methods of screening, appraising, evaluating and making decisions on opportunities are introduced, showing how to select between high-potential and low-potential value opportunities. Frameworks and tools for opportunity selection, assessment, evaluation and decision-making are introduced, and the need for an effective business model to create and capture value is explored.

Part III: Planning and Developing Opportunities

Chapter 5. Planning to Realise Opportunities

The purpose of this chapter is to provide a practical and action-based guide to creating a venture plan, which may be applied to any opportunity, whether for a new business venture or within an existing organisation. The core is the development of a viable business model, which creates and captures value by investing available resources. It addresses the process of planning for new ventures and opportunity exploitation, connecting the decision to focus on a specific opportunity with the actions required to do so. Planning is considered as a future-oriented thinking and acting process of continuing dialogue between stakeholders, including investors, the venture team, suppliers and customers, in which the enterprise becomes a negotiated entity. A storyboard approach is demonstrated to develop a venture plan from the initial opportunity map and as a means of individual or team-based planning. The need to create a robust business model is explained and the process of project planning, from idea to reality, is outlined. Essential aspects of the business plan are identified and a short section provides an overview of the key financial aspects of planning: investment, cash flow, break-even, risk and return. The importance of setting goals, targets and success measures as integral parts of the plan, and of identifying key themes, strategies, activities and tasks, is explained and underpinned by a practical exercise. Establishing resource requirements, to access different types of resource, potentially including knowledge, finance, human capital, plant, technology, land, permissions and licences, networks, access rights and distribution, is considered.

Chapter 6. Developing the Opportunity

This chapter builds on Chapter 5 by showing how an opportunity can be developed beyond the planning stage. The principles of Design Thinking are applied to the development of a new venture. The importance of creating and defining an identity for the venture is described. Market development and strategies to attract and build up customers and develop sales and revenue streams are explored. The use of internet based tools and social media in the venture creation process are considered. The skills and approaches involved in presenting the business proposal to investors, supporters and partners, including selling, communication and influencing strategies, are considered and developed. Guest contributions and case studies illustrate practical examples of these approaches.

Part IV: Acting on Opportunities

Chapter 7. Enactment: Making Opportunities Happen

This chapter covers the final quadrant of the Opportunity-Centred Entrepreneurship map: acting on opportunities to make them happen. It demonstrates how to act on an opportunity by implementing the venture plan and by applying skills of entrepreneurial management and strategic thinking. It shows how knowledge of critical success factors and ways to avoid the causes of failure can be applied in early-stage business ventures.

The chapter aims to enhance your awareness and ability to translate ideas and intentions for opportunities into action. Enacting the opportunity involves a process of real-time, dynamic learning in conditions of constant change and uncertainty, in which the models, tools and ideas from previous chapters are applied in making the venture happen. Essential activities in an early-stage business and reasons for success and failure of businesses are considered. The practical theory approach is applied to establish both 'what works' in businesses and what happens when it doesn't work, and to demonstrate how this can contribute to organisational sustainability.

Chapter 8. Putting It into Practice: Where Do We Go from Here?

The final chapter proposes ways to continue the journey, personally, practically and academically, through developing ideas and strategies for personal career planning in the context of the future development of entrepreneurship. It explores how to develop entrepreneurial career options at different life stages, and includes activities intended to assist in personal career planning.

A number of emerging themes are proposed as being significant for the future development of entrepreneurial research, learning, policy and practice. These suggest possible topics for further study, including independent studies and dissertation projects. The themes include the role of science and technology entrepreneurship and innovation, and the implications for corporate and public sector organisations; the importance of an international and multicultural approach to entrepreneurship as a means of democratic, economic and social empowerment; the need for environmentally sustainable forms of entrepreneurship; the role of lifelong learning and education in entrepreneurial development; the vital importance of female entrepreneurship; and the role of the informal business sector and the relationship between criminality and entrepreneurship. The chapter closes with a challenge to the reader: what are you going to do to create your entrepreneurial future?

Appendices: toolbox

The toolbox contains a series of conceptual and practical tools for opportunity assessment, development and planning, and to support personal learning. They are referred to in the appropriate chapters by means of learning activities which use them.

The book follows the two related themes of personal development and opportunity development. Personal development is concerned with the growth of your own entrepreneurial awareness, skills and confidence.

Tables 1.3 and 1.4 enable you to identify and locate the practical activities in each chapter which will help you in developing your understanding and capabilities in these two themes. The personal development tools and exercises are listed in Table 1.3. These activities are in Chapters 1, 2, 8 and the toolkit. The tools and exercises for developing opportunities are listed in Table 1.4. These run through Chapters 3–7 and the toolkit. Finally, Figure 1.3 provides a detailed map of the questions addressed in each of the four quadrants of the Opportunity-Centred Entrepreneurship approach.

Tables 1.3 and 1.4 enable you to identify and locate the practical activities in each chapter which will help you in developing your understanding and capabilities in these two themes. The personal development tools and exercises are listed in Table 1.3.

Table 1.3   Personal development tools and exercises

Chapter 1
1. Are you an enterprising person?
2. Investigate an issue of global concern which affects you
3. What does entrepreneurship mean to you? Setting learning goals

Chapter 2
1. Career options exercise
2. Life and career goals
3. Mapping your starting point for entrepreneurial learning
4. Reflecting on decision-making
5. Enterprise awareness
6. Entrepreneurial mindset
7. Personal organisation
8. Interpersonal interaction skills
9. Leadership and entrepreneurial teamwork
10. Mapping your contacts
11. Networking activity
12. Review your entrepreneurial learning map

Chapter 8
1. Generating study topics from the eight emerging issues in entrepreneurship
2. Entrepreneurial career stages
3. Reviewing your goals and motivations
4. Develop your career plan
5. So what are you going to do?

Toolkit
Entrepreneurial learning model
Entrepreneurial and managerial capabilities
Career plan

Table 1.4   Tools and exercises for developing opportunities

Chapter 3
1. Recognising and creating opportunities
2. Do you think of yourself as a creative person?
3. Take a walk through your neighbourhood
4. Recall a 'special moment' from your experience
5. Developing ideas for pop-up businesses
6. Reflecting on a special moment
7. Moment of truth exercise
8. Defining demand, innovation, feasibility, attraction
9. Seeing an existing need as a creative opportunity
10. Develop a solution to the problem you identified

Continued

11. Draw a resource map
12. What intellectual property could your idea potentially produce?
13. Review questions on opportunity creation

Chapter 4
1. Future thinking exercise
2. Using the market focus funnel
3. Evaluation report for the opportunity
4. Types of opportunity
5. Assess the impact of economic, environmental, political, social and technological factors on the opportunity
6. Using the pentagon model for opportunity assessment
7. Identifying value created by an opportunity
8. Review questions on opportunity evaluation

Chapter 5
1. Future thinking exercise
2. Creating a storyboard for the opportunity plan
3. Creating an identity for the opportunity
4. Business model – basic questions
5. Review the Pizza Base business model
6. Develop a business model for your opportunity
7. Complete a marketing matrix for your opportunity
8. Design the sales order process for your venture
9. How will the business ensure consistent quality and service for its customers?
10. Develop a simple people plan for the venture
11. Prepare a financial plan for the venture plan
12. Review the resources required in the venture plan
13. Identify the most useful contacts for your venture
14. Prepare your venture plan and a short presentation
15. Critical questions on venture planning

Chapter 6
1. Draw a mind-map of your networks of contacts
2. The four modes of innovative working
3. How can you apply innovation function analysis to your opportunity?
4. Creative thinking using the 'Idea Space'
5. Design the customer's experience of your enterprise
6. Critical questions on developing the opportunity through innovation

Chapter 7
1. Moving from planning to acting and reviewing success
2. Review the six essential activities for an early-stage business
3. Gathering information on business success
4. Consider your opportunity in relation to reasons for business success and failure
5. Apply the practical theory framework to a business
6. Entrepreneurial management
7. Autonomy – HP case study

Continued

8. Entrepreneurial and management capabilities: self-assessment
9. Entrepreneurial strategy questions
10. Resource-based, relational and opportunity-based strategies
11. Critical questions for acting on opportunities

Toolkit

Opportunity assessment questionnaire (pentagon model)
Business action plan template
Finance planner
Business model

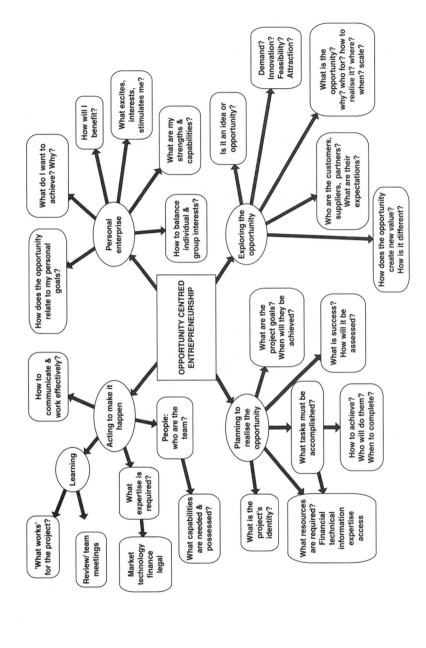

Figure 1.3 Opportunity-Centred Entrepreneurship map

Chapter

Personal Enterprise: Connecting Opportunities and Personal Goals

2

Chapter Contents

- Introduction
- What is entrepreneurial learning?
- A model of entrepreneurial learning
- Assessing the fit between ideas and personal goals
- Developing entrepreneurial effectiveness
- Personal organisation

- Interpersonal skills and interaction
- Being a leader: forming and leading entrepreneurial teams
- Networking, influencing and selling: vital skills in seeding opportunities
- Critical questions to consider from this chapter

■ Introduction

The purpose of this chapter is to help you explore and develop your capacity for personal enterprise. It explores the human dimension of the entrepreneurial process: how people learn to work in entrepreneurial ways and become entrepreneurs, why they select the opportunities they do and the connections between learning and selecting opportunities. It offers you ways to relate these ideas to your own development.

The chapter explains the important concept of entrepreneurial learning and key elements which relate to this. A model showing *entrepreneurial effectiveness* as an outcome of the learning process is introduced to help you reflect on your own personal experience and development. There is a series of exercises to help you map your personal learning to date. You can use these to take stock of, identify and plan your future entrepreneurial learning and development. These involve reflection and self-assessment of your personal values, goals, motivations, self-confidence and capabilities.

The learning goals of this chapter are intended to enable you to:

- relate your own learning experiences to a framework for entrepreneurial learning
- identify and reflect on your values, goals and motivations to help develop your confidence to take entrepreneurial actions
- assess your entrepreneurial capabilities and skills
- develop a learning map to summarise and plan your entrepreneurial development.

Working through this chapter will help you to develop an enhanced awareness of your entrepreneurial learning at a personal and social level, and to think about how this connects with the types of opportunity which you can select. This chapter covers the first quadrant of Opportunity-Centred Entrepreneurship, which focuses on personal enterprise and includes the questions shown in Figure 2.1. Activities in the chapter encourage you to reflect on the importance of self-confidence, motivation and achievement in entrepreneurial working. The chapter explores personal goals, motivations and ways of assessing the 'fit' between these and ideas. Personal skills and capabilities are assessed in relation to changes in roles and skills at different stages of the entrepreneurial venture. You will be asked to consider your preferred role in forming and leading entrepreneurial teams. The social skills required in entrepreneurial working to seed opportunities through networking, influencing and selling are explored. This chapter links with Chapter 8 at the end of the book which considers entrepreneurial career planning.

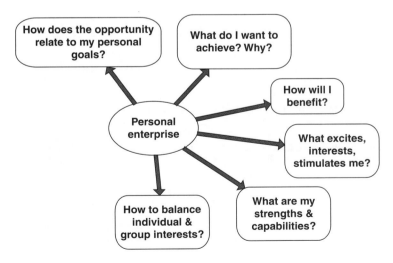

Figure 2.1 Relating opportunity to personal goals

■ What is entrepreneurial learning?

If we accept that people can learn to work in entrepreneurial ways, the question is: how? There has been extensive research on entrepreneurial learning since the late 1990s, as charted by Peter Erdelyi (2010), and this continues to emerge as a dynamic field of knowledge and practice (Figure 2.2). There is no single defining theory of entrepreneurial learning, but rather a range of overlapping areas of theory, practice and policy.

Entrepreneurial learning is the process of becoming an entrepreneurial person and of learning to generate and act on opportunities. This is different from many educational experiences of 'being taught' as it involves active discovery-learning, experience to gain practice and social learning to work with other people. Entrepreneurial learning is a personal journey which connects individual development with the skills of bringing opportunities to fruition and the ability to work co-operatively with other people. Everyone starts from a different individual background, personality and abilities, and their learning is a unique set of experiences which enables them to become distinctive in the way they do entrepreneurial things. There is no single stereotype or blueprint for the 'entrepreneurial person', and the individual learning experience is an important feature of this chapter. Personal enterprise, or developing an 'entrepreneurial mindset', is the core of this individual experience of entrepreneurial learning.

This chapter is based on research which explores how people learn to work in entrepreneurial ways and identifies significant processes and experiences in their learning (Rae, 2005). It also draws on recent work in the United Kingdom on entrepreneurship education which developed a model of entrepreneurial effectiveness (QAA, 2012). These sources are used to develop the entrepreneurial learning model included in the chapter.

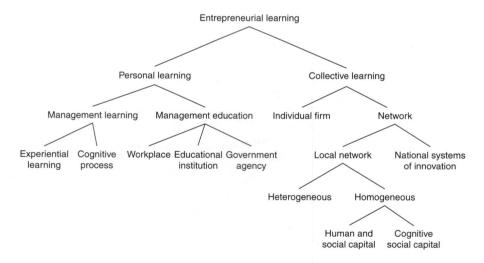

Figure 2.2 A classification of the entrepreneurial learning literature (Erdelyi, 2010)

Entrepreneurship consists of interrelated processes of creating, recognising and acting on opportunities, which combine innovating, decision-making and acting. Learning in this way is an emergent process of *sense-making*, as Karl Weick (1995) termed this process, through which people develop the ability to think and act differently. Learning comprises knowing, doing and understanding why (Mumford, 1995). Through learning, people construct meaning through experience in a context of social interaction and create new reality. Both entrepreneurship and learning are behavioural and social processes, so they are not only about 'knowing' but also acting, and they are not simply individual, but constantly involve interaction with other people, so social learning is an inescapable dimension of the process. The term 'entrepreneurial learning' means learning to recognise and act on opportunities. This can be achieved by working with other people, and by initiating, organising and managing ventures in social and behavioural ways.

■ A model of entrepreneurial learning

Figure 2.3 introduces an entrepreneurial learning model. This is based on Wenger's (1998) theory of social learning, which connects individuals with their social context. It centres on people's *lifeworlds* as they develop their entrepreneurial identity and capability through social learning (Berger and Luckmann, 1967). The model includes three major themes of:

- *Personal and social emergence*: becoming an entrepreneur
- *Contextual learning*: using your experience to find and work on opportunities
- *Negotiated enterprise*: interacting with others to create ventures

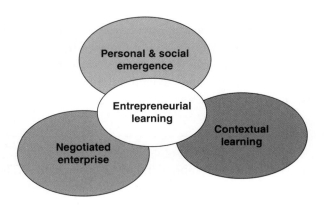

Figure 2.3 Three major themes in entrepreneurial learning (Rae, 2005)

Here is a short example which illustrates the three major themes.

Gracia's story

Personal and social emergence: becoming an entrepreneur.

When I was growing up in China, my mum had her own business. Maybe this was quite unusual but it meant that she worked very hard, and I learned that to get what you wanted you had to do that. It was a service business, doing industrial cleaning contracts, and from an early age I used to help out in the office, run errands and that sort of thing. There was always a lot to do so you had to be productive, not just sit around like many of my friends, texting and chatting all day! I started taking responsibility when my mum was not there, to make sure everything got done and by the time I was 18 I was running the office most of the time, because she could trust me. So really I grew up thinking of myself as a business person; it was our business.

Contextual learning: using your experience to find and work on opportunities.

My mum's business was very 'arms and legs'; it depended on the margin between what you got paid for a worker's time and what you paid them, but there was always pressure from the client to pay less, with competitors who would be trying to undercut us. So I was looking out for business opportunities with higher profit potential, where we could do better based on what we knew. As China got more prosperous, I could see that there were more people with expensive houses and apartments but little time, so there was an opportunity for a high-quality domestic cleaning business which could offer specialist services and a trusted brand. I talked to other business people with high-pressure jobs and found out that for a really good service they would pay well; it was not price-sensitive and there was a growing market.

Negotiated enterprise: interacting with others to create ventures.

I decided to start the business, but it had to be more than me. We needed a professional image, with our own office, personalised marketing and investing in an excellent customer experience. So my mum matched my investment in the start-up costs, and a friend who is experienced in personal services would run the office side while I find the clients and get us known. Also we are attracting the best cleaners who want to work for us because they can do a quality job and get paid more for it. It may seem a simple business but we're a strong team who enjoy doing it well and the business is really thriving!

Each of the three themes is developed in more detail by 11 sub-themes. These are shown in Figure 2.4. The toolkit includes a set of reflective questions integrated into the entrepreneurial learning model to help you use this in developing your personal awareness of entrepreneurial practice. Work through this once you have read this chapter.

Personal and social emergence: becoming an entrepreneurial person

'Becoming an entrepreneurial person' and creating an entrepreneurial identity is an outcome of personal and social emergence, including:
- narrative construction of identity – our changing story of who we are
- identity as practice – what we do shapes our identity
- the role of the family – how family relationships influence us
- tension between current and future identity – how dissatisfaction can lead to entrepreneurship.

Opportunity recognition arising from contextual learning

Recognising and acting on opportunities is an outcome of learning within our social context, including:

- learning through immersion within an environment such as career or work experience within an industry or community
- opportunity recognition and innovation through participation – developing ideas from experience
- practical theories of entrepreneurial action – finding out 'what works for me'.

Negotiated enterprise

Starting and growing a new venture is an outcome of processes of negotiated enterprise, which include:

- participation and joint enterprise – working with others on the venture

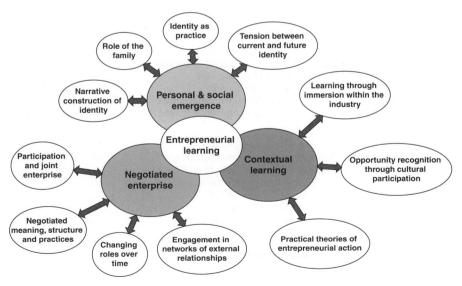

Figure 2.4 The entrepreneurial learning model showing sub-themes (Rae, 2005)

- negotiating meaning, structures and practices – developing shared beliefs about the venture
- engaging in networks of external relationships – building and managing relationships with people around the venture
- changing roles over time – roles growing with the venture.

Entrepreneurial learning, like entrepreneurship, is an emergent and dynamic activity, which means it is continually changing through the situational interactions of many influences, such as economic, technological, financial, social and other factors. Because it is dynamic and constantly changing, static models and approaches may be of limited value in understanding it. So, for example, this chapter introduces a set of entrepreneurial capabilities which are intended to help you to reflect on and plan to develop your own skills. This is valid as part of a learning process, at one moment in time, but any list of skills can only be generic and incomplete and will not reflect new developments and changes. Entrepreneurial learning can be likened to a never-ending journey, in which the only certainty is the need for continued curiosity and learning.

Every journey has a starting point and direction of travel, even if the destination is not fixed. This chapter uses the journey metaphor to help you in planning your entrepreneurial learning (Figure 2.5):

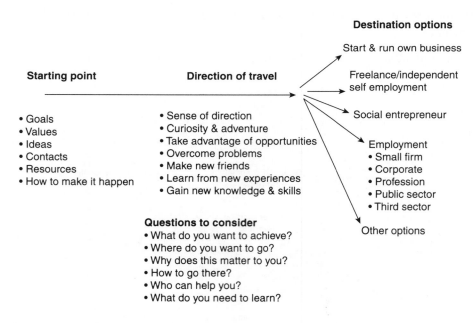

Figure 2.5 Entrepreneurial learning journey

1. Starting point: mapping where you are now, your goals, preferences, intentions, capabilities.
2. Establishing the preferred destination and direction of travel
3. Planning the route of how to go there.

The learning journey shows examples of preferred destinations, in terms of work and career outcomes. These can be combined and are not mutually exclusive. Think about the four main options of starting and running your own business; self-employment (selling your skills as a service); social entrepreneur; and employment in different types of organisations. Use Table 2.1 to assess what you see as the advantages and drawbacks of each of these? Which of them are most attractive to you? Why do you think this is? Are there any other options which are relevant to you?

This is a simple exercise but its aim is to help you to reflect both on the options and on your preferences. For example, one person might see the options of starting their own business or self-employment as offering independence, being able to put their ideas into practice and linking effort with reward. Another might consider these to be risky, with no guarantee of income and requiring too much effort. Both views could be equally valid, but the difference is that the first sees the independence in positive terms as an opportunity and recognises that they have the self-efficacy to generate the end result they seek. The second is more acceptant that things could go wrong and likely to seek security in an employed role. Employed options can have greater rewards of career development and assured income but lesser independence. However it is an error to assume employment automatically brings security, since rapid change can make apparently stable organisations vulnerable. This was the case with Nokia, which was outpaced by the development of 'smarter' phones after a long period during which it dominated the mobile phone market, but it failed to innovate and move its services onto a

Table 2.1 Assessing career options

Career option	Advantages	Drawbacks	Attractiveness
Start and run own business			
Self-employed			
Social entrepreneur			
Employment:			
• Small firm			
• Corporate			
• Public sector			
• Profession			
• Third sector			
Other options			

new technology platform, for example. So it is probably more sensible to think in terms of a working life including periods of self-employment, entrepreneurship and employment at various stages.

Goals and direction

It is normal to think of a goal as a fixed point, an ideal state to attain. Some people are highly goal-oriented, often competitive and setting themselves high standards to achieve. Setting goals can provide a mental focus and stimulus to perform, but they do not work for everyone and, in themselves, they do not predict success. Goals can be viewed as mileposts along a line of travel. It is possible to travel in that direction without considering the mileposts, and for other people it is the direction which is important. For example, the person whose direction is becoming a social entrepreneur, a designer or medical researcher may set goals against which they can measure success and achievement, or simply follow that direction. Being able to define a goal as a well-formed outcome of visualising the end result, knowing how you would measure successful achievement and planning the timescale involve careful thought.

Having considered the attractions of different career options in the previous activity, think about your direction of travel. Do you have a fixed goal, or a direction you want to move towards? Or are there multiple options to choose between?

Questions to think about before you start your journey:

- What do you want to achieve?
- Where do you want to go?
- Why does this matter to you?
- How to go there?
- Who can help you?
- What do you need to learn?

Activity

Think about what you want from your life.
Do you have a life or career goal? Or a direction of travel? Write this down.
Think about why this is meaningful to you: what makes you value this outcome?
How would you measure or assess your success in this?

Having established a destination or direction of travel, we can map the journey from the starting point. We use mind-mapping, or cognitive maps, as a core technique for developing learning and opportunity maps in Opportunity-Centred Learning. This is a variant of the approach developed by Tony Buzan (2003). It is a fast and flexible means of getting ideas and information from your brain onto paper or screen to enable you to make creative connections between them.

Activity: mapping your starting point for entrepreneurial learning

To develop a simple learning map, put a bubble to represent yourself in the centre of a piece of plain paper. Then draw six branches from the bubble and label these as follows (Figure 2.6):

1. Goals or direction – what do I want?
2. Values – what's important to me?
3. What ideas & interests do I have?
4. How to make these happen?
5. Who do I know as useful contacts?
6. What resources do I have?

You can vary these labels as you prefer.

This provides a very basic learning map template. Try using it by thinking about what you want to accomplish and writing these as short goals on your map. As you do this, you'll have other, related thoughts. Log these as they fit best against the other branches. Add twigs off the branches for linked ideas. Practice this approach during this chapter and it will be further developed for opportunity mapping and planning later in the book. There are many digital apps you can use for mind-mapping which run on computers, tablet and phone devices.

As you work through this chapter, start to take notes to help make sense of your own learning journey. You can use the opportunity mapping approach to map your learning and ideas for your development by creating branches and twigs and making notes of your thoughts on each of the questions as you go along. In this way, you can build up your personal entrepreneurial learning map. An example is shown in Figure 2.7 to help you get started. Allow several periods of time for this, to reflect on each theme in turn.

If entrepreneurship can be learned, can it be taught? If you are reading this book as part of an entrepreneurship course, then either you or your tutor probably assumes that it can.

Figure 2.6 Entrepreneurial learning map

Figure 2.7 Example of entrepreneurial learning map for start-up business idea

However the extensive research into entrepreneurship education suggests that while education can provide cultural and personal support, knowledge and skill development about and for entrepreneurship, the 'art' of entrepreneurial practice is learned from experience, rather than from the educational environment alone. So learning must take place through action in the 'real world', rather than being a purely educational and theoretical process (Jack and Anderson, 1999). Gaining practical experiences and 'learning by doing' is a key part of the entrepreneurial learning process.

There have been many new contributions to the field of entrepreneurial learning and opportunities. Saras Sarasvathy (2001) introduced the concept of effectual entrepreneurship which has become highly influential. It is based on the notion of: 'starting with what you have: who you are, what you know, who you know'. This approach brings entrepreneurial thinking within everyone's grasp, and finding out about effectuation should be part of your journey. Rather than being goal-oriented, and reaching the goal through a given set of 'means', effectuation uses the resources available to the entrepreneur at the time in flexible and creative ways to achieve new and different goals.

■ Assessing the fit between ideas and personal goals

The ideas we work on and which we can develop into opportunities are likely to be those which have greatest personal meaning for us. This tends to result from personal interests, experiences, concerns and an emerging sense of direction and goals. So, although there might be a wide range of opportunities which objectively exist, only those which fit our personal priorities and interests are likely to be explored. Effectuation theory also suggests it is those which are readily available and feasible at a given time that are most likely to be selected. It is worth understanding how we focus on particular types of ideas, and why we are more likely to select these than others to create opportunities. For whilst economic theory might suggest that rational decision-making would play a major part, many opportunities are selected for quite different reasons, much more closely aligned with personal experiences.

Activity

Think back to how you make major decisions about your life, such as where to go to university or college, which course to select, future careers or your choice of leisure interests.
Which of these factors tend to dominate in making such choices?

- What friends say and choose to do
- Views of your family
- Personal interests
- Previous experience, education and employment
- How you feel about the situation
- Logical analysis
- What is the 'right' thing to do based on personal values
- Sense of curiosity and adventure
- Potential for personal benefit – 'what's best for me'

All this exercise may suggest is that the factors which influence our choices and decisions in other areas of our lives are likely to be similar to those which generally affect our choice of ideas and opportunities; in fact we may not realise a choice is being made. It is worth reflecting on whether any of these influences are too dominant in your decision-making; for example, do you pay too much attention to the opinions of friends or family? Are you governed more by feeling or curiosity, and what part does rational analysis play in making decisions?

Example: Vicky, Cetus Media

Vicky is the owner of Cetus Media, a small business she started after leaving university to offer social media, public relations and press marketing to organisations. In her narrative, she explains the background and how her personal story led her into this business venture.

I studied journalism at Uni, I'd always been interested in writing, news and media. I saw my career starting in newspaper and probably moving on to magazine journalism and editing. I did a few placements and got some articles published, but by the time I came to graduate in 2010 the industry was changing beyond recognition.

The recession had really hit both advertising and sales right across the industry. A lot of titles were losing money and people being let go, so career opportunities were few and far between. I just couldn't see how to get started. Even established regional daily papers were going weekly. There was huge uncertainty and it didn't feel like print journalism had much of a future.

It was clear that the action was happening online, with people reading much more from the Internet, and social media such as Facebook and twitter starting to take off in attracting people to media stories. It probably started with the Huffington Post, with journalism going online. I started doing my own blog, dabbling really to find out how to do things, and found I could locate interesting stories and comment on them which then attracted more interest as people started to follow me. Rocket science it was not, but I found that having journalism skills helped me to research, develop a story and then publish something that people would want to read.

It sounds logical in hindsight, but in the year after I graduated there was a fair bit of personal angst and soulsearching – had my degree been a waste of time? I found online journalism enabled me to write, publish and be read but the problem was, how do you get paid and make a living? There are a lot of people living on thin air in the online media and it doesn't pay the bills.

I was waitressing to make ends meet, and overheard a conversation with some business guys about how they didn't really 'get' social media, and how could they use it to help promote their business? This probably happened a couple of times and it made me think that there could be a market for my skills. So the next time it happened I just smiled and said 'I could help you with that!', they stared open-mouthed as they didn't expect this from a waitress, but we met to talk it through.

So the idea for my business came out of this – helping business people to understand social media, to develop a strategy for using it and to shape and communicate their message. That includes writing and placing features about my client businesses. I also advise and coach them on how they can use social media themselves, mainly twitter and LinkedIn. Then I write a regular column for a business journal on using social media for marketing, so I finally broke into print journalism that way. But that helps to promote my business and I do business club sessions on how to stay ahead in using social media. As there is continual change, people are prepared to pay and come along to find out what's new.

So I didn't really expect to be running my own business, but I found a market for my skills and it meant I could give up waitressing! I think I have more control over my career as an independent business than if I was working as a journalist. Being confident to see the opportunity and present yourself as the person who can help, and understanding that providing a business service has a value which clients will pay for, really were essential steps for me.

Vicky's story illustrates how people can find opportunities to use their skills which are different to those they expected from their educational or career pathways, and how economic and technological changes create new demand. Also, her narrative shows her awareness of the wider context of the industry sector and the economy, and how she connected these factors with her personal learning, opportunity recognition and development.

■ Developing entrepreneurial effectiveness

There has been much interest in developing frameworks for entrepreneurial education and skills, by organisations including the World Bank, the European Union and national governments. In the United Kingdom, a guidance document for enterprise and entrepreneurship education in Higher Education was developed with input from leading educators, including this author (QAA, 2012). It includes the outcome of *entrepreneurial effectiveness* being developed through a learning process including awareness, entrepreneurial mindset and entrepreneurial capabilities (Figure 2.8). It is introduced here to enable you to use it to plan and reflect on your own development. To do this, you need to make it individual and relevant to you by working through it.

Entrepreneurial effectiveness

This is an all-round state of achieving independent self-direction in being able to progress individual goals and projects. Entrepreneurial effectiveness means being able to work in enterprising and entrepreneurial ways. This can be achieved through developing enhanced

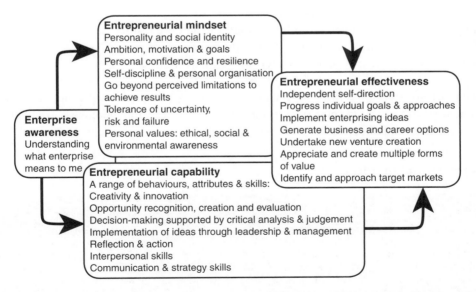

Figure 2.8 Entrepreneurial effectiveness: mindset, awareness and capability (QAA, 2012)

awareness, mindset and capabilities to enable you to perform effectively in taking up opportunities and achieving desired results. Effective performance means adapting and applying an entrepreneurial mindset and capabilities to the relevant context, and exercising judgements about the best actions to take within given environments. Let's look at what awareness, mindset and capabilities are about.

Enterprise awareness is understanding 'what enterprise means to me'; that is, why and how it is relevant and useful in your life. Developing an entrepreneurial mindset is learning to think in entrepreneurial ways, being self-aware of your own enterprising and entrepreneurial qualities, and developing the motivation and self-discipline to apply these flexibly in different contexts to achieve desired results. This can be developed by actively participating in enterprising learning and activities.

Activity

1. Enterprise awareness: in what ways do you think of yourself as an enterprising person?
2. Can you think of examples of entrepreneurial behaviour from your experience, either by yourself or by others? Also, think of examples in the media or from actual businesses.

An entrepreneurial mindset includes:

- awareness of your personality and social identity
- understanding your motivation, personal ambition and goals
- personal confidence and resilience
- self-discipline and personal organisation
- being able to go beyond perceived limitations and achieve results
- tolerance of uncertainty, ambiguity, risk and failure
- personal values: ethical, social and environmental awareness

By being self-aware and comfortable with 'who we are', our self-confidence, rapport and relationships with others in their roles as customers, investors and employees are likely to be more productive and effective.

Entrepreneurial mindset

Activity

Look back to the entrepreneurial learning map you drew earlier.

1. How would you describe your own entrepreneurial mindset?
2. What motivates you to achieve what you set out to?
3. How confident do you feel in being able to accomplish goals you set for yourself?
4. What helps you to increase your confidence?

Entrepreneurial capability

Developing entrepreneurial capability means gaining skills, knowledge and confidence through experience. This can be through a combination of formal education as well as practical experiences – ideally, both are needed, and many enterprise courses involve experiential entrepreneurial learning, either simulated (e.g., business games) or real-life practice.

This section outlines the capabilities which contribute towards entrepreneurial effectiveness. Capabilities include skills and also the knowledge and understanding needed to apply them in completing specific tasks. Skills are behavioural and can be learned, although each individual has differing degrees of innate ability and readiness to learn them. They are not dependent on personality, which is individually variable, although both personality and mindset influence the readiness and personal style we bring to learning and practising the skill. Also, it is an error to disaggregate entrepreneurial capability into a list of skills, knowledge and attributes and then to equate possessing these with the ability and motivation to become a successful entrepreneur, since this is dependent on more than simply possessing skills.

Entrepreneurial capability includes this range of behaviours, attributes and skills:

- Creativity and innovation – Chapter 3
- Opportunity recognition, creation and evaluation – Chapters 3 and 4
- Decision-making supported by critical analysis and judgement – Chapter 5
- Implementing ideas through leadership and management – Chapter 7
- Reflection and action – Chapter 8
- Interpersonal skills – the current chapter
- Communication and strategy skills – Chapter 7

There is a self-assessment tool for entrepreneurial capabilities in the 'toolkit' section at the end of the book. You can use this at any time – have a look now. But each of these capabilities will be covered in a chapter as you work your way through the book, so it will make most sense to complete that section of the self-assessment at the end of that chapter. This chapter considers personal organisation and interpersonal skills as essential capabilities around which to develop a wider range of skills.

■ Personal organisation

Being personally organised and effective is at the core of entrepreneurial working. This involves being clear and focussed on goals and priorities and being able to manage time and personal resources to achieve. In turn, this generates confidence in the ability to achieve desired results. This can present personal challenges; for example, a creatively oriented person may be more concerned with developing ideas and appear less organised and aware of turning up on time to meetings with clients.

The skills listed here are all useful and necessary in developing entrepreneurial activities. Each of us will be more comfortable and effective in some of these areas than in others.

- Set and plan to achieve personal and business goals
- Take personal responsibility for managing projects and achieving results
- Plan and use time productively to achieve goals and ambitions
- Apply energy, perseverance and determination to achieve results, especially within challenging situations
- Apply self-awareness of personal strengths and limitations to achieving goals
- Seek creative and effective solutions to challenging and complex problems
- Manage stress and pressure which may result from conditions of uncertainty and change
- Reflect to learn 'what works for me' from experimentation and feedback

Activity

Read and reflect on the list of personal organisation skills.

- Which of these do you feel most confident and effective in?
- Think of examples of when you have used these well.
- In which ones do you feel less comfortable?
- Again, think of examples when these have not gone well and you could have performed better.
- Note down the skills where you think you could gain greatest improvement.
- Think of real situations where you can practice this: what can you do differently?
- Who could you ask to give you feedback on your progress?

■ Interpersonal skills and interaction

Enterprise and entrepreneurship involve the ability to build effective relationships with others in a wide range of situations. The idea of the lone, 'heroic' entrepreneur acting against the world is largely a myth. As well as working within entrepreneurial teams, well-developed interpersonal skills form the core skillset for building a wide range of relationships and networks both within and beyond the venture team. Being able to interact effectively with potential partners, investors, experts, customers, suppliers and others who will become essential to the business is vital. The skills mentioned here are typical of those involved in creating and building relationships to develop the opportunity.

- Grow and maintain networks of social and industry contacts, to build support for ideas
- Find out what is important to people as stakeholders, understanding and responding to their perspectives
- Use social skills to build rapport, trust and long-term relationships with people
- Influence and persuade people to understand, accept and trust my point of view to gain support for ideas, concepts or solutions
- Negotiate and conclude agreements with people to make things happen

- Lead individuals and groups to achieve common goals
- Coach and provide feedback to team members on their behaviour and performance

Activity

Read and reflect on the list of interpersonal interaction skills.

- Which of these do you feel most confident and effective in?
- Think of examples of when you have used these well.
- Which of these have you not had relevant experience of using, or do not feel confident about?
- Again, think of examples when you could have performed better.
- Note down the skills where you think you could gain greatest improvement.
- Think of real situations where you can practice this: what can you do differently?
- Who could you ask to give you feedback on your progress?

Both these capabilities are included in the self-assessment section in the toolbox.

Roles

Thinking about personal organisation and interpersonal interaction also helps in understanding the issue of roles and leadership in working on opportunities in the entrepreneurial venture.

In developing an opportunity and creating and subsequently managing a business venture, a number of roles may be assumed by an individual. A role is a socially defined identity that comprises certain functions, attributes and types of behaviours used in accomplishing the tasks which normally accompany the role. Here are some of the roles which the creator of an entrepreneurial business may play, or be expected by others to play:

- *Inventor*: creates a new product.
- *Innovator*: applies a new technology.
- *Entrepreneur*: starts a business to exploit a future opportunity.
- *Manager*: builds and runs a business organisation.
- *Marketeer*: creates a market for a new product or service.
- *Leader*: leads and inspires people to achieve business goals.

The difficulty with viewing entrepreneurial work as a series of roles is that they are static, whereas entrepreneurship is a dynamic process which will involve some or all of these roles being played during the first few years of a business. It should not be assumed that the founder of the venture can or will play all of them as it develops, or that he or she has the personality preferences or capabilities to excel in a particular role. A venture often requires multiple contributions, and roles will be taken on by others within a team in which flexibility is important. It is more helpful to identify the skills and capabilities which may be required by a business at particular points and periods in its development, than to be over-concerned with individual roles, which often overlap and change. The concept of entrepreneurial teams has become influential, and in the development of an enterprise the range of capabilities needed in the team should be considered (Shepherd and Krueger, 2002).

◼ Being a leader: forming and leading entrepreneurial teams

Increasingly entrepreneurship is viewed as 'co-creation', or the result of several people working effectively together rather than just one 'lone entrepreneur'. So a business or a project of any scale is usually the product of an entrepreneurial team, in which people must learn to work effectively together. Within this group, one person may well emerge as the leader, but without the combined efforts of the team, success will not be achieved. Such teams may be long-lasting in a business, or project-centred and short-lived, such as for organising an event. Therefore it is essential to cultivate skills of leadership and teamworking to develop a venture which can grow, and for individuals to appreciate the distinctive contributions they can make to a team.

An important application of your entrepreneurial capabilities is in considering what contribution you can make to an entrepreneurial team. An entrepreneurial team is a group that has come together to exploit an opportunity, usually by setting up a new venture. The ideal entrepreneurial team is likely to have:

- complementary skills and expertise;
- compatible goals and motivation – people want to achieve the same things;
- compatible personalities and working styles;
- trust, honesty with each other and mutual respect; and
- effective leadership.

There are differing approaches to entrepreneurial leadership, some of which focus on defining personality traits and what might be classified as 'the *great man* school of leadership'. However, more helpful approaches have also emerged, including distributed leadership, where the cultural norm is that everyone in an organisation can demonstrate leadership, an approach that is of value in the flat, non-hierarchical entrepreneurial organisation. One such approach originates from the Sloan School of Management at Massachusetts Institute of Technology, where entrepreneurial leadership is taught. The model of leadership developed at Sloan includes five core leadership capabilities (Ancona, 2005):

- *Visioning*: fostering individual and collective aspiration towards a shared vision.
- *Analysing*: sensemaking and strategic planning in complex and conflictual settings.
- *Relating*: building relationships and negotiating change across multiple stakeholders.
- *Inventing*: inventing new ways of working together – social and technical systems.
- *Enabling*: ensuring the tools and resources to implement and sustain the shared visions.

This activity aims to help you reflect on your approach to leadership, and the contributions you could make to an entrepreneurial team.

Activity

Leadership and entrepreneurial teamwork

- What do you think are the top three personal and interpersonal capabilities you bring to an entre-preneurial team? Look back at your self-assessment of personal organisation and interpersonal skills from this chapter to help you think what these might be.
- Do you prefer to be the leader in a group, or would you prefer to support someone else in a leadership role by being a team member?
- What aspects of personality, roles, capabilities and expertise would you look for in others to complement your own?
- How could the Sloan leadership capabilities help you think about how distributed leadership can work in a group?

■ Networking, influencing and selling: vital skills in seeding opportunities

As suggested in the section on interpersonal capability, networking is highly important in finding, exploring and resourcing opportunities. Building on the previous section on leadership, leaders need to engage with a wide range of people and to develop broadly based personal networks. You may find it helpful to look back at your self-assessment in this capability.

Entrepreneurial effectiveness depends to a significant extent on being able to develop and utilise networks of contacts. This is not about simply being an avid user of Facebook, having many followers on twitter or a world-class contact directory, although any of these may well be useful in generating and maintaining contacts. Effective networking is constructing and participating in a world of social connections, in which new opportunities can be created and existing opportunities are taken forward. Even reserved people, who may feel less comfortable in social gatherings, can do this.

The development of social media creates infinite possibilities for generating networks, contacts and social capital, and business opportunities to accompany these. Yet many of the same principles apply online as they do in person. A sensible rule is not to behave online in ways you would not in person. Effective entrepreneurial networking, both interpersonal and online, depends on a number of behaviours which are outlined here.

- Create a distinctive and confident identity, both online and in person. People need to know who you are, what you are about, and what is interesting and memorable about you (personal and social emergence). They also need to be able to find and contact you.

- Be strategic, purposive and focused in your choice of networks and investment of time in them. These include LinkedIn groups and online communities. Which ones are useful and which are not?
- Get to know decision-makers, resource holders, experts, influencers and most useful people in your chosen networks.
- Practice conversational skills of listening and asking questions, finding out about people's needs, interests and their networks (interpersonal interaction).
- Manage contacts. Keep a contact database or business card folder up to date, and categorise groups of contacts, for example, all the news media people you know, as they will be useful when you want to get media coverage.

Activity

- Draw a map of the contacts in your network.
- Use the map in Figure 2.9 as a starting point. You can use these headings if they are relevant to you, or change them to fit.
- In which groups are most of your contacts?
- Which are informal and personal?
- Which are more formal and business-oriented?
- How do you think you need to develop your range of contacts?
- This will be revisited in Chapter 6.

Remember that human relationships depend on trust and reciprocity, so be prepared to do favours for people and to keep your promises. This builds up 'favours in the goodwill bank'. Successful entrepreneurs often 'give without the expectation of receiving in return' and find that goodwill consistently repays them. Renew and keep warm the contacts you value and

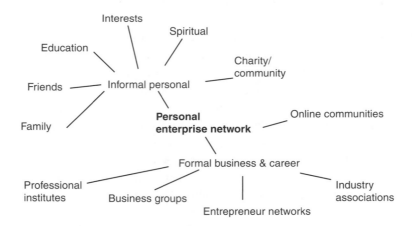

Figure 2.9 Mapping personal enterprise networks

want to maintain, but be selective. By participating in separate networks, covering a range of industries, and expert-professional, interest, cultural, even international domains, you will be the point of convergence and be able to introduce people from one network to contacts in another. When you need information, advice or access to a resource, then use your network – once you have developed it.

Networking building activity

This is an action-learning approach which can help you to develop further your skills and confidence in entrepreneurial networking. You can use a combination of online and face-to-face activities in doing this.

- Identify an idea, need, opportunity or question you want to explore. Think about how you will introduce this in an interesting way to new contacts.
- Use your contacts or other research (e.g., Internet search, business interest group, Chamber of Commerce) to identify a network where you can find out more about the opportunity. This should not be a network in which you have previously participated. It may be an expert, professional, trade, industry or interest group.
- Online social media, such as LinkedIn groups, and face-to-face contact can both be used to locate and participate in networks, but actually meeting and being comfortable with people is also vital.
- Negotiate your way into the group. If it is a group which holds face-to-face meetings, arrange to attend the next possible meeting.
- Talk to at least six people you have not met before. Find out about their areas of interest and points of connection with your own interests. Ask who they know who could help you further with your enquiry.
- Review your success in starting a new network and exploring your opportunity.
- Keep your promises to your new contacts.

One important reason for participating in networks in this way is to represent your business idea, and to make sure both that people are aware of you and that you can find opportunities for influencing, finding prospective new clients and other forms of relationship development. It is not about selling, because social contacts generally find it embarrassing to receive unsolicited sales pitches at parties, and few people are good at delivering them. The aim is to identify prospective clients who may be interested in what your business can do, to create a relationship of rapport and trust with them and to obtain their details, promising to contact them later. The next day, you can contact them and suggest a meeting or, if this is not possible, ask questions to find out about their needs, listen attentively and only open a selling conversation if that is appropriate. The effective entrepreneur is always alert to the possible sales opportunity!

■ Critical questions to consider from this chapter

Look back over your work in this chapter, including your learning map following the entrepreneurial learning model in the toolkit, your self-assessment of entrepreneurial capabilities, the leadership and entrepreneurial team exercise and your development of networking skills.

Use the following questions to update your entrepreneurial learning map, to reflect on your learning so far, and to plan your continuing development.

- How would you describe your entrepreneurial mindset or identity to someone else?
- What are your personal values, goals and motivations?
- How would these affect the types of opportunity you would explore?
- What are your most developed entrepreneurial capabilities, and how could you apply these to your best advantage?
- Which capabilities do you most need to develop, and how could you achieve this?
- Do you see yourself as an entrepreneurial leader, and if so how can you develop in this role?
- What expertise, personality and capabilities would you look for in other people as team members, to complement your own?
- How can you develop the networks you need for your opportunities and business?

Part II
Creating and Exploring Opportunities

This section of the book includes two chapters which address the second quadrant of Opportunity-Centred Entrepreneurship: creating and exploring opportunities. Together they show how entrepreneurial opportunities can be created, identified and developed through a semi-structured process.

Chapter 3 focuses on how to create and recognise opportunities, with particular emphasis on personal and social creativity. The purpose is to explore the relationships between creative thinking, awareness and recognition of opportunities. Chapter 4 then builds on this by taking a more analytical approach to show how opportunities can be explored, assessed and evaluated. The two chapters provide a detailed exposition of the questions in the second theme of Opportunity-Centred Entrepreneurship, creating and exploring opportunities, which is shown in Figure 3.1.

Creating and Recognising Opportunities

Chapter Contents

- Introduction
- Creating and recognising opportunities
- Creativity and innovation in entrepreneurial opportunities
- Openness to opportunity
- Creative moments
- Recognising opportunities in the external environment
- Creative problem solving

- Opportunity and problem mapping
- Creative thinking to generate innovation
- Opportunity building: matching needs and resources
- Current and future scenarios for opportunity creation
- Intellectual property: protecting ideas
- Critical questions to consider from this chapter

■ Introduction

The learning goals for this chapter will enable you to:

- identify and define problems as potential opportunities
- generate ideas and solutions to problems using creative thinking techniques
- explore creative moments in opportunity recognition
- use mapping techniques to explore problems, opportunities and resources
- define and follow a structured process of creativity from idea to innovation.

The chapter explores the roles of creative thinking and situational awareness in generating ideas and transforming them into opportunities through associative thinking. Creating and exploring opportunities is a process of generative curiosity – by being curious and investigating ideas and situations, new insights and possibilities are developed, as shown in Figure 3.1. Gaps, needs and problems can be identified and analysed as starting points for creative problem solving and opportunity recognition in the external environment.

The role of 'the moment' is introduced as a way of understanding and using creativity in both personal and social dimensions. The use of future scenarios and time perspectives in opportunity recognition are explored. Opportunity, problem and resource mapping are introduced as core techniques, and the connections between creative opportunity and innovation are explored. Finally, the importance of protecting intellectual property rights in the entrepreneurial process is summarised. Use is made of practical business examples and 'cameo' mini-cases to illustrate the concepts. The chapter is activity based, and you will be prompted to develop ideas and identify potential opportunities to explore and work on.

The outcome from this chapter is for you to learn how to develop ideas into opportunities by using mapping techniques, and then to plan how to undertake detailed market investigation of the opportunity which you will later use by applying the exploration tools and techniques to be covered in Chapter 4. These will enable you to use this information to assess and evaluate the potential of the opportunity.

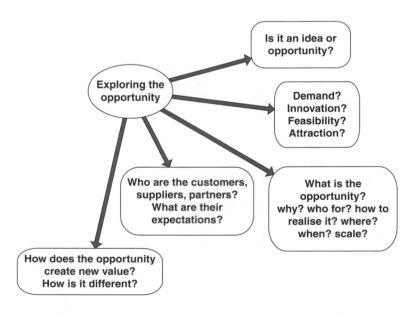

Figure 3.1 Creating and exploring the opportunity

■ Creating and recognising opportunities

Creating, finding, developing and exploiting opportunities are central activities in entrepreneurship (Shane, 2003). There has been extensive debate on whether opportunities already exist and are there to be *discovered* by the 'alert opportunist'; whether the unconnected elements of an opportunity need to be *recognised* and connected by the entrepreneur as acts of associative cognition; or whether they are the result of individual creativity and are *constructed* by the entrepreneur. All three of these statements are valid; existing opportunities can be perceived as market gaps and filled, whilst emergent opportunities can be worked on and developed. Neither of these need involve more than the application of some creativity in making them happen. But there is undoubtedly a fourth category, where we might think that the opportunity arises as an original idea from the mind of the creator. Yet true originality may be much less common than you might think. Very often it is the recycling of existing knowledge and resources in novel ways.

Kirzner (1997) suggested that people discover and recognise opportunities which are held to already exist, whilst Shane (2003) proposed a general theory of entrepreneurship based on the nexus, or connection, between individuals who discover opportunities and the entrepreneurial process of opportunity exploitation and execution. There is both purely 'opportunistic' behaviour, which centres on the short-term exploitation of currently available opportunities, and the creation of future new opportunities which do not yet exist, through innovation, generally over a longer timescale. Studies of opportunity recognition in successful US entrepreneurs suggested that they identified many opportunities and were highly alert and sensitive to opportunity (Hills and Shrader, 1998). The opportunities they selected were mainly problem and solution oriented, the identification of opportunity was a multi-step process rather than a single event and opportunities were often interrelated and sequential. Such opportunity recognition was often based on prior experience within an industry, with long-term exposure to markets and customers.

The debate over opportunity recognition was summarised by Gartner et al. (2003), who compared the economic perspective, in which opportunities are held to exist objectively and be discovered, with Weick's (1979) enaction theory in which individuals make sense of their world through scanning, interpretation and action. They termed this the enactment perspective: 'opportunities would be the result of what individuals do, rather than ... of what they see'. This reinforces the importance of individual prior knowledge and experience, and the contribution this makes to the ability to recognise opportunities.

As Kirzner argues, short-term opportunities do exist and await discovery by the alert entrepreneur. However the circumstances that can give rise to new opportunities before they emerge can be recognised by people with the imagination, experience and judgement to do so, and that they can create and enact the opportunities which they assess as worthwhile. The vital skill lies in recognising and exploring the future opportunities with the greatest long-term potential which the entrepreneur can gather the resources to exploit.

Activity

1. Do you think that entrepreneurs generally recognise opportunities which already exist?
2. Do you think that entrepreneurs are more likely to create new opportunities which do not already exist?
3. What are the advantages and disadvantages of each of these approaches to opportunity recognition?
4. What do you think are the differences in entrepreneurial mindset which may make an entrepreneur more likely to recognise existing opportunities, or to create new ones?

■ Creativity and innovation in entrepreneurial opportunities

Just as many people do not consider themselves to be entrepreneurs, even though what they do is entrepreneurial, so also people may not think of themselves as creative. Yet entrepreneurial creativity is less about individual genius and more about situational awareness, open-mindedness, and being able to learn, practice, sometimes copy and develop new ways of thinking and working. Some people are individually creative, others are much more socially creative – that is, they will gain ideas and insights from sparking off other people in chance conversations or working together on tasks and problems. So social creativity, or 'co-creation', creative teamwork and collaboration in entrepreneurship are highly important. For the writer, for example, the best ideas are almost always stimulated by meeting and conversation with other people, in which possibilities, current examples and resources are connected by the shared minds of the people involved.

Creativity and innovation are often associated with entrepreneurship, but although they are linked the terms are not synonymous and their respective meanings are important, since entrepreneurial opportunities require both creativity and innovation to progress from idea to solution. The creative act can be defined as 'bisociation', or combining two (or more) unrelated pieces of information to form a new third idea (Koestler, 1964). Creativity is the association of ideas, information or materials to form new concepts – or as Schumpeter (1934) described, 'new combinations'. Creativity sees the world in new ways, through free expression, by developing new and original ideas and concepts. This involves divergent, associative and non-linear thinking which may appear illogical to others. Creative art, for example, is judged by aesthetic criteria and subjective perception, so creative activity does not require practical or financial value.

Creativity has several important roles in the entrepreneurial process. It enables people to develop completely new ideas and to envision possibilities of 'new reality'. Imagining future demand and a business or a product which does not yet exist is a creative act. Creativity enables people to imagine the future and to construct future scenarios for business ventures. This is strategic creativity, by imagining and then enacting a new reality. However there are at least two other significant roles for creativity. One can be described as tactical creativity; it involves thinking and acting in creative ways to exploit opportunities or to manage and develop the business, often dealing with problems of limited time, expertise or resource. Entrepreneurial working is applied creativity, and entrepreneurial people are frequently creative in practical ways, in devising new product ideas, routes to market and solutions to problems, and it is certainly worth developing and using skills of creative thinking and working. Figure 3.2 illustrates different ways of applying ideas.

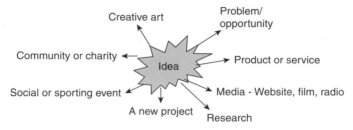

Figure 3.2 Idea and potential application routes

The other aspect is the application of creative skill within the business, for example, in designing or producing creative media, products or experiences. This opens up the area of innovation, or the application of novelty to create value by problem solving, using technologies in new ways or devising new processes and applications. Innovation processes and techniques are covered in Chapter 6 on developing opportunities.

Activity

1. Do you think of yourself as a creative person?
2. Are you more likely to have new ideas and insights:
   – When you are on your own?
      – Socially, when you are with other people?
3. How readily do you put your ideas into practice?
4. What stops you acting on more of your ideas?

■ Openness to opportunity

The intentional search for creative ideas and opportunities may be of limited effectiveness. Rather, it is about being open to new insights and possibilities when they arrive. Per Blenker and colleagues (2012) in Aarhus Business School developed the idea of 'entrepreneurship as everyday practice'. So in learning entrepreneurship, being critically aware of the world around us, noticing new and interesting ideas and being observant of approaches which do not work is a fundamental starting point. Observation, listening and paying attention to the latent and potential opportunities around us is a transferable and lifelong skill.

Activity

• Take a walk through your neighbourhood or downtown area. Look at the businesses which are in operation.
• Which businesses appear to be attracting customers and thriving?
• Which businesses appear to struggling or closing?

- What customer needs exist and are not being met very well?
- Why do you think these are happening?
- What opportunities can you see for doing things better than existing businesses?
- Can you see any vacant shop, pub or other premises you think have potential for starting a new business? Take a photo or keep details for later.
- What ideas does this give you?

Practising these skills of observation, talking to people and monitoring business health and assessing opportunities can help you to build up a knowledge base of ideas. This helps to develop your skills of situated learning as a basis for recognising potential opportunities. You can scale it up to assess businesses in a given industry sector, district and up to national and international level by using publicly available information on how real businesses perform.

Example: David Friel, the Entrepreneur Handbook

David Friel started his career running a web development business, before deciding to study for a degree in International Business. As a student, he realised that there was a major gap in the online information and expert resources available for entrepreneurs. From this developed the idea for the Entrepreneur Handbook. This aims to provide entrepreneurs with the highest quality expert information and education as an online ecosystem. David raised the initial investment aged 23 and launched Entrepreneur Handbook which went live in 2012.

The website features themes on business start-ups, marketing, finance, law and other areas. The content is built up from short articles by an extensive range of entrepreneurs, business experts and specialists. This resource base is continually growing and is attractive and immediately accessible, with a database of information on an international spectrum of business issues. In the first 11 months, the site grew to over 4,800 visitors monthly and has many recommenders on social media.

David aims to grow Entrepreneur Handbook into a global brand, with expansion initially into regional markets in Europe and North America, reaching 11 countries in the first year. One project is the Startup Map of the World, featuring a global library of start-up resources.

Entrepreneur Handbook is a free resource, funded by sponsors and other activities, including film production. It becomes more attractive as its user base increases. David sees it as simply his first venture. He is planning Founder Elite as an online members' club for start-ups, and Founder Academy, an online learning platform based on video and interactive content.

The initial growth and impact of Entrepreneur Handbook demonstrated David's energy and ability to market and connect the business with people and groups who recognised its potential. It is an invaluable resource for entrepreneurship students and practitioners (www.entrepreneurhandbook.co.uk).

■ Creative moments

People often talk about 'Eureka' or 'lightbulb moments' in relation to coming up with ideas and recognising opportunities. This section explores why what goes on in 'the moment' is significant, and how it relates to entrepreneurial creativity. It explains how we can capture ideas from such moments, why they can be significant turning points and the wider significance of moments in entrepreneurial learning and working.

There are many types of moments in the entrepreneurial experience, often including moments of learning and creativity. Here are common types of entrepreneurial moments.

Creativity: inspirational moment of association forming a new idea
Innovation: recognition of how an idea can be applied to a practical situation
Opportunity: recognition of a potential or actual position of advantage
Problem: a disadvantage, mistake or setback which must be addressed
Encounter: social interaction, meeting or social connection
Insight: gaining a realisation of new knowledge
Intuition: 'knowing' at a subconscious or 'gut' level
Judgement: making a decision or choice
Resolution: intention to act

Activity

- Recall a 'special moment' from your experience – something you remember which made an impression on you; this may have been good or bad
- Can you remember what happened?
- What makes it special/memorable for you now?
- How did it affect you at the time?
- What did you do as a result?

Two little ideas are introduced here:

Serendipity – you have the 'happy accident' of finding something useful or desirable whilst not consciously looking for it. But subconsciously, your brain may have been recognising patterns which led you to the discovery.

Ephemerality – a situation which is brief and temporary, and may not be recreated.

Discovering opportunities can involve both serendipity and ephemerality, but ephemeral opportunities may be too short-lived to be worthwhile.

What is 'the moment' and why is it significant?

Special or significant moments occur in many aspects of everyday life. A 'moment' is a point in time when we are consciously aware of what is going on, either within our mind or around us, and are aware and able to remember what we thought and our responses. Moments can be 'turning points' in our life stories. They are transitory; some are remembered for an event which has significant meaning or enduring consequences, but most are incidental and pass by. A moment is a conscious attention span, rather than a fixed time interval, such as the 'blink' identified by Gladwell (2005).

Two factors combine to make the concept of the moment increasingly important in entrepreneurship. One is the constantly unfolding and unpredictable economic and business context which has emerged since the financial crisis of 2008, creating a complex and risky business environment for entrepreneurs in the 'new era' as described in Chapter 1. This is paralleled by the rapid emergence of the virtual entrepreneurial economy, connected by a continuous digital media flow of messages, images and data, supported by continually evolving technologies. These are accelerating and enlarging the scale of entrepreneurial opportunities. This 'always connected' environment stimulates constant momentary interactions. This makes our mental processes of perception and decision-making in the moment increasingly important, since how we respond instantly, without really thinking, is often critical. The processes of entrepreneurial creativity, opportunity recognition, learning and decision-making all occur in the moment as increasingly important facets of entrepreneurial working, which are not well understood. There is also growing research in cognition and neuroscience which can inform us, some of which is referred to in this chapter.

Example: Ephemeral entrepreneurship

During the economic crisis, mainstream businesses such as shops and restaurants found survival difficult as demand and customer confidence slumped. A creative use for redundant retail premises was to set up 'pop-up shops', or 'flash retailing', selling limited-run clothes, creative products, food and other merchandise. These enabled start-up entrepreneurs to 'have a go' and try out business ideas which bring life to depressed high streets by using very short rent periods. They can also be controversial by competing with existing businesses. In Italy, people opened their houses and flats as mini-restaurants as alternatives to highly taxed trattoria. Pop-up has created new business opportunities, with specialists offering property and design services for retailers. Pop-ups last longer than a moment, but they show the scope for ephemeral entrepreneurship which can provide customers with 'instant' choices and opportunities.

Activity

- Think back to the vacant shops and business premises you looked at earlier. Yes, you did need to do that activity!
- List all the possible ideas for a pop-up business you could try in one of these. As well as shops, cafe, street food, fashion, make-up and creche might be possible. Think of activities you and friends could provide, with existing resources and at low cost.
- What do you think there could be an unmet need for?
- Who would you aim to attract as customers? What would instantly appeal to them?
- Which available shop or location would be ideal?

- Draw a simple opportunity mind-map to develop the concept (refer to Figure 3.3). Use these headings for the branches:
  - Ideas
  - Needs
  - Customers
  - Attractors
  - Location

This activity aims to prompt you to think creatively about ephemeral entrepreneurship. Hold onto the idea you've started to create, as this will develop during the chapter.

The moment in creative thinking and entrepreneurship

There are existing theories of creativity and recognition of entrepreneurial opportunity associated with the moment. These include Wallas (1926) who referred to moments of 'illumination' in the four classical phases of creativity, moving from unconscious preparation and incubation to illumination (the 'light bulb moment'). This may be followed by a reaction of emotion (such as joy, elation), action (moving to immediately write, draw or record the idea) and by conscious thinking on its implications: practicality (Will it work? What are its applications? etc) or, as Wallas described, verification.

This was later developed by Lumpkin et al. (2004) into a creativity-based model of entrepreneurial opportunity recognition, centred on a moment of 'insight'. Kneller (1965) suggested 'first insights' precede 'the moment of creation', occurring after a period of conscious preparation and an interlude of non-conscious activity. Inspiration and opportunity recognition often stem from the insights gained by making perceptual connections between previously unassociated ideas and information, and Penaluna et al. (2009) concluded, 'most creative ideas are achieved through insight'.

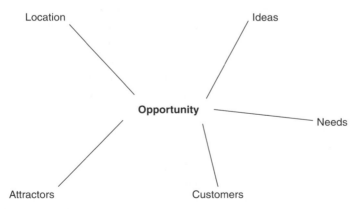

Figure 3.3 Simple opportunity-generating map

The late Jason Cope (2005) proposed that 'critical events' create 'metamorphic' fundamental learning during 'dynamic temporal phases' of entrepreneurial learning. He also suggested that one-off critical learning events could stimulate challenging, 'deep' reflection and create higher-level entrepreneurial learning, and that proactive generative learning could enable entrepreneurs to anticipate and apply prior learning to critical events.

Entrepreneurship can centre on serendipity: fortunate chance events coupled with sagacity or wisdom. Dew (2009) developed a conceptual framework for entrepreneurial serendipity in opportunity discovery which connected the systematic exploration of existing knowledge with pre-discovery intuition, spontaneous recognition and serendipitous discovery of something the entrepreneur was not looking for.

Finally, Kollmann and Kuckertz (2006) argued that the entrepreneurial event was of 'utmost importance' within the entrepreneurial process, and developed a framework for four 'archetypes' of opportunity recognition and exploitation, and a list of categories of entrepreneurial events. They suggested two classes of entrepreneurial events:

> The more confident part of the entrepreneurial population regards the starting point of the entrepreneurial process to be *the very moment* when the entrepreneur starts to *act* entrepreneurial and tries to take advantage of a certain business opportunity. However ... entrepreneurs of a more sceptic nature ... need proof of concept provided by the market ... and only start when customer interaction has happened. (45)

Understanding the moment in entrepreneurship

How do we understand 'what's going on' in the moment? In our daily experiences of 'being' in the moment, we are perceiving, generating meaning, both consciously and unconsciously, and acting in response, through speech and behaviour, in interconnected ways. The human brain is highly complex and developed, but three interconnected mental processes are critical: *perceiving* what is happening, *generating meaning* from these perceptions, and *acting*. Most perceptions take place at an 'unconscious' level, with selective conscious attention, awareness and memory of perception. Meaning is constantly being generated from the interconnections between perceptions and memory, with decisions to act being formed and executed. There is a complex and constant interaction between unconscious mental activity and conscious awareness, in which 'realisations' occur and conceptions of learning are generated in moments which may be remembered.

Figure 3.4 illustrates, in a very simplified way, these three essential and interdependent processes and the complex interactions which occur constantly. They occur both consciously, with selective attention being paid to a small proportion of the sensory data being perceived in the mental 'foreground'; and unconsciously, with awareness of a much wider range of experiential data taking place as 'background'.

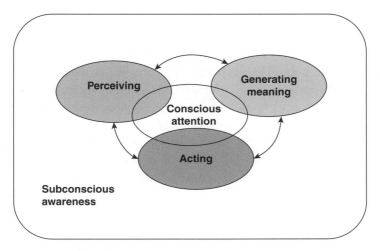

Figure 3.4 Momentary perspective: 'Being' in the moment

Activity

- Think back to the *special moment* you remembered earlier in this chapter.
- This asked you to recall your perceptions (what happened?), meaning (why it was special?) and activity (what you did?).
- What do you recall was taking place in your conscious awareness?
- What do you think you were subconsciously aware of, either at the time or subsequently?

So back in the High Street, people are walking past shops, adverts and market stalls. They see much and are subconsciously aware of a vast range of sensory data, but will become consciously aware of only limited stimuli and connections. What would make them notice a new pop-up business? By being colourful and breaking the pattern of 'the same old shops', it is more likely to be noticed and to stand out. Using different emotional and sensory messages, such as music or pleasant aromas of fresh coffee, can also do this.

Subconscious awareness is important in all aspects of life, including entrepreneurial activity. If you recall decisions you have made, many take place without much conscious thought. Intuition – 'gut feel' or instinct, when you 'just know' – and tacit knowledge, gained from prior experience, together with emotion, are all highly significant in how we recognise opportunities, make decisions, respond to events and many other actions

Entrepreneurial cognition has tended to over-emphasise conscious rationality, and under-plays these subconscious processes. Subconscious mental processing is more rapid than conscious (Banks and Isham, 2009), so the result of 'thinking about' how to respond will be slower and more likely to follow rather than occur in the moment (I've got to think about it...'). This applies in the selling process and in 'closing the deal'. Conscious reflections on the meaning may continue to flow long after the creative moment itself.

Time and memory are important aspects of the lived experience in the moment, as conscious awareness connects with experiences of past recollections and anticipation of future possibilities. As well as chronological 'clock time', there is also narrative or Kairotic time. Kairos was the Greek word for a moment of indeterminate time in which something significant happens, or the optimum moment for something to happen. We create a timescale in a narrative to make sense of past and planned events by selectively perceiving what is most significant and making connections between them. For entrepreneurs, acting at the right time is crucial – too early and you lose money, too late and others will have seized the opportunity. Kirzner characterised the entrepreneur as an 'alert opportunist' for whom acting at the best time was vital.

For example, the optimum time to open a new business or to launch a new product. For your pop-up business, when would be the best time to launch it? And to close it?

In Western retailing, for example, a high level of sales occur in the November–December period before Christmas. So gift and food pop-ups could do well in this period.

Figure 3.5 suggests how meaning is generated in the moment within a perspective of narrative time. This may look rather abstract, but it applies constantly in entrepreneurial working.

Activity

Imagine you are presenting your case for your pop-up business to persuade the property owner or agent to give you a short tenancy period to use the property, at a low or even free rental. This is a 'moment of truth'.
   How will you do this?

This activity puts you into the moment when you need to tell a persuasive story (your narrative) using your prospective imagination about how, in a short period of the future, you will provide a product or service to attract customers and make money. You will draw on your

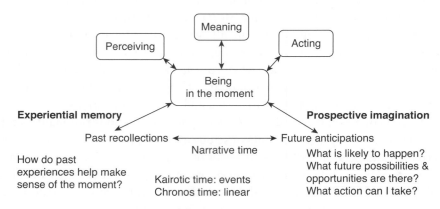

Figure 3.5 Time perspective and being in the moment

experiential memory to persuade the owner how you can do this and show them benefits, such as demonstrating you will enhance the property's commercial value. You will connect together the key events into a convincing timescale (Kairotic time). Meanwhile the owner will be perceiving you and your story, not just listening to what you say but aware of your body language, authenticity (are you believable?) and confidence. They will be generating meaning and deciding how to respond. Their decision will be informed by lots of subconscious awareness, and their 'gut feel' and emotional response to you may well be the decisive factor. You want to influence them to act by agreeing to your tenancy.

A critical outcome of the moment is the decision to act. People often become consciously aware of the decisions they have already made unconsciously, and 'spur of the moment', impulsive, intuitive and conditioned responses may over-ride considered logical analysis. Decisions arise from a complex set of underlying factors and cognitive structures, such as personality, sense of identity, emotion, beliefs and moral sense of 'what is right', as much as rational judgement. Many responses are conditioned by experience and learned behaviour: sometimes crudely termed the 'no-brainer'.

The intention of this section was to increase your awareness of critical moments in entrepreneurship, and of how you – and other people, such as co-workers and potential customers – are likely to respond. Seize that creative moment and follow your intuition!

■ Recognising opportunities in the external environment

An opportunity was defined in Chapter 1 as: 'the potential for change, improvement advantage and value creation arising from our action'. The opportunity may be an existing one which we can identify now, or it may be a future one for which we recognise the potential. This section addresses the following types of opportunity:

- 'gaps in the market' or a mismatch between supply and demand
- current and future opportunities
- solving of a problem, such as by developing and applying a solution
- a new product, service or experience people would find useful.

Is an idea the same as an opportunity? This appears to be a simple, but essential question. An idea is a creative connection between two or more pieces of information. An opportunity can exist where there is a need, problem and either actual or potential demand for a product, service or experience. The idea may identify the customer demand – but very often it will not. There have been many ideas for new products where insufficient demand existed and could not be created. The Museum of Failed Products in Michigan, USA, includes many examples.

It is also possible to identify needs and to think creatively about them without being able to solve the problem or to fulfil the demand. If the idea is not technically or otherwise feasible it is not yet a real opportunity. These factors help to define three of the four essential features of an opportunity:

Demand: there is a need, problem or potential demand to be satisfied.
Innovation: there is an idea for the product, service or experience to be provided.
Feasibility: the idea is technologically feasible, it can be realised and provided with available resources.

These can be investigated objectively, but we need to add a fourth, based on more subjective judgement, which in practice often makes the vital difference between opportunities which are exploited and those which are not:

Attractiveness: the potential reward and the level of interest to the entrepreneur.

Together these produce the DIFA (demand, innovation, feasibility, attractiveness) method of defining whether an opportunity actually exists.

Example of DIFA

Adam and Ivy were hospitality students in a regional city with a big Christmas market which attracted many visitors. They found a small, vacant shop unit which they could rent on a short licence and which had space for a food preparation area and serving bar inside with stools and a few pavement tables and chairs, and decided that there would be an opportunity for a distinctive street-food business selling savoury and spicy hot snacks and drinks for the winter season. Their DIFA looked like this:

Demand: Many seasonal visitors and shoppers looking for quick, warming food and drink during the cold weather. Up to 10,000 people pass within 50 metres of the shop in peak periods; 80 customers spending £3 average each will more than break-even each day

Innovation: Many alternative vendors but healthy, tasty and novel snacks and drinks will be a distinctive offer.

Feasibility: Pop-up cafe with three-month licence, November–January, selling pre-prepared own recipe snacks or bought-in products, heated using simple facilities. They had the skills and resources to do this.

Attractiveness: Unique offer in the market. Opportunity to try out own recipes and promotion and build business experience

Activity

Go back to your pop-up business idea.
  Can you define these four features:
  • What is the demand? Who is this from?
  • What is innovative or different from what already exists?

> - How is the idea feasible? Could you get what you need to make it happen?
> - What will make it attractive to you, customers, the property owner?
>
> The factors which give rise to opportunities can be divided between, on the one hand, 'supply-side' or 'push' factors, based on the availability of technology, resources and economic and policy changes which provide the ability to create new opportunities, and on the other, 'demand-side' or 'pull' factors based on market need. In both cases, changes in these factors over time create spaces for new opportunities.

Supply-side or push factors

- technological advance, new possibilities and innovations
- new products or processes becoming available
- legislation, market liberalisation, compliance and standardisation
- increase or decrease in cost and availability of resources
- increase or decrease in transaction and process costs
- supplier and distributor capabilities
- availability of skilled people.

Demand-side market and customer needs, or 'pull' factors

- demand for innovation or novelty
- social and consumer trends, for example, rising expectations, increasing or decreasing disposable income, less free time, changing consumer tastes and changing demographic factors
- demand for value for money
- the effects of competition, for example, rising or falling prices
- potential advantages, for example, saving of time or cost, convenience
- demand from supplier and distributor chains
- reduction in risk, uncertainty or variability.

These lists are not exhaustive, but they indicate the range of factors which affect and give rise to opportunities, and provide an initial framework for opportunity analysis. As shown in Figure 3.6, the entrepreneur operates in the space where supply and demand converge, by connecting supply-side resources with market opportunities to create new value.

■ Creative problem solving

Business opportunities can be based on devising a solution to a problem which affects enough people to make the solution viable, following the old maxim of 'find a need and fill it'. These activities lead you through a systematic approach to defining the problem before starting to look for solutions. The activities can be completed by one person or by a team of two or more people working together. More people collaborating will bring more ideas!

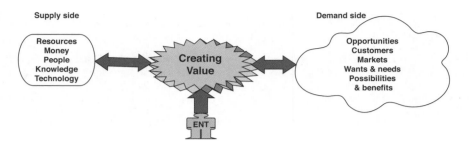

Making creative connections between needs/opportunities and capabilities/resources

Figure 3.6 The entrepreneur: creating new value by connecting supply and demand

■ Opportunity and problem mapping

We can apply a technique called 'opportunity mapping' in several different ways. This is the same as the technique introduced in Chapter 2. It can be used for defining problems, exploring opportunities, establishing resources, planning and developing an opportunity.

Opportunity mapping, like mind mapping, is a creative way of connecting ideas together by association rather than by step-by-step logical thinking. It can be used with pictures as well as words and gives great flexibility in the way information is expressed and processed. Opportunity mapping works by enabling us to generate thoughts quickly, creatively and intuitively, by 'free association' rather than sticking to a logical process. It can be used by one person, but is more productive when used by a small group – for example, to sort the results from a brainstorming session where a group of people 'freewheel' to come up with as many ideas as possible.

Opportunity mapping has a range of applications in entrepreneurial working, including:

- reviewing and making connections between ideas, experiences and resources
- creating and developing new concepts
- developing ideas, strategies and plans for projects and business ventures.

Activity

Seeing an existing need as a creative opportunity

Think of a problem which continually recurs, or a repetitive unmet need. It could be something you have noticed, which affects or annoys you.

If you cannot think of anything, choose one of these real problem-based opportunities:
- how to find part-time jobs in term-time for students
- how to use resources such as old mobile phones, CDs, personal computers or textbooks which are no longer required

- how to reduce the number of solo-occupied cars in city rush hours.
- Now go through the following stages to define the problem by answering as many of the questions as you can; guess or estimate to fill in the gaps. You can use an opportunity map to chart your responses.
- What is the problem you have identified?
- What are its results or effects? How can you assess its scale or measure it (e.g., number of people affected)?
- Why is it a problem? Why does it happen? What factors cause it?
- Who is causing, and who is affected by, the problem? How do those causing the problem benefit from it?
- Where, when and how does it happen?
- What are the costs – financial, time, resources – that are incurred?
- What are the potential gains from solving it?

At this point you can review the problem and consider:

- Is the problem capable of being solved? Is a solution feasible?
- Does solving it offer a big opportunity? What benefits or value could be created?
- Is the problem interesting and useful to solve?
- Is this an isolated, individual problem or a recurring one which affects many people?
- Could resources potentially be found to solve the problem?

Asking questions like these can screen out problems on which it may not be worth investing further time, and identify those which are *systemic* and recurring and so are worth trying to find solutions for.

The result is a map which connects the key ideas and information associated with each branch or sub-topic. This can then be used to develop the opportunity further. The important stage is in moving from *implicit* understanding (information in people's heads) to explicit information on paper where different pieces of information become connected, leading to fresh ideas, insights and possibilities. Figure 3.7 suggests headings on the branches as starting points for your opportunity or problem map.

Figure 3.7 Starting point for a problem or opportunity map

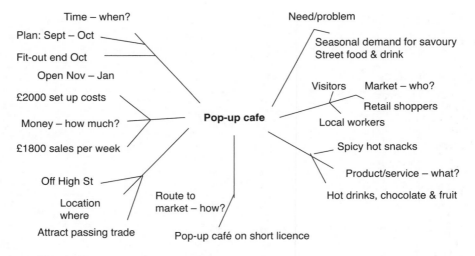

Figure 3.8 Opportunity map for pop-up café.

Figure 3.8 shows as an example the opportunity map for the pop-up café example from earlier in the chapter.

■ Creative thinking to generate innovation

Creativity generates new ideas by bringing existing knowledge together in new ways, opening the door to innovation. Opportunity mapping can be a useful way of associating information visually to produce new ideas, as we will see in the next section. A new concept only needs two or three elements, which may already exist separately. So a customer need and a technology can be combined to create a new product innovation. If we think of creative resources that we can use, these can include knowledge, technology, materials, skills, production and distribution capacity and many others. There are numerous examples; think of the increasing applications being found for wi-fi technology, mobile phone applications, social media and so on.

Creativity can result from 'breakthrough' thinking: taking something out of its existing context and applying it in a new situation. Most innovations are adaptive – small-scale incremental improvements on existing products, such as the latest model of the Apple i-Pad, for example. Radical or 'disruptive' innovations, which create entirely new concepts and which can transform their industry, are much rarer and generally higher risk. However any successful innovation requires other ingredients, which include a clear focus on the customers: how will the innovation benefit the customers' life or business, what will it do for them and what value will it create for them? It makes sense to involve customers in the creative process, to find out about their needs, problems and desires, and what innovation they would value.

■ Opportunity building: matching needs and resources

Activity

Use the approaches shown so far in this chapter – of analysing the problem, thinking creatively and opportunity mapping – to develop a potential solution to the problem you identified earlier.
   Review whether it includes the four key features of an opportunity in the DIFA model:
   - *Demand*: what is the need, problem or demand to be satisfied?
   - *Innovation*: what is the product, service, process or experience?
   - *Feasibility*: is it technologically feasible?
   - *Attraction*: is it worth doing? Why?

There are three important points here, each connected with how we recognise opportunities.

We perceive, recognise or create opportunities in our subjective consciousness. This is part of our learning process. Ideas are not the same as opportunities, since an idea is simply a creative thought, which may not be practical or viable in any sense. However an opportunity can be acted on and made to happen. So turning a business idea into a business opportunity involves demonstrating that it is feasible, viable and worthwhile – it can be done and is worth doing. The same opportunities are not apparent to everyone, and some people will perceive the same opportunity more quickly than others through imagination and foresight. Opportunities can start off as individual, unique perceptions or social shared insights, either by people co-creating it in the moment, or people who are quite unconnected coincidentally recognising the same opportunity at around the same time.

As we observed in relation to the moment, time is an important dimension in recognising and working on opportunities. Opportunities can be transient and ephemeral, occurring through combinations of such forces as technological change, social and market trends or even the weather. The 'opportunist' trader at the seaside will sell ice-cream on sunny days but switch to waterproofs and umbrellas when it rains. So opportunities are time-limited, and if we recognise one then the decision to work on it or not should be made quickly, since others may already have noticed it or will become aware of it. Inevitably this leads to competition where the first or best comes to dominate. Future-based rather than current opportunities give greater scope for strategic innovation and developing something new in a 'white space', unoccupied future market niche, rather than an intensively competitive existing market.

Third, just because we recognise an opportunity that does not mean it is a 'good' opportunity for us. We live in an opportunity-rich society. Being opportunistic and pursuing every opportunity will quickly exhaust personal resources of money and energy. 'Good' opportunities, those which we should select and develop, are likely to be ones where we already have some relevant skills, knowledge, experience and understanding, where we have an interest or fascination which excites us and where the opportunity is in harmony with, or at least compatible with, our personal and business or career goals. And it is only an opportunity we can exploit if we can gain access to and harness the necessary resources – of finance, information, technology and people – to do so.

So here are some basic questions to use in assessing and filtering an opportunity you have identified:

- Is it an idea or an opportunity?
- Is it a current or future opportunity?
- Has anyone else already noticed or seized the opportunity?
- Is the opportunity distinctive and different from existing approaches?
- Is the opportunity compatible with my goals, interests and experiences?
- Is the opportunity feasible?
- How can I gather the resources which would be needed?

One important process in developing an opportunity is to match the need, problem or demand with the resources needed to make it happen. That does not mean the entrepreneur needs to own or control the resources, but rather that they be able to find them and connect them with the project in a negotiated way, for example, by offering the resource owners the opportunity to participate as investors or partners in the venture. The resources which may be required to exploit an opportunity could include:

- knowledge – skills, expertise, specialist know-how and information
- technology – existing technical capability or capacity
- physical equipment and plant or materials and components
- finance – investment capital and start-up capital
- human – skills, expertise and capability which is required in the venture
- access – permission, licences, distribution networks
- intellectual property – patents, brands, trademarks, design rights, copyright
- capacity – facilities which need to be bought-in or sub-contracted.

Opportunity mapping can be used to create a resource map of the resources and capabilities needed to develop the opportunity. An example of a resource map from the pop-up café is shown in Figure 3.9.

Activity

- Draw a resource map for the opportunity you have identified, using the categories of knowledge, finance, technology, materials, access, intellectual property and any others which apply.
- Review it to identify where these resources currently exist and could be located.

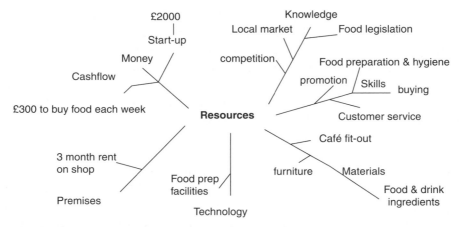

Figure 3.9 Resource map of the opportunity

■ Current and future scenarios for opportunity creation

Acting at the right time is a critical factor in opportunity recognition.

Current opportunities are those where customer demand already exists and the innovation is feasible now; the idea may be a new one, an adaptation of an existing one or a simple replication. Generally, current opportunities are less innovative than future opportunities, or may not be innovative at all. The opportunity may result from the market growth being greater than existing businesses can fully exploit, making competition possible or exploitation of a defined market niche feasible. A new market does not have to be created. Current market opportunities involve less uncertainty, but it is certain that increased competition with possible price-cutting will result. The technology already exists and is known, and the risks and costs can be defined with greater certainty.

However if one new firm is able to enter the market, then it is likely that others will also do so, potentially leading to price-cutting and over-supply. Competition is almost inevitable with existing opportunities, although introducing an innovation which gives a clear cost or customer advantage into an existing market, especially one which is growing, can be a viable strategy.

Opportunities have an optimum 'moment' for being initiated and a period in time at which they can best be exploited, when the need can be created or is self-generating, the resources and technology can be brought together, and the potential return is greatest. We can use creative thinking about the future to imagine opportunities which do not yet exist, but which are possible or emergent, because the resources required to make them happen are or will become available. Future thinking is inherently innovative, yet risky, demanding confidence and the availability of significant resources into the future.

Potential market opportunities arise where the demand may not yet exist but can be stimulated, where the technology either already exists or will become available in the foreseeable future, and where the innovation, or idea, has not yet been applied. Future opportunities require prediction of future market, customer and other trends. The further into the future an opportunity is projected, the higher the degree of uncertainty or risk there is in implementing it. Significant investment may well be needed, and it may be difficult to quantify how much is required. However the entrepreneur may also have the potential to gain a much higher return from being first to exploit the opportunity, to gain a market lead and possibly to secure intellectual property rights on the innovation.

Amazon.com in Internet-based media retailing and Sky in satellite pay-TV are two examples of future opportunities which were exploited successfully. In both cases the potential was identified by the founders significantly in advance of their competitors. Substantial investment was made in establishing the technological, market and product bases for the businesses. Establishing a controlling position in a new industry which they created was the goal, rather than short-term return or profitability. When the businesses were launched they provided a unique service which was impossible for rivals to copy quickly. The founders continued to invest substantially in the businesses to build up market dominance over a period of several years, this being considered more important than short-term profitability. Both businesses developed a market, product and technological dominance which competitors who entered the market later with similar offers were unable to rival.

These are examples of successful future opportunity exploitation. However, future opportunities can have significant disadvantages, in particular the uncertainties giving rise to risk, the uncertain time period before implementation and break-even or profitability and the uncertainty over the investment needed to support this. There are many cases of unsuccessful attempts to create and exploit future opportunities, and the reasons for failure are important to learn from.

■ Intellectual property: protecting ideas

A vital area to consider in exploring opportunities is whether the ownership of the idea can be protected. The area of idea ownership is termed intellectual property (IP). This is neglected as being complex and expensive by many businesses and early-stage entrepreneurs, which can bring at least three serious disadvantages for them:

1. By failing to protect their ideas, they lose the value which comes from being able to secure their unique rights to use them.
2. Potentially, others can then register and exploit them instead and deny the owner this right.
3. If you are accused of infringing IP owned by another party then this can be extremely costly. IP litigation is used by US-based organisations as a tactic to suppress competition. An example is the case where Apple accused Samsung of copying its designs and distinctive features from the iPhone to use on Samsung smartphone products. This was upheld by US patent laws in 2012, and Samsung incurred a heavy fine.

If you create new ideas then the ways in which these are expressed can be protected. New products, processes and techniques can also be protected. IP relates to the following forms of intellectual property rights (IPR):

- patents
- trademarks
- design protection, including registered design and design right
- copyright
- trade secrets.

Full details of intellectual property in the United Kingdom can be found on the Intellectual Property Office website, and this provides excellent online IP for Business tools and guidance 'which can help you create value from your ideas, turning inspiration into sustainable business success' (www.ipo.gov.uk).

In summary:

- *Patents* protect original discoveries and inventions, such as processes and products, which must be new, inventive and capable of industrial application. An application is filed and a full patent may be granted after a search and examination has been carried out by the IP Office. Once published, the patent gives the holder exclusive rights to use or licence the innovation for up to 20 years. It is vital not to disclose the invention to a third party, or to use it, before the patent is applied for, and the application must include full disclosure of all details since nothing can be added subsequently. The patent process is complex, and the use of an expert such as a patent agent or lawyer on a confidential basis is likely to be necessary. UK patents only provide protection in the United Kingdom or, by extension, within 23 European states, and beyond these areas other national patents have to be taken out. If a patent is infringed the holder needs to defend it, although insurance cover may be taken out against the costs of this. The process of securing, renewing and defending patents is complex and costly, especially for the solo inventor, but it is vital if the rights to a valuable invention are to be protected. Imagine how you would feel if you invented something and another organisation patented it, preventing you from using it; this has happened.
- *Trademarks* are signs, such as words, logos and pictures, which distinguish the products and services of one organisation from another. They include product and organisation brands such as Virgin, McDonald's and Orange. Registering a trademark prevents others from using the same mark in relation to the types of products and services for which it is registered. International registration can also be applied for. This is vital to protect logos and icons in the online space for example.
- *Design protection* includes *Registered Design*, which is the total right of ownership to use the design. It covers the appearance of a product or part of a product, which must be novel, individual and not generic. It can be granted on submission of photos or drawings of the design with an application and fee, and lasts for 5 years with extensions to 25 years. *Design right* also exists as intellectual property when the design is unregistered, but

provides less cover. It provides an exclusive cover against copying for up to 5 years, but only within the United Kingdom.

- *Copyright* is similar to *design right*, giving creators of all creative works the right to control use and publication for between 25 and 70 years, depending on the type of work. In both copyright and design right, it is up to the creators to record and retain proof of their origination of the work and the date this took place, so that they can subsequently defend their right to the work.

All these categories of IPR can be sold, licensed or given by the owner to another party; needless to say, the future potential value of the rights should be considered carefully before taking such a step, and professional advice obtained from a legally qualified IP expert in cases where there is substantive potential value. Just think that J.R.R. Tolkein, author of *The Lord of the Rings*, sold the film rights for a tiny proportion of the eventual value of his creative work, and many songwriters, authors and designers have never received more than a nominal payment from the exploitation of their work.

Trade secrets are unregistered intellectual property, which include confidential processes, techniques and recipes – for example, the secret ingredients of Coca-Cola. They can be protected by confidentiality agreements or by being handed down verbally from one family generation to another, effectively depending on trust. But once the secret is disclosed it is impossible to assert ownership, protect the product or prevent copying.

It is important for innovators to assess what unique intellectual property they are creating, and how their rights to its ownership can be protected most effectively. The future value of the opportunity and the ability to exploit it nationally or internationally may well depend on the strength of intellectual property. Also, it is not enough simply to register the patent, design or trademark. If it is infringed it is necessary to defend ownership, which is inevitably costly, especially on an international basis. However in a number of countries, intellectual property rights are almost impossible to assert or defend, since international trade agreements are not enforced, and copying and counterfeiting of products are widespread. China, Russia and a number of other developing countries are territories in which it is very difficult to enforce intellectual property rights.

Activity

- What intellectual property could your idea potentially produce?
- In which category or categories of IPR would this fall?
- How could you go about securing your IPR?

■ Critical questions to consider from this chapter

- What are the four essential features which distinguish an opportunity from an idea?
- How are creativity and innovation different? In what ways do they relate to the entrepreneurial process?

- What factors are most important in creating an opportunity?
- How can you translate a need or problem into an opportunity through creative thinking?
- How would you use opportunity and resource maps to develop your thinking on an opportunity? Which branches would you use?
- How can you make the most of a creative moment?

Opportunity Exploration and Assessment

■ Introduction

This chapter builds on Chapter 3, which covered creating and recognising opportunities. Having identified an opportunity, this chapter demonstrates how to use a systematic approach to explore, evaluate and assess entrepreneurial opportunities. Just as not all ideas are opportunities, not all opportunities are timely, viable or worth pursuing. So the approach, techniques and skills which can be used to identify the most promising and to select the 'best' opportunities are critical for entrepreneurship, since the majority of potential opportunities may well be rejected for various reasons, in order to focus attention and resources on the best. A critical question is how the opportunity can create and capture value, and the multiple types of value which apply. This is a first stage towards developing a business model, which will be expanded in Chapter 5.

This chapter uses a process, framework and tools for opportunity selection, assessment, evaluation and decision-making, using criteria to distinguish 'high-potential' and 'lower-value' opportunities. These enable the higher potential opportunities to be identified and progressed, whilst less promising opportunities can either be adapted and reconsidered or abandoned. The approach, in comparison with the creative stance in Chapter 3, is more rational and analytical, based on the need to gather and appraise firm evidence of an opportunity which can be used to present a convincing business case to investors or partners.

The learning goals for this chapter will enable you to:

- assess what is known about an opportunity, and what new information is needed
- apply market research skills to the structured exploration of opportunities
- assess and evaluate potential opportunities in relation to decision-making criteria
- understand multiple forms of value, how they are captured and created, to start to develop a business model
- prepare a report to evaluate and inform decision-making on the opportunity.

During the chapter you should continue to work on the example of an opportunity which you selected in Chapter 3. The outcome of this chapter is to assess the potential of this opportunity, a consideration of the strategic options, and identification of the networks and resources which are likely to be most useful in acting on it. This information will be brought together in the form of an opportunity evaluation portfolio of information, or a report, which provides an essential contribution to the venture planning process in Chapter 5. This type of report is often required to demonstrate to potential investors, partners and others that there is a substantive opportunity capable of being exploited.

Activity

Future thinking

Consider the opportunity you have identified in relation to time perspectives from now into the future, over a time period up to three years.
- Is the opportunity current, or one which will exist in the future?
- If it is in the future, how many years ahead will this be?
- Is it currently being explored or exploited by others?
- Do all the conditions exist for it to be exploited? Which do not?
- Are you bringing a significant innovation or advantage to exploit the opportunity?
- What assumptions about future conditions are you making? (e.g., demand, innovation, technology, resource availability, social trends etc.)
- What factors could change to affect these assumptions?
- What are the most significant risk factors in the opportunity? How could these be reduced?

■ Exploring opportunities: market and related investigation and research

Exploring the market is an essential process for any opportunity, especially if it is in a sector or activity which is new or unfamiliar to the entrepreneur, since much can be learned about the potential market and customers. The fundamental task is to establish what we already know about the opportunity in the intended market, and to identify what is not known, but needs to be known. This is a process of moving from assumptions, which are often flawed ('everyone will buy this product!'). This section applies market research thinking to show how the opportunity can be explored in increasing depth. Students and graduates are likely to have more up-to-date academic research skills than many people in business, and being able to apply these skills to researching opportunities is a valuable type of skills transfer. This activity will provide information which can be used to assess and evaluate the opportunity, and to demonstrate to others that an opportunity exists or can be created. The market focus funnel in Figure 4.1 visualises the market exploration as a progression where we move from an overview to detailed and specific probing. You may recognise this as an example of moving from divergent to convergent thinking.

Using the market focus funnel

To work through this model we need to gather information at several different levels: the overall markets available, the target market, the customer segments available, and the target segment. We may already have assumed that there is a given market and target group of customers. However in developing an opportunity, it often becomes apparent that the initial target market is not the most attractive or rewarding. Therefore even if a single potential market has been identified, it is worth moving back up the funnel to ask 'What are all the

• Identify potential markets
• Market characteristics:
   • Total value, growth, accessibility
• Decide on target market
• Identify customer segments within market
• Identify segment characteristics:
   • Total value, growth, accessibility
• Decide on target segment(s)
• Identify customer needs, preferences,
• Decision making factors, pricing
• Identify media, promotional & sales channels
• Develop marketing plan

How will you identify the market potential and customer requirements for your opportunity?

Figure 4.1 The market focus funnel

markets available for the product?' or, as one entrepreneur challenged his team, 'What is the *sales universe* for this product?'

If you are unfamiliar with marketing theory, the definition we are using of a market is the demand for a product or service within a given geographical, social or industry boundary. Segments are defined as the discrete customer groups within the market. These have a number of characteristics that enable different segments to be identified at increasing levels of precision.

Example: E-books

The electronic book (e-book) is not a recent invention, with the underlying technologies dating back to the 1960s developed at Brown University in the United States. However it took the development of the Internet and the agreement of the Open eBook format as a common standard to create the conditions for mass-market acceptance and growth. Yet despite early eBook devices (such as the failed Microsoft Reader) being introduced from the late 1990s, it was slow to take off in this way until first Amazon launched the Kindle in 2007 and Apple introduced the iPad in 2010. Both developed business models which enabled them to sell digital downloads of e-books to owners, and other reader devices were also introduced. These did not achieve the same success in the market until Samsung introduced the Android-based tablet as a serious competitor to the iPad.

During 2010, e-book sales at Amazon outstripped first its hardcover, then paperback sales. The format also enabled authors to write and self-publish e-books themselves, bypassing conventional publishers who entered the e-book market quite slowly and conservatively. An example is E.L. James, who self-published her 'Fifty Shades of Grey' erotic thriller and subsequent works as e-books, gaining a big cult following which enabled her to close a major publishing deal. Many other writers are taking advantage of the ability to self-publish, although few are likely to achieve similar success. There are many business ventures which have either started as a result of e-book opportunities, or existing businesses which have recognised that the growth in e-book publishing is unstoppable.

- The market for e-books can be segmented by using the following characteristics:
- Type of book: fiction: mainstream, crime fiction, thriller, romance, sci-fi, dark, erotica, etc.
- Non-fiction: comedy, history, true crime, sports, cooking, business, etc.
- Reader format: Kindle, iPad, Kobo, Sony Reader, Android reader (e.g., Samsung, Google)

- Internet download format: PDF, EPUB, TXT, RTF, DOC, HTML
- Preferred purchase channel: Amazon, iBooks, online library, eBook, BookBoon, MP3, file-swapping, other
- Average purchase value: free; less than £1, £1–2.99, £3–4.99, £5–£10, £10+
- Average monthly spend: less than £5, £5–£10, £10–20, £20–30, £30–40, £40+
- Age group: under 10, 10–15, 15–20, 20–30, 30–40, 40–55, 55+
- Social media sites and media channels most used: facebook, twitter, satellite or digital TV; websites; BBC radio; independent radio; magazines, newspapers
- Gender: male or female
- Ethnic group: white, Afro-Caribbean, Indian, Chinese, Arab, other

From these characteristics the target segment for a new online eBook magazine and catalogue business could be defined as: Female aged 30–55, Kindle owner reading mainstream, crime, romantic fiction is currently buying increasingly by download from Amazon, spending £20+ per month, using twitter and browsing news online, in any ethnic group.

Detailed consumer research could then take place with this group to identify their likes, dislikes, dissatisfaction with existing channels and their buying criteria for the new product.

Questions to use in conducting market research

The following questions are intended for use within the market focus funnel, in order to gauge the size and value of the market and to move from the 'big picture' of the potential markets to the characteristics of the target customer segment in the chosen market. An important point is that you are very unlikely to have all, or even most of this information when you start exploring the opportunity. What the questions do is give you a 'prompt' to suggest the type of questions you can ask to better understand the opportunity in the market-place. So even though you may be unlikely to find all the information needed to answer every question, the result should make you better informed both about the opportunity in the chosen market and what is still unknown.

Analysing the industry

- What is the structure of the industry at present: globally, nationally, regionally, locally? What is the buying chain from supplier to end user?
- Who are the dominant firms which supply the market? How do they exercise control over the market? What 'rules' or barriers to entry exist?
- Who are the existing suppliers which the new venture will compete with?

- What are their strengths and weaknesses?
- How can the new venture be differentiated from existing suppliers?
- How are competitors likely to respond to a new entrant to the market?
- Who else is known or likely to be working on a comparable opportunity? How far advanced are they? What advantages and disadvantages do they have? How fast can others replicate it?

Potential markets

- What are all the potential markets for the opportunity?
- What is the size of each market: global, national, regional, local?
- Can we find out the total value of each market in sales per year?
- Which of these markets are growing, static or declining?
- What channels and distribution platforms are these markets accessed by (e.g., wholesale distribution, retail, Internet, direct delivery, personal selling etc)?
- What share does each distribution channel have, which are increasing or decreasing?
- How intensive is the competition in each market?
- What percentage share of each market could be achieved within (say) two years?
- Which is the most attractive market to enter? (based on size, value, growth)

Target market

- How many customers are in the target market? Is this population increasing or decreasing?
- What is the anticipated lifetime of the market in years?
- What are the key factors which drive demand and price in the market?
- Who are the dominant sellers in the market?
- What are their market shares by per cent, their competitive strengths and weaknesses?

Customer segments

- How can the market be segmented, for example, by geography, industry sector (business/ institutional), socio-economic group, age range, occupation, interests (consumers), average spend and media consumption?
- What are the customer segments?
- Which of these are most attractive in terms of under-met needs or aspirations, growth in size/spend and affinity with product?
- How will the product be priced?
- What are the costs of gaining and selling to a new customer?
- Is the customer relationship loyalty-based or transaction-based (one-off)?
- Is the product or service a unique, desirable, essential or a discretionary commodity?

Target market segment

- Who are the target customers?
- What is known about these customers?
- What do they want or need? What do they like and dislike?
- Why would they want or need the product or service? What benefits and value-added will they gain from it?
- How far are these wants and needs met at present? How well are they met?
- What advantages over competitors can the business offer customers?
- What problems or dissatisfaction do the customers experience?
- What are their buying criteria: what, how and from whom to buy?
- How do target customers prefer to access information about and to buy the product or service? (e.g., by retail store, mobile phone, TV shopping channel, online, home visit)
- What selling and distribution channels will be used to reach the target customer segment?
- What is the average spend per customer per transaction and per year on this product?
- What percentage of the annual spend by this segment can the business secure?
- What factors do they see as 'value for money' and 'quality'?
- What are their 'affinity habits' – what related purchases do they make?
- What are their listening, viewing, Internet browsing, social media, reading, visiting habits?
- What factors will affect customer retention, repeat and added-value purchases?

Gathering this information is a process of market research. You will probably not be able to answer all of the questions, but the research process will generate useful information and reduce the uncertainty and risk associated with the opportunity. At the top three levels of the funnel this is mainly through secondary research. This can be done through the Internet and by using information normally held in university and business libraries, official publications and statistics, and Mintel and other market research reports can be used. The references section in the appendices lists useful sources. At the bottom level of the funnel, secondary information will only provide limited intelligence, so primary, direct research will be needed to generate the very specific information needed to really build up detailed understanding about the segment characteristics, to get to know the customer, and to be able to make informed decisions. A market research project that targets individuals or groups of people in the segment will be required. Corporate and well-resourced entrepreneurs may commission market research specialists to undertake this, whilst students, start-up entrepreneurs and smaller firms can normally do it themselves, which takes time but facilitates direct learning from the customer.

The methods available for direct market research can include:

- direct one-to-one interviews
- focus group meetings

- informal conversations at trade shows, network events etc.
- e-mail and electronic survey (e.g., SurveyMonkey) questionnaires
- social media, for example, via twitter, LinkedIn and facebook
- telephone interviews
- postal survey questionnaires.

Direct, personal contact requires the greatest investment of time, but also yields a higher level of qualitative knowledge about the customers and the opportunity than is achieved through remote questionnaires. Also, an initial list of prospective customers can be developed by retaining details from positive responses.

From the research process, a detailed picture of the market, the segment and the customers can be built up. This can be used to start developing the opportunity as a business model and provide vital information for the venture plan. This will be expanded in Chapter 5. Not all questions are applicable to every opportunity, and not all of the information is ever available. However the important point is for the entrepreneur to be posing the important questions for the business, trying to find the best information and deciding at what point there is enough information on which to make decisions.

Activity

This activity asks you to consider how you would use the market focus funnel as a research tool, and to apply it to a specific opportunity as described in this section. The objective is to gather as much relevant data as you can, which can be used to evaluate the opportunity in the next chapter and to reduce uncertainty. You probably have limited time and access to information, so you will need to be selective and focused in your research.
- How would you go about applying the market focus funnel to a real market opportunity?
- How would you gather the primary market research information?
- What information sources would you use?
- If you are working on a specific opportunity, then decide on the most relevant questions to investigate that opportunity. There are 44 questions of which you should aim to answer at least 30.
- Then conduct initial research using the funnel approach, and go down the funnel gathering data on as many of these questions as you are able. If you cannot find the information go on to the next question. Some of the questions in the final section on 'the customer and the new venture' ask you to start making initial decisions on the business in relation to customers.
- Keep the information you gather in the headings of the potential and target market, customer segment, industry analysis. This information will be used later in Chapter 5 to assess the opportunity.

■ Evaluating the opportunity

Having gathered information to assess the opportunity, the next stage is to use this to evaluate it. The purpose of opportunity evaluation is to assemble the known information about the opportunity, and use it to investigate essential, strategic questions. The answers will inform your decision-making on whether to go ahead with a venture to act on the opportunity, and in planning how to do so. Opportunity evaluation aims to reduce the risk of project failure by researching thoroughly all the relevant information on the factors which affect the project. It also aims to ensure that the opportunity identified offers attractive rewards, and that opportunities with lower potential are not progressed. The opportunity assessment (pentagon) tool included later in the chapter is designed to help you to make informed judgements about the potential value of opportunities.

The market focus funnel and accompanying questions can be used to gather detailed market information on the opportunity. Through bringing this information together, critical factors such as these can be identified:

- the reasons for a perceived opportunity; what and where it is
- the market opportunity for the business; its size, value and duration
- key market segments and customer groups, preferences and distribution channels
- the industry structure, driving forces and competition
- the dynamic effects of change on the industry
- who may support or invest in the business
- the options, resources and key factors for the business project.

This can be presented as a report which sets out the key information showing what the opportunity is, and what is known about it. Potential venture team members, sponsors, investors and partners can consider this and decide whether to go ahead with further development and planning of the project. This information can then be used as the knowledge base for the business proposal, which will be explained in Chapter 6.

The opportunity evaluation report can take the form of a portfolio of information, structured under the following headings:

- *The opportunity*: from opportunity map and DIFA summary
- *The market and customer information*: from market focus funnel
- *The industry and competition*: from market focus funnel
- *Impact of change*: from pentagon model (covered later in this chapter)
- *Investment and return*: from pentagon model

This covers the critical factors required to assess the viability and future prospects for the venture. A balanced decision on each opportunity can be taken, based on the relevant factors from these studies and other information. The evaluation reduces uncertainty through research and exploration, and can help to ensure that only higher potential opportunities that offer an acceptable degree of risk are progressed.

Activity

- Refer back to using the market focus funnel and the activity.
- If you were able to complete the activity, use the information to start to put together an evaluation report for your opportunity, under the headings 'opportunity' and 'market and customer information'.
- If you did not complete the activity, do it now:
- use the funnel approach to identify the target markets, available customer segments and target segment for your chosen opportunity
- work through the questions
- gather as much market information as you can about the target segment(s)
- identify what information is missing, and how you would collect this, for example, by primary market research.

You will return to and add further material to the opportunity evaluation report as you work through the activities in the chapter.

■ Types of opportunity

There are many different types of opportunity, and it is essential for the entrepreneur to be aware of the nature of the opportunity and its characteristics. Each type of opportunity involves actual or potential market demand, as explored in the market research process you have completed. This section presents eight general types of opportunity, and summarises the advantages, disadvantages and critical points for exploration of each one. None of these types are intrinsically 'better' or 'worse' but they do have distinctive characteristics which need to be considered early in the evaluation process. Innovative opportunities tend to bring together combinations of two or more types. This can make them more attractive and differentiated and hence potentially more innovative and rewarding. However one type will normally be dominant, and the combination may make them more complex to manage and possibly risky. The eight types are:

- knowledge
- technology
- product
- service or experience
- social market
- cultural, social or lifestyle
- physical resource
- trading and commodity.

Knowledge opportunities

Knowledge opportunities exist where specialist information, know-how or expertise can be applied to create value. The 'knowledge economy' arises from knowledge opportunity, and can be based on scientific, medical, market or other research, specialised skill or ability. Experienced professional and technical people often set up niche consultancy practices to use their specialist expertise, and these can be considered as knowledge opportunities. Knowledge resources can have major new markets, and knowledge opportunities are continually expanding. Universities, research institutes, consultancy practices, publishers and many others are players in the knowledge economy.

There are tensions between the drive for freely available information on the Internet and the business need to create commercial value by selling knowledge, and the related issues of ownership and protection of knowledge. For these reasons, successful exploitation of knowledge opportunity requires clear identification of the application of the knowledge, the target customers and the value of the knowledge to the customer, and a business model which enables income to be generated and captured.

For example, there is a huge drive towards 'open access' publishing. Traditionally, academic research has been published in scientific and other journals where the work is peer-reviewed, and authors and reviewers are not paid. Publishers then require subscriptions from libraries, organisations or individual who want to access the work. This model has been profitable for journal publishers, but it prevents access by most citizens and small firms. Open access means that research grant-awarding bodies require researchers to publish via open access journals or websites. Here, either the author or the institution pays a publication fee, and the work is available free to all readers.

Technology-based opportunities

Technology-based opportunities apply a technology to solve a problem, meet a need or create a new product or process. The technology may be physical, such as an engineering or manufacturing process or product, a chemical, biological or information-based technology, or a combination of these. Biotechnology, physical, material and earth science, organic and inorganic chemistry and computer programming are all examples of technology-based opportunity.

Whilst there are links and overlaps between the technology and the knowledge associated with it, it is the application of technology through innovation which provides the opportunity. The development of the science and technology base continues to provide growing opportunities for technology-based innovation. The issues associated with technology-based opportunity again include the importance of securing intellectual property, for example, through patenting, and of identifying both applications and potential customers.

Technology-based opportunity is usually highly skill and resource intensive, requiring significant research and development support and budgets. However the large organisations which have these resources often do not have the entrepreneurial approach required to exploit the opportunities, and there is significant potential for innovation by entrepreneurs who can aim to develop opportunities and to gain partnership or support from corporate organisations. Recent years have seen significant growth in spin-off and spin-out companies from universities and research institutions to enable technology applications to be commercialised.

Example: Wilson Solarpower

Wilson Solarpower developed a new system for generating economical and clean electricity from Concentrated Solar Power (CSP) which offered fundamental advantages over existing solar energy technology. Formed as Wilson Turbopower in 2001 as a spin-out company from Massachusetts Institute of Technology (MIT) it applied patented research on gas heat exchange technology using rotating discs. The indexed-rotation regenerator heat exchanger was the first major innovation in this field for 80 years and presented an enabling technology which significantly improved the efficiency of heat exchange systems in industrial, power generating and military applications. The major new opportunity seized by the company was in using CSP to generate compressed hot air to drive turbines derived from the earlier research, providing low-cost power generation with no water required for cooling. The system uses modular components allowing an installation to be rapidly scaled-up to meet energy demand in domestic, industrial and military sector applications. (www.wilsonsolarpower.com)

Product opportunities

Product opportunities are where existing products can be used to meet market demand as they are, or can be, adapted by incremental innovation where new markets can be found. This means that significant product innovation may not be required, but market development is needed to research, prepare the market and promote the product. It is also necessary to be able to source the product, either by manufacturing or by buying-in. It is advantageous if the product is exclusive and sought-after, and the source of supply can be restricted or is intellectual property that can be protected through patents or design rights. Otherwise, if successful, it will quickly become a commodity product and be copied by other firms at lower cost; trading and commodity opportunities are covered later. Product opportunities of this kind are often best exploited by alert traders who are able to spot product/market opportunities, respond quickly and move on as competition increases and prices fall.

Examples are often seen in the fashion world, where premium designer ranges are shown at fashion shows and highly priced for a limited market. But imitation and copying rapidly takes place of the successful designs and derivative, low-cost clothes manufactured in Asia rapidly appear as ready-to-wear on websites and with mainstream clothes retailers.

Service opportunities

Service opportunities exist where there is actual or potential demand for a service by business or public organisations, individuals or groups. The 'service economy' grew steadily in the United Kingdom from the 1980s, when it overtook the manufacturing economy, and it covers a very wide range of activities. Services can include, for example, health, child and social care; office services; personal and social, telecommunications and computing, education and training; and financial, legal and property services. A service is intangible; there is no physical product, and whilst knowledge and especially Internet technology are increasingly likely to be used in providing the service, they are generally not significant outputs from it. A service opportunity can include a new business model which provides a service more effectively or at less cost than competitors.

There are a myriad of small and large service providers, from the freelance secretary/personal administrator who runs a support service for self-employed consultants, to firms such as Regus who provide serviced office accommodation for small firms, and self-storage facilities to serve a growing market. There are clear advantages to service opportunities. Barriers to entry are often low, as is the level of investment required. By being innovative, spotting a gap in the market and working hard to build up a customer base through providing a personal, consistent level of service, a level of success can be achieved so long as there is scope to develop the market niche and the business is well managed.

Service businesses have much to commend them, and they are the backbone of the small business economy in developed countries such as the United States and United Kingdom. However most are destined to stay small, which often reflect the founders' goals. There is a continuous flow of both start-ups and closures in this sector. Most service ideas are hard to protect and can be copied if the model is successful. The most important aspect of a service business is providing a high-quality experience which meets customers' needs. Service firms have to work hard to provide distinctive, memorable experiences and build up a repeat customer base. Many attempt to build recognisable brands and grow through such strategies as franchising, but few break through to become large businesses. It is often hard for a service business to grow significantly. Many exist because of the founder's ability to provide or supervise the work directly, but they may be unable to make the transition into managing others to provide the service or run the business day-to-day.

The economics of the service firm depend on the net profit margin between the sales revenue and the fixed and variable costs, in which staff costs are one of the largest elements. Competition tends to force margins down, and it is difficult to build up retained profits to grow organically or by acquiring other businesses without external investment. Service businesses which grow significantly tend to be those where innovation can both increase customer service responsiveness and choice whilst lowering costs; an industry sector which is growing rapidly; or those with entrepreneurial management who are able to gain external investment to fund a growth strategy.

Social market opportunities

Social market opportunities exist in the space where people and communities have needs, generally for services, which are not met effectively by profit-based businesses. There may be state-based services which are either inadequate to respond to demand or where these may be withdrawn to reduce public spending. Social market opportunities tend to reflect partial or total market failure for free-enterprise services, for example, in areas such as child care, affordable housing, access to health care, education and small loans. Generally the users would be unable to pay the full costs, so funding is required from a combination of public, private and charitable sources. Social market opportunities are increasingly the subject of social enterprises and social innovations which recognise that needs have to be met with new economic models. Social innovation is a rapidly growing movement in which new technologies and approaches are applied to social market needs. Social innovation is explored in Chapter 6 (see the Open Book of Social Innovation, NESTA 2010).

Credit unions are an example of a social market opportunity. They provide an alternative access to savings and small loans for people who find it difficult to become customers of orthodox for-profit banks. Credit unions are owned by their members, effectively as co-operatives, and only members can deposit money, and after a period can make loans. Credit unions are often very small, and they can fail, but they fulfil a growing need for access to financial services, often for people and communities which are unattractive to mainstream banks. Yet they can also offer more personalised services. In the United Kingdom, Credit unions managed over £900 million in savings from over 1 million people, with loans worth £676 million in 2013 (Association of British Credit Unions Ltd, 2013).

Lifestyle, social and cultural opportunities

Lifestyle opportunity originated within the service sector, but has grown so rapidly worldwide that it merits its own category. Lifestyle opportunity is where customers are provided with an experience which makes their life easier or pleasanter. The fields where such opportunities arise include leisure, tourism, hospitality, culture and entertainment. These are all areas of discretionary expenditure, where people wish to consume or experience sports, food and drink, films, music, drama, dance and other pleasures. It should not be confused with what is sometimes described as a 'lifestyle business', which an owner-manager runs to finance his or her lifestyle rather than to grow.

Advantages of lifestyle opportunities are that in a growing economy demand increases as people have additional money to spend. A downturn will reduce some types of consumer spending but other parts of the leisure economy may remain healthy. Consumer fashion and taste play a major part and can be fickle, with people becoming bored with an experience and moving on. Businesses such as restaurants are especially prone to this, but others such as personal fitness gyms and dance studios can have a more durable appeal if they meet their customers' expectations for service and innovate in ways they appreciate. The ideas of 'cultural diffusion' and 'growing the fan base' apply to the appeal which creative and lifestyle businesses need to offer their customers. Repeat business, referral and word-of-mouth promotion is vital for most lifestyle opportunities but social media – specifically facebook and twitter – have become vital aspects of service business marketing.

There are many examples of lifestyle opportunity businesses. The 'Blockbuster' home video rental chain grew from offering the widest range of visual media products (video, DVD and computer games) for rental in urban/suburban outlets, and being able to meet the demand for a wide selection of recent and older film releases of all genres. Blockbuster made many independent video rental stores irrelevant, and themselves moved online but too late, threatened first by the growth of the postal DVD rental service, and then by downloading and online movies. Blockbuster went into administration and then closed in the United Kingdom in 2013. Lovefilm, owned by Amazon, shows how they were replaced by easy-to access DVD rental and movie download service.

Physical resource opportunities

Physical resource opportunities include the exploitation of land, water or naturally occurring resources. This includes extracting basic resources, such as oil, gas and minerals. It also includes land use such as agricultural production, and land, property and real estate development. Although this is a wide range of types of opportunity, in all cases the source is the ability to create value based on a natural or physical resource, either renewable, such as wind power and agriculture, or finite, such as mineral extraction.

Advantages of physical resource opportunities include the rapidly increasing demand, pressure for access and consumption of resources as the world population, energy needs and economic development grow, driving price increases in oil, mineral and water costs. Greater innovation in the exploitation of resources enhances opportunity and the value created, as in the controversial area of genetically modified crop production. However, advances in the technology of food production have led to declining incomes for many farmers worldwide, and a challenge for many rural economies is how to add value and diversify to reduce their dependence on economically marginal food production, as shown in the Tyrrell's case in Chapter 1. Physical resource opportunities tend to involve long-term investment, with significant capital employed for long periods in land ownership, resource extraction or renewable power generation. Risk management is always a major factor in physical resource businesses, whether caused by natural factors such as weather or geology, or economic and social factors such as falling demand, changes in taste or opposition to a particular policy or practice, such as mineral extraction.

The rapid growth in the production and consumption of bottled drinking water is an example of physical resource-based opportunity. In most developed countries, tap water meets acceptable standards for drinking, yet sales of much more profitable bottled water continue to grow rapidly for reasons of fashion, taste, convenience and perceived health benefits. In the United Kingdom, major retailers were found to be filtering normal tap water and selling this in bottled form as a basic-price product.

Trading and commodity opportunities

Trading and commodity opportunities are based on buying and selling in relation to market conditions of supply and demand. They encompass a wide range of trading opportunities, including wholesale and retail, energy (gas, oil, electricity), chemicals, raw materials, semi-manufactured items, food and agricultural produce and any commodity which can be bought, traded or sold, including securities, currency, stocks and purchase options. Trading requires the ability to predict and act on market trends, with exposure to risks of changing market demand and pricing. The potential for profit can be very high, but excellent information and significant reserves are required to support trading activity and to cover potential losses.

Online trading has revolutionised and expanded trading opportunities. eBay shows the way in which individuals can trade, creating a market and online business in the most specialised items and commodities. One example of trading opportunity was Enron, which owned a national gas pipeline network in the United States. The CEO, Kenneth Lay, recognised the pipeline network was an opportunity to buy gas where it was cheap and sell where it was needed. He created spot markets for energy, financial models for trading in energy futures and promoted deregulation which changed the industry. For a period it paid off. Enron was named one of the 'most admired' companies by *Fortune* magazine and ranked No. 1 in innovation. It collapsed through over-expansion, lack of financial control, corporate mismanagement and fraud on a grand scale.

Activity

This section has discussed the different types of opportunity in general terms. Specific opportunities may overlap between two categories, or possibly more. Use Table 4.1 to consider the opportunity you are exploring and write your responses to the following points:
• Which of these type(s) of opportunity do you think it is?
• If it falls into more than one category, which is the dominant type?
• What do you think are the advantages, disadvantages and specific points for exploration of your opportunity in relation to this type?

Table 4.1 Types of opportunity grid

Type of opportunity	Advantages	Disadvantages	Points to explore
Knowledge			
Technology			
Product			
Service			
Social market			
Lifestyle, social, cultural			
Physical resource			
Trading/commodity			

■ Assessing the environment for your opportunity

The developed world is an opportunity-rich environment, although this was depressed by economic recession after 2008. In economically developing countries, there are also many opportunities but access to the resources, technology and other means of exploiting them can be more limited, sometimes costly and challenging. Yet it is also clear that fast developing countries such as China, India and Brazil with growing economies can offer many more attractive growth opportunities than mature European and North American markets. This section summarises the main factors which affect the context, or 'bigger picture' within which specific opportunities are explored and which are likely to be outside the entrepreneur's control. It is necessary to assess the relationships between economic, environmental, political, social, technological forces and entrepreneurial activity. You may have done a STEEP or PESTEC analysis on a Business Studies course; this approach is similar, but is focused on analysis of the environment for the opportunity. These factors may in themselves create opportunities and will either positively or adversely affect the ability to exploit the opportunity.

Economic factors

These include the economic stability of the country or market, the conditions of economic growth or recession, predictability or volatility in demand, pricing, level of inflation, exchange rates of the currency to be used and availability and cost of investment or loan finance. These factors have shifted markedly in recent years, even in previously 'stable' markets such as Southern European states within the Eurozone, which makes business management very challenging.

Environmental factors

The natural and physical environment includes factors such as climate change (increasing unpredictability of weather patterns), lack of rain and water shortage or excessive rainfall, and availability of natural and physical resources. Geographical factors, including the concentration of population in urban areas or distribution in rural districts, transport and communications such as road networks, airports, fast rail links, telephone and data networks, and levels of congestion may all be significant factors. The cost of data transmission via high-speed broadband or mobile phone network, and transport, either through delays caused by congestion or charges such as tolls for road use, are increasingly important but may present new opportunities for alternative logistics, communication and distribution businesses.

Political factors

Political factors include the level of political stability, and the extent of support for enterprise development at the local, regional, national and supranational levels. The level of legislation and regulation and the ways in which this is administered, the transparency of government processes and the presence or absence of corruption in government are all relevant and have a major bearing on the ease and attractiveness of operating a business venture. The time taken to start a new business in different countries varies considerably, from less than a day in the United Kingdom to several weeks even in other EU states. Certain countries are much more conducive to enterprise than others; registering and starting a new business in France or Germany, for example, is relatively bureaucratic and time-consuming when compared with the United States or United Kingdom, caused by regulation and procedures which were not designed with free enterprise in mind and have the effect of reducing opportunity entrepreneurship. Factors such as political influence and official corruption continue to be significant in some post-Soviet and developing-world states.

Social factors

The cultural acceptability of entrepreneurship is changing markedly in many societies, but this is only one factor. Others include demographics; many developed societies have ageing populations, in contrast to the 'youth' of many developing countries. Health and diseases such as HIV/AIDS have had a major effect on many African and Asian countries. Levels of education, including literacy, numeracy and language, are important factors. Generational change brings changes in taste, fashion, media awareness and use of communications technologies in all countries, providing new market opportunities for such products and services.

For example, when the ten accession states joined the European Union in 2004, the levels of education, linguistic fluency and enterprising culture in some of the new states such as Estonia and Lithuania, especially among young people who had grown up in the post-Soviet era, were appreciably greater than in some of the existing EU members. The potential for entrepreneurial development both within those countries and by their citizens in other EU states is very significant. The development of Finland's economy in recent years illustrates the potential for relatively small states with high levels of education and entrepreneurial culture as they emerge from state control. It is increasingly clear that the high social costs, employment protection, legislation and taxation levels in some older European states make them relatively less competitive and attractive for entrepreneurship, and reform continues to be needed. The EU 'Lisbon Agenda' set out in 2000 with an intention to create a much more open and enterprising climate within the EU in which entrepreneurship and innovation would drive economic growth, yet by 2013, little progress had been made in achieving the desired economic changes across the EU and there had been major reversals and tensions arising from the recession and financial crisis.

Technological factors

These factors include the level of technological development in the market. They include: access to fast communication media such as Internet, broadband and mobile phones; the support for technological development and innovation such as research institutes and universities with relevant expertise; enablers and constraints to the implementation of technology. Industry clusters and networks are major factors in technological development, and the role of these is considered later in this chapter.

The interaction between time and technology is important. There is a 'product lifecycle' between innovation and obsolescence, and in certain economies and industries this can be very short; for example, fashion drives rapid innovation in mobile phone and computing devices such as the iPad. Other markets have different rates of obsolescence for different products, so that some product lifecycles may be longer in less developed markets such as Africa, where low-cost utility rather than fashion is important.

Summary of contextual and environmental factors

Economic

- How economic trends affect the opportunity, for example,
  - currency/exchange rate fluctuations
  - economic growth or decline in demand; boom or recession
  - cost and availability of lending and small business finance
  - debt deters investment or spending
  - strength of demand for key resources, for example, people, land, materials, fuel
  - taxation

Environmental

- Restriction and cost of resources, for example, fuel, waste disposal
- Transport, planning, environmental compliance

Political

- Stability or volatility
- Political support for entrepreneurship
- Legal framework, impact of future legislation and its effect on business, for example, compliance costs
- Harmonisation of laws or standards
- Ethical or corrupt ways of doing business

Social and cultural

- What are the relevant demographic trends?
- What cultural influences affect it? For example, fashion, lifestyle, media?
- Acceptability of entrepreneurial activity
- Growth in social market opportunities

Technological

- How is new technology affecting the industry?
- What are the key innovations now and in the near future?
- How is the Internet affecting the market?

Activity

The impacts of these factors will differ according to the type of opportunity. A physical-resource-based opportunity will be especially affected by environmental factors, for example. These factors may enable or constrain the opportunity. Some factors may not apply in a significant way to a given opportunity.

Assess the impact of economic, environmental, political, social and technological factors on the opportunity you have identified, using Table 4.2 to log your responses.

Table 4.2 Environmental analysis of the opportunity

Factor	Advantages	Disadvantages	Points to explore
Economy			
Environment			
Political			
Social			
Technology			

■ Opportunity evaluation, assessment and decision-making

Clearly some opportunities are 'better' than others, and it is necessary to have methods for comparing, assessing and evaluating opportunities to enable the most attractive ones to be selected. This means that we can screen and select opportunities to identify those with higher or lower potential and use this information to decide which to invest effort and resources in, and which to avoid unless we can find ways of increasing their attractiveness as an investment of financial and entrepreneurial resources. This section introduces a framework for opportunity assessment and evaluation called the pentagon model, because it includes five dimensions. The assessment questionnaire and further information on its use is included in the toolbox.

The pentagon model: assessing five key dimensions of opportunity potential

These five key dimensions show how the potential of any opportunity can be assessed. By using these, an opportunity can be evaluated as an investment proposition and decisions reached on its attractiveness – initially by the entrepreneur, and by other investors. The five decision-making dimensions, which are called the pentagon model of opportunity assessment, are shown in Table 4.3 and described thereafter. The information necessary to complete the questionnaire in the toolkit should be available from the activities already completed.

Investment

Resources must be invested to realise any type of opportunity. The nature of the investment is likely to be a combination of the following:

- Financial: capital belonging to the entrepreneur; venture capital from an investor; equity or loan finance. This may be used for start-up capital, to fund working capital or for business expansion, and may be invested in fixed assets, product or market development or working expenses prior to break-even.
- Non-financial resources such as productive capacity, staff time and capability. These represent an 'opportunity cost' since the resources could be used alternatively for a different reward.

Table 4.3 Five dimensions of opportunity

Investment of resource	from none to high
Risk and uncertainty	from certainty to unpredictability
Return and value created	from none to high
Impact of innovation and change	from none to great
Timescale	from now into the future

- Intangible resources such as knowledge, information, expertise, intellectual property rights.
- Reputation, such as branding, partnering, social capital and credibility.

The size of the investment as well as its nature is significant and needs to be calculated: how much is required, over what period? What proportion of the entrepreneur's own resources does this represent, and what additional resources are required? If so, who will contribute them, and on what terms? Finally, what does the investment actually buy? Is it tangible assets which have a disposal value or simply an opportunity? This leads on to the concept of risk. Intangible factors such as branding can have considerable value: for example, a product endorsed by a corporate brand (such as an Apple iPhone app) will have much greater market attraction than one without such support.

Risk and uncertainty

It is essential to evaluate the degree of risk involved in exploiting an opportunity. Risk arises from uncertainty, so if complete certainty should exist, there is no risk; conversely, complete unpredictability of outcome produces very high risk. In a financial market, a UK or US government bond has a guaranteed rate of return and offers much greater certainty and hence less risk than, for example, a bond from a country or corporation with a low credit rating, or a newly floated biotechnology stock where the outcome is highly uncertain and there is a high risk. Entrepreneurs are often stereotyped as risk-takers, but this has little bearing in fact; successful entrepreneurs seek to minimise and avoid risk as far as possible, preferring other investors to carry the financial exposure. However entrepreneurs frequently operate in conditions of rapid change and uncertainty which give rise to unpredictable outcomes. Also, where the venture innovates and introduces change into the marketplace, it introduces new risk factors because the outcome is to some extent unpredictable. The aim is to identify what factors lead to uncertainty, and how far these can be reduced.

Identifying the risk factors

The variable factors which cause risk need to be identified. They may include:

- *Knowledge*: lack of information about market factors and likely demand
- *The economy*: fluctuations in macro-economic factors such as market stability, debt, currency exchange and interest rates
- *Technology*: will the technology work as planned?
- *Financial factors*: are the financial costings and plans realistic and achievable?
- *Competition*: how will competitors respond?
- *Customers*: will they buy and pay as expected?

- *Supply chain*: will suppliers and distributors deliver as expected?
- *Human elements*: does the venture team have the management skills, experience, credibility and expertise to manage the venture, based on their track records?

The potential risks to the venture should be identified and then be divided into *controllable* and *uncontrollable*. The former are those that can be reduced or eliminated. Examples include lack of market or product information, where focused research can take place to fill gaps; technology which can be demonstrated and tested; customer, supplier or distributor dependability, where research, credit rating and negotiation can take place; and skills gaps where staff recruitment can reduce risk. *Uncontrollable* risks are a function of factors in the economic and market environment together with the completely unpredictable. For each of these there is a need to establish:

- How serious is the risk – could it destroy the business?
- How likely is it?
- What are likely to be the earliest warning signs of the risk arising?
- What contingency plans can be drawn up to respond to the event?
- How can the effects of the risk on the business be minimised or insured against?

In these ways the risks to the venture can be established and either they can be prevented or their effects can be assessed and plans to deal with them made. But risk can never be predicted or eliminated entirely and managing risk is an integral aspect of entrepreneurial management, which will be addressed in Chapter 7.

Return and value created

The return on the investment, or reward, may vary from nothing – a total loss of the investment – to high, which may be a return of several hundred per cent. An assessment of the acceptability of the return should take into account the following factors:

- The amount invested; it may be acceptable to lose a small investment completely.
- Return in relation to risk: the higher the risk, the higher the return which will normally be expected.
- The timescale over which the return will come. Risk tends to increase further ahead in time.
- The form of the return, for example, as capital growth of the investment or as a flow of income. An asset such as property or equity in a company may show both capital growth through a rise in its value and an income flow from dividends or rentals. But negative returns (losses) in both capital and revenue are possible.
- The exit strategy from the opportunity, for example, as liquidation of assets, sale as a going concern, flotation, value anticipated and timescale for exit.

The matrix in Table 4.4 shows the basic dimensions of risk and reward. In this simple model, clearly position 1 is the optimum, offering a high return at low risk. Both positions 2 and 3 are less attractive, 2 offering low risk but at low return and 3 offering high return but at high risk. Position 4 is clearly to be avoided since the prospects are of high risk and low return. Such a two-dimensional model may be used for quick personal investment decisions, but it is of limited application in appraising complex business opportunities, where many other factors, such as the characteristics of the industry sector, apply.

Impact of innovation and change

Exploiting an opportunity both creates change and is affected by other changes in the dynamic market environment. Innovating and introducing a completely new concept or product, such as the iPad or e-book, introduce fundamental changes into the market. Disruptive innovations such as these change the value creation process of the industry, making existing products or businesses obsolete, creating new markets and altering the power dynamics of the industry. An enhancement to a current product is a moderate, incremental change, and a replication of something that already exists represents little or no change.

It is necessary to assess the impact of change caused by the opportunity. Will exploiting it drive and lead a change process, or is it passive, causing little change but being affected by external change? Strategic and disruptive innovation can reduce competitors' power and create new markets. A process innovation which enables a new business to offer lower prices than existing suppliers will attract existing and probably new customers, thus changing customer expectations and behaviour; the introduction of low-cost air carriers expanded the air travel market, polarising customer expectations between low-cost, no-frills service and high-cost standard service. A disruptive innovation may make previous standard products obsolete, as with the impact of e-mail on the fax machine, or MP3 formats on recorded music CDs. The impact of such changes can be felt throughout the supply chain, affecting suppliers, resellers, customers and sources of finance, as well as competitors. A new venture offering innovation also invites copying and retaliation from competitors.

The impact of introducing innovation and change into the market is to some extent unpredictable, because they increase risk rather than reducing it. Any business is also subject to external changes such as macro-economic factors and market trends that influence customer

Table 4.4 Risk and reward

	Seek to increase ⟶		
High risk	4	3	Seek to decrease
Low risk	2	1	
	Low return	High return	

behaviour; supply and demand changes leading to price fluctuations; technological advance; and changes in the legislation, regulation and so on, which can be assessed under the heading of risk.

Timescale

The timescale for the venture needs to be assessed. Achieving the right timing is often a critical factor in entrepreneurial decision-making, and points to consider here include:

- Is the timing of entry leading 'the rest' of the market, which may give an advantage but also require greater investment? Is it entering the market at the same time as competitors, or is it trailing others into a mature or declining market?
- What is the duration of the opportunity – from short to long term?
- What is the lead time needed to enter the market?
- When will the investment achieve a return?

Return and timescale are connected, because the essential distinction is between rapid profit opportunities which may be quite short term, and longer-term businesses which will take longer to establish and to achieve a return. Someone considering a soft drinks business could simply aim to buy and sell cold drinks to people in the summer as a profit opportunity, or might see a longer-term opportunity to offer new flavours and types of drinks with an innovative, appealing brand.

The return on the investment together with the expected timescale needs to be established as realistically as possible. 'Best case', 'most likely' and 'worst case' scenarios can be built into these forecasts to forecast:

- the investment required over the timescale
- the sales revenue to be generated as a cash stream and when this starts
- the gross and net profit margins on sales
- the break-even point
- the return on capital employed
- growth in the asset value of the investment.

The time period is highly significant. It may be that in establishing a new venture a loss is made in year one, requiring further working capital, break-even is achieved in year two and a profit is made from year three. The longer the investment period, the higher the rate of return needs to be. The nature of the gain to the investor needs to be clear, in terms of returns from trading profits and growth in the value of the investment, which can be realised through an exit strategy and sale of the equity at some point. Most businesses take longer to launch and consume more start-up capital than projected, as will be shown in Chapter 5 on venture planning. Computer spreadsheets make forecasting straightforward so long as accurate and realistic data can be obtained.

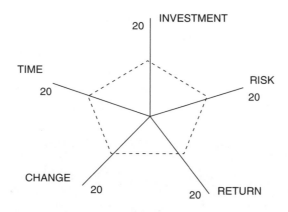

Figure 4.2 The pentagon model of opportunity assessment

The five dimensions of the pentagon model are shown in Figure 4.2 and can be used to evaluate the prospects for successfully exploiting an opportunity and therefore to decide whether the opportunity is an attractive one. The decision-making process is complex, and it is likely that almost every entrepreneur would weigh up a venture in a different way. The process is more complex than the simple bivariate '2 x 2' matrix shown in Table 4.4 which relates 'risk to return' alone. Therefore, having a standard method has advantages because it enables opportunities to be compared, and different approaches or business models applied to the same opportunity. The dimensions can be changed, so, for example, a social enterprise using this approach might well modify the 'impact of change' dimension to 'impact on community'. The questionnaire in the toolkit enables each dimension to be scored on a 20-point scale.

Using the questionnaire, a profile can be drawn on the pentagon model. Each dimension is given a scale from 0 to 20. Zero is 'none' and 20 is 'high'. Any given opportunity can then be given a series of values along the score. These in themselves will involve a series of objective (factual) and subjective, interpretative choices being made, involving available information, past experience, prospective judgement and so on. They may be relatively unscientific, but they represent decisions which would be made, often on the basis of 'gut feel', intuition or experience, by an entrepreneur. The scores along each dimension then represent a distinctive pentagon.

Opportunities that have characteristics of greater risk, higher reward, bigger investment, larger scale change and medium/longer-term timescales can be described as more 'aggressive' or ambitious in the venture strategies which would be required to launch them, and will have a large profile when drawn on the pentagon. Those with lower degrees of investment, risk, reward, change and short-medium timescales can be described as more 'defensive', with a tightly grouped profile on the pentagon. There are also many combinations which have elements of both.

A defensive profile, scoring low in most aspects, would not require sophisticated entrepreneurial strategy or skills. An aggressive profile, scoring higher, indicates that a strategy to exploit it would require much more advanced management capability to be successful. Each opportunity therefore has its own profile, representing a view at that moment of its potential. If a venture is launched to exploit the opportunity, each of the variables has its own dynamic and may shift in either direction at any stage in the life of the venture.

Activity

- Look at the opportunity assessment questionnaire in the toolkit and read through the questions in each dimension.
- Apply the pentagon model to the opportunity you have developed.
- Do you have all the information required? If not, what additional information would you need to gather to be able to answer the questions? You can either make estimates, and complete it again when you have more reliable information, or you can work on it as you develop the opportunity over the next few chapters.
- If you have completed the market research in the market focus funnel, will this provide the information needed to complete the assessment?
- How could the opportunity be changed to increase its attractiveness as an investment?
- Add the completed pentagon to your opportunity evaluation report.

Assessing high- and low-value opportunities

The aim of opportunity assessment and evaluation is to distinguish between opportunities with high potential for creating value and those with lower potential, which are less attractive investments for effort and resource. The terms 'value creation' and 'value capture' are explained in the section on business models in this chapter.

There can be no one way of establishing the potential return with a high degree of certainty. Instead, tools are used which give a degree of predictive judgement based on experience. Even venture capital funds with extensive experience in investing in many enterprises know most of the investment decisions they make will turn out to be ones that, in hindsight, they would not have taken because the ventures fail or under-perform. Their funds gain an investment return from the small number of businesses which perform very well and aim to exceed the losses made on the poor performers. In assessing opportunities, prospective judgements are made about the potential for venture growth and success, based on many variables, and aiming to reduce risk and uncertainty as far as possible, to a manageable level. But judgement and intuition still entail an element of risk that is inevitable and comes with the territory.

Why are some opportunities not worth exploring?

The purpose of opportunity assessment is to select the most promising opportunities which are worth developing further, by investing initially time and then financial and other resources in them. In this process, the majority of opportunities will be screened out for various reasons, either because they are less attractive, fundamentally flawed or the combination of time, attractiveness and resources is not right to pursue them. It is easy – but dangerous – for the entrepreneur to be so emotionally engaged and passionate about 'their idea' that they cannot bear to abandon it. But an essential skill is being able to stand back and take a balanced view about the prospects for making it a success. Here are some common features found in opportunities which are not likely to be successful, and should normally be abandoned.

- It replicates what is already being done, with insufficient innovation of value to the end user
- The potential market is too small, not well defined, or shrinking
- Initial target customers will not commit to the project
- Alternatives are already being developed which offer greater advantages
- The entrepreneur does not have specific expertise or knowledge in the industry sector, technology or service
- Initial resources to invest cannot be identified
- A prototype, pilot or test version cannot be shown to work
- A realistic break-even point cannot be established with confidence
- The degree of risk is too great

■ In search of the better business model: capturing and creating value

A vital component of the successful opportunity is the development of an effective business model. Creating a business model will be covered in more detail in Chapter 5, but at this stage the essential features need to be understood as part of the process of opportunity exploration.

A business model represents the ways in which the opportunity creates and captures value. An important principle is that there are multiple types of value as shown in Figure 4.3.

The opportunity creates value in a range of forms through the activities and steps taken to exploit it. A viable business model requires that a proportion of the value created is captured by the business, to meet the costs and to be able to redistribute and reinvest this in the business. So whilst we might normally think in terms of purely creating and capturing financial value as traditionally being paramount and more important than other forms of value creation, this is a simplistic 'old entrepreneurship' view. Financial value only arises in most cases as a result of what may be quite complex forms of non-financial value creation. Financial value includes:

- profit stream and share dividend
- return on capital employed
- balance sheet valuation of the business assets and liabilities
- valuation of shares

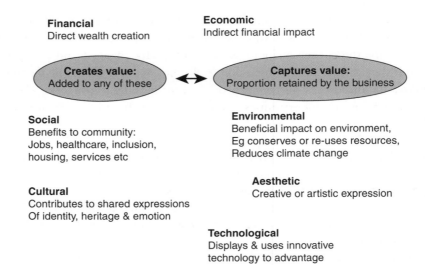

Figure 4.3 Creating and capturing multiple sources of value

Example

London staged the Olympic Games in summer 2012. This had required a major programme of investment to create the events stadia, Olympic Village and transport links on a vast area of land which required regeneration in East London from 2002 onwards. The costs of staging the Games grew far beyond the initial estimates and there was much criticism of whether the Games were 'affordable'. Yet the events were highly successful, even though the question of what direct return the project provided on the investment remained uncertain. It undoubtedly created and captured significant value in all categories.

Financial: Income from direct ticket sales, sponsorship, commercial activities and licensing.

Economic: Stimulus to construction and employment in other industries in a depressed area at a time of recession. Increase in visitor numbers and spending, partly offset by reductions elsewhere during the events.

Cultural: Olympic Flame journey through the United Kingdom engaged much of the population with a 'feelgood factor'. Opening and closing ceremonies viewed worldwide, promoting the United Kingdom in a new way, and created massive goodwill towards the events and the country. Brought competitive sports teams together from all countries to celebrate the best in sporting achievement.

Social: Created employment and housing with 'legacy' of sports facilities for future events. Significant boost to sports in schools and communities with health benefits.

Aesthetic: Opening and closing ceremonies showcased excellence in British culture. Sporting performances provided brilliant spectator and broadcast entertainment. Architecture, design and construction of facilities created a 'public good'.

Technological: Innovative use made of wide range of technologies in design and construction, events management, ticketing, security, broadcasting, with events screened remotely in many town and city centres.

Environmental: Regenerated derelict land; environmentally sustainable construction, event management and transport.

This example shows that financial value capture is just one important part of a wider map of value creation and control. The non-financial value can be measured through both financial and non-financial indicators – for example, for social value, the value of jobs and housing created, and health impacts from increased participation in sports can be projected.

Activity

Focus on your opportunity.
1. What value can it create in each of the following ways? Think radically and flexibly about the categories.
- Financial
- Economic
- Social
- Cultural
- Aesthetic
- Technological
- Environmental
2. What indicators could you use to measure the non-financial value?
3. How can the opportunity capture a proportion of the financial and non-financial value it generates? That is, by ensuring it is attributed to the opportunity alone, not distributed more widely.

An important balance is the 'value created' by an opportunity which may be free to the user and society, and the 'value captured' as a result of this, and how this is done.

Example: Wikipedia

The Wikipedia Internet encyclopedia site is used by over 400 million people each month worldwide as a resource, and many also provide their time and expertise free to update and extend it through collaborative content creation. It is the fifth most visited website worldwide and does not carry advertising, being free of any commercial links, so what is the business model?

The Wikimedia Foundation represents a worldwide, volunteer-driven movement which values knowledge as being free, shared with every human being worldwide through openness and diversity, information as accurate and unbiased, independence protected.

In 2010–2011 its revenue, exclusively from grants and donations, was $24,784,000 with an increasing third of this from over 500,000 small, online donations. Wikimedia has set itself ambitious strategic targets for increasing its global reach and inclusivity to 1 billion users and to engage many more people in the global south. It expected its revenues to double to $50 million to finance this. By 2013 they had reached over $48 million.

(https://wikimediafoundation.org/wiki/Home)

Within existing industries, there are opportunities to introduce new business models which create superior value or cost efficiency. Over the past ten years many of these have used Internet and mobile phone technologies to create new ways of exchanging ideas and social value. Some have radically reduced transaction costs, for example, in marketing, financial services and retailing. Examples of new business models which have challenged or transformed existing industries include Apple in mobile phones, computing and media purchase. MoneySupermarket.com became market-leaders in promoting and retailing financial services and products online in the United Kingdom. There are also many examples of new business models being introduced as a key aspect of an innovative service or product which did not already exist. Examples of these include eBay in creating new markets for online auctions and trading.

What such businesses have in common is their success in creating a business model which is both more convenient and attractive as well as cost-competitive than those used by existing players in the industry, and using this to offer customers a service with distinctive features – usually cheaper, possibly also faster, more convenient, personalised or with features that existing providers simply did not offer. Whilst these are successful examples, there are many cases of less successful or failed attempts to introduce a new business model, and the model itself should be seen as one highly important aspect in the overall business concept, rather than the 'whole deal'.

Here are suggestions for recognising opportunities for a better business model in an existing market:

- Look for industries which are dominated by large, high-price and high-profit operators who provide indifferent service.
- Analyse the business process being used: where is the value being created for the customer? Where are the costs being incurred?
- How can you provide what the customer really wants whilst eliminating as much of the costs as possible?
- Think radically about how essential activities can be provided at less cost, for example:
  - online and automated rather than by people
  - using advanced technology applications more effectively to deliver cost and speed or service performance improvements

- offshore in a low-cost economy
- in bulk by a specialist provider.
- Engage the customer in 'co-creating' the value by doing some of the work rather than providing the service for them
- Develop the new business model, comparing it with the competition to find vital features where it provides superior cost efficiency, and other features the customer will value over existing providers.

Example: Glassesdirect.co.uk

James Murray Wells recognised that high-street chains of opticians were charging £150 for spectacle frames and lenses which actually cost a fraction of the price. They were providing eye examinations and prescriptions at a fixed cost which encouraged customers in, and then charged a high profit margin for the supply of the frames and lenses or contact lenses to support their expensive retail premises and staff costs. In 2004, Wells set up Glasses Direct to offer a low cost alternative and sell glasses at prices starting at around £15.

Glassesdirect uses Internet technology to radically reduce transaction costs and offer much lower prices to customers. The website asks customers for their eye prescription from an optician and offers a wide range of spectacle frames and lens options. At their central laboratory they assemble frames and lenses sourced direct from the manufacturers and send the finished spectacles to the customer, with credit card payment online. The customer can save as much as 60% of the cost in comparison with high-street opticians. By eliminating the premises and staff costs, stripping out all unnecessary costs and trading on the requirement that opticians had to provide a prescription that customers could use online, Glassesdirect pioneered a new, low-cost business model which took the competition by surprise – and about which they could do little to respond.

Glassesdirect grew continuously from 2005 onwards, and won a series of awards for entrepreneurship and business growth to over £40 million in turnover as well as building up a strong media profile and planned entry into the US market. The parent company acquired the Sunglasses Shop as a European eyeware business.

■ Critical questions to consider from this chapter

At this stage you should aim to bring together the information you have collected for your opportunity evaluation report, to collate this and review it.

- Overall, what is your assessment of the opportunity?
- What has the application of the tools covered in this chapter revealed about the strengths and limitations of the opportunity?

- What have you learned from working through the opportunity evaluation process? How can you use this to refine/improve the opportunity?
- How can you use the concept of multiple forms of value in creating a business model for your opportunity?
- How would you identify and gain access to the networks relevant to your opportunity?
- Do you intend to go to the next stage of venture planning, and do you have sufficient information to do this? If not, what are the gaps and how could you fill them?

Part III

Planning and Developing Opportunities

This section of the book addresses the third quadrant of Opportunity-Centred Entrepreneurship: planning and developing opportunities. As in the previous sections, it includes two chapters. Chapter 5 covers the reasons for and approaches involved in planning for opportunities. This builds on the previous section on creating and exploring opportunities. Chapter 6 then delves further into the essential processes which are involved in developing an opportunity, moving from planning to action. These include applying design thinking to the venture, innovation, online marketing and raising finance.

Planning to Realise Opportunities

Chapter Contents

- Introduction
- Why plan and how to plan
- Creating a storyboard for the opportunity
- Defining an identity for the venture
- Creating a business model

- Building the venture plan
- Establishing and accessing resources
- Planning as a dialogue
- Presenting the plan: pitching the idea
- Critical questions to consider from this chapter

■ Introduction

The purpose of this chapter is to provide a practical guide to planning how to realise the opportunity. In many cases this will take place through planning to form a new business venture. However, many opportunities can also be realised to achieve growth within existing organisations and social enterprises, or in less formal ways such as one-off projects and within community groups. 'Opportunity planning' is not always synonymous with business planning and can be undertaken independently in relation to any opportunity.

The learning goals of this chapter are to enable you to:

- generate the information to use in preparing a plan to exploit an opportunity
- develop a business model to show how the business will generate revenue

- create a plan for a new venture
- critically evaluate a venture plan and business model
- prepare to present a venture plan to potential stakeholders.

We spend much time thinking about, anticipating and sometimes dreading the future. All these activities involve the fundamental human capability of imagining and planning what has yet to happen. This is essential in working with opportunities and business ventures, yet the terms 'business plan' and 'business planning' are often viewed as irrelevant and unhelpful processes. This chapter will focus on why planning is important and how to plan in a realistic way which connects readily with acting on opportunities.

Entrepreneurs and innovators are habitually fascinated by future possibilities and how to realise them. The entrepreneur, in creating a new opportunity or venture, is using imagination in a practical way. This involves achieving a balance between creative and rational thinking, but the conventional approaches to planning often overemphasise the rational and miss out the inspirational. The approach to opportunity planning explained in this chapter aims to engage both creative and rational dimensions.

There is a huge amount of literature on 'how to write a business plan', which this chapter does not aim to duplicate. Guidance on writing a business plan can be obtained from many banks, business support agencies and other sources listed in the resources section. However, many business ventures are set up without a written plan, and research does not show a clear relationship between business success and having a business plan. It is increasingly argued that the orthodox advice to 'write a business plan' quite often misses the target (e.g., Bridge and Hegarty, 2012).

This chapter therefore takes a different approach. It offers a flexible and imaginative, future-oriented approach to planning the opportunity, in which working on the 'design' for the venture and producing a viable business model are necessary skills and activities. A key task for the entrepreneur is to gain support for the business concept from third parties, be they investors, partners, customers or suppliers. Creating a credible and persuasive plan is generally an essential stage in achieving this. Experience of working with many entrepreneurs in new and small businesses shows that they are often asked to produce a business plan by a third party, such as a bank, potential investor, customer or grant-providing agency, and the plan is written to unlock these resources. The chapter covers the questions in the third quadrant of Opportunity-Centred Entrepreneurship, shown in Figure 5.1.

■ Why plan and how to plan

Why plan? A professor of entrepreneurial studies often remarked wryly to business owner-managers that 'men make plans to make God laugh!', because the unexpected always happens. The serious point is that planning is about future-thinking and envisaging the future as you intend it to be. However, while we must try to implement our plans and make them happen,

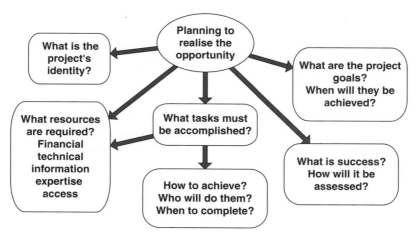

Figure 5.1 Planning to realise the opportunity

as will be covered in Chapter 7, the reality is that predictions are inherently unreliable guides to the future which we cannot control, and what we intend through a plan will generally be different in reality. Business plans usually end up being wrong.

This may seem like a good argument for not planning but, as with democracy, what is the alternative? The alternative is to not plan, to run the business on an emergent, contingent basis, by muddling along from day to day, being reactive or at best opportunistic. This is how many people, and indeed small business owners, do behave. The problem with this approach is that success, if it is achieved at all, becomes dependent on chance, circumstance and 'being in the right place at the right time'.

There are strong reasons for planning as a key aspect of the entrepreneurial process. Planning makes us think strategically and purposively about what we intend to achieve and how to realise this: it is planning for success as a clear statement of what the venture aims to achieve. Through planning, we can envisage different scenarios. This enables us to anticipate and prevent problems. Planning helps us to think ahead and to stay in control rather than simply reacting tactically to events, and it enables us to monitor the variations between the plan and reality and to re-plan accordingly.

Planning is necessary because in making the connections between having defined, explored and evaluated the opportunity through the activities in Chapters 3–4, we are now engaged in realising it. Opportunity planning involves future-oriented thinking and acting. This chapter introduces a simple but effective approach to planning to realise an opportunity in three stages. The first involves creating the story of how the opportunity will be realised. The second is to develop a business model to show how the opportunity will work in practice. The third is to shape the venture plan, using much of the work developed through the activities in previous chapters. To do this, we have to shift our thinking into the future. This builds on the work in Chapter 3 on creativity and opportunity mapping.

Planning:
- Envisage future
- Creative thinking
- Decision-making
- Prioritising
- Rational thinking - detail

Finance:
- Budgeting
- Costing & pricing
- Cash flow & working capital
- Estimating risk

Marketing & communicating
- Presenting, selling & influencing
- Written communications
- Handling questions
- Training & educating

Making it happen
- Leadership & direction
- Implementing
- Problem-solving
- Review progress, measure, follow-up

Figure 5.2 Planning skills: who has these in the business?

Activity

Future thinking

- Sit back for a few moments and allow your body to relax and your mind to wander.
- Think about what you would *like to happen* in the future. This could be about anything – not necessarily business, work or career oriented. You could imagine your next holiday, where you want to live, your ideal evening out.
- What do you see? What does it feel like? What are sounds and sensations you experience? Spend some time thinking about 'what it would be like'.
- Have a piece of paper, preferably blank and unlined, and a pen or pencil to hand. Use this to note down the ideas in your mind. These might be words or pictures. You could draw a mind-map of what you imagine.

This exercise might seem strange or unproductive at first. However time spent developing your ability in 'future thinking', about what you would like to happen, which we can term 'vision', or about 'scenarios' or 'contingencies' which could happen, will be worthwhile. Humankind is, so far as we know, the only mammal able to think prospectively and imagine the future. This is probably the most valuable capability we have in entrepreneurial working, so it is worth investing time in developing these skills; even if it seems like 'daydreaming', it can be productive. Everyone can think creatively, and does so in different ways. Walt Disney, for example, had a creative space in his office where he went to develop ideas.

■ Creating a storyboard for the opportunity

This section uses future thinking to imagine how the opportunity can develop, using a 'storyboard' approach to develop prospective future-thinking and vision. One of the problems of conventional business planning is that it has become dominated by highly rational and often numbers-based thinking, which creates an illusion of certainty through detail. There is nothing wrong with rational planning in its place but it should be seen as one outcome, rather than the whole point of the planning process.

Instead, we can think of a plan as being like a good story. A story creates a new and different reality which may be the future, the past or an alternative version of today. A story has a plot or storyline, characters, actions and movement. It is narrated in a way that holds the listener's interest. Even if the story is a fantasy, if it works it is 'believable' or credible and convincing in its plot, characters and narration. Increasingly the academic literature, both on entrepreneurship and business management more generally, is taking storytelling and narrative seriously (Hjorth and Steyaert, 2004). We can use the 'art' of storytelling to develop our ideas for the opportunity and to communicate these to other people more effectively than through a detailed plan alone. If you aim to use a venture plan to gain partners, investors or customers then it is essential that you create and tell a story which they can believe in.

Shaping the story

- The story has a structure including a beginning, a middle and an end.
- There is a plot or storyline which involves change and movement, so we do not know at the beginning what will have happened by the end.
- The story has characters – believable people who make things happen – and things happen to them which they do not expect.
- There is a storyteller or narrator.

Example: Blue Fish Creative Media

Here Tony tells the story of how he set up Blue Fish Creative Media with his associates:

Blue Fish was established by myself, Mike and Darryl in 1991. We had lost our jobs when the design agency we worked for went into liquidation. We decided to start on our own, selling our motorbikes and renting a single room to work from. During this pioneering stage we worked ludicrous hours to get off the ground – survival was the name of the game. We spent every waking hour in the office. We didn't believe we were working hard enough unless we were working past midnight, we'd often work until 3 a.m., supplying our clients with pizzas and Coke whilst they checked and signed off text. We'd take on any work, agree to any turnaround and built our reputation for service with a huge number of people.

We turned over £57k in the first year, then we turned over £220k in the second year and made £50k profit. But we were all working long hours and became busy fools, like prisoners in our own company, and we realised we wouldn't continue to enjoy work if we carried on like that. We knew we had the seeds of something good but needed help in getting to the next stage. We had to work out what we had done wrong and more importantly what we were doing right. So for the first four or five years we were messing around, trying to find our feet, establish our credentials, starting to understand how we made a profit or a loss. After five years we had seven people, turning over £400k.

We went to see our accountant. He ripped our business model apart and showed us how we make a profit. We assumed we made a profit on buying print and marking it up, but we were only charging 18 per cent of the hours that we worked. We analysed everything to see exactly what we were doing; we now know what our key performance indicators are. He showed us how to double our salaries and our profits but halve our hours within two years and we did it.

We all agreed we wanted to be out of the business by the time we're 50 with about £2m each, so we wrote a 20-year plan of the profitability levels we had to hit to get ourselves out of the business. We've put in a strong management team who can run the business for us; they can either buy us out or we could sell to a third party with the management team in place.

We're bang on target, we've set ourselves 30 per cent growth targets and this year we'll do just over a million, from £782k last year. We've set a target of around £1.3–1.5m next year but the main thing is the profitability levels. Now we work 40–50 hours per week, never more than that. Salaries have trebled, we've doubled our fee rate and profitability is still going up – we know where it all comes from now.

Tony's story tells us why they formed what has become a successful business, what they wanted from it, a good deal about how the business has changed and how the founders have learned, and what their strategy and goals for the business are. This is a story, not a business plan, which communicates something of the innovative, sometimes manic nature of their business that you would not gain from a conventional business plan. But they needed a plan to enable them to define and then realise their ambitions. They have gone on to become a highly successful design and digital media business, focusing on creative branding, identity and digital media work.

Activity

Creating a storyboard for the opportunity plan

The purpose of this activity is to think creatively about how you will realise the opportunity in the future. It can help you to generate strategic thinking to inform the opportunity plan, by starting to create the story of your opportunity. You can use several sheets of blank paper to create the storyboard and draw mind-maps and 'rich pictures', putting down key words and ideas using marker pens. Alternatively you can draw it on a digital device or tell the story orally and use a voice recorder.

Where you aim to be

- Think about what the end result of making the opportunity into reality will be.
- What will you have achieved?
- What will it look and feel like?
- How will customers or users experience it?
- What will you be doing?
- How will you know if it is successful?

Where you are now

- Now go back to the beginning, where you are now.
- What is the opportunity, and the potential as you see it?
- What is your current situation?
- Why do you want to make the opportunity happen?
- Who is working with you?
- What resources do you have?

How to get there

- Now work on the middle. You have an image of the end. What will you need to do to get there?
- What are the actions, the stages in the story that move you from current to future reality? What is the flow of events which need to take place?
- What help and resources are you going to need?
- What are the good things and successes you think will happen?
- What could be the bad events and misfortunes which might take place?

Now you have a storyboard for the opportunity. This may be a voice recording, in which case you can play it back and write down the key ideas into a story, or it may be three or more pages of a written and drawn storyboard. This can be the basis for your opportunity plan; you can always come back to improve and work on it. Like any story it will improve every time it is told and this is certainly true of venture plans.

This activity aimed to help you to future-think about the opportunity and how you can make it happen. Future-thinking is creative strategic thinking, focusing on what you intend to achieve, where you want to take the opportunity and what this means for you and others involved with it. The storyboard conveys the narrative of the opportunity, the progression from now to the future and being able to identify the activities, events, people and possibilities which are involved in going from 'now' to realise the future goals. This material can be translated and used in a more formal plan which will be prepared later in this chapter. It aims to help you to develop a vision for what realising the opportunity will achieve, and the first thoughts on a strategy for how to get there. These will be used in the opportunity plan which will be prepared later in this chapter.

The introduction to this chapter mentioned that an opportunity could be realised within an existing organisation, outside a formal organisation, or through creating a new business venture. The question is what type of organisation is needed to make the opportunity happen – formal or informal, existing or new, single or joint venture (e.g., two existing organisations may form a new, jointly owned one). Any plan, decision and action to make an opportunity happen is a 'venture' in the sense that a venture is 'an undertaking of a risk, a risky enterprise, a commercial speculation' according to the *Concise Oxford Dictionary*.

One feature of planning is that as well as being creative, it is a way of forcing out questions and decisions which need to be made, and of 'problem solving in advance' by identifying potential problems and finding ways of preventing, eliminating or dealing with these situations.

■ Defining an identity for the venture

One vital aspect of an opportunity is to establish a unique identity for the project, product or new business venture. It will take different forms depending on the type of opportunity and the strategy for its exploitation. Creating an identity is essential because it moves the opportunity from a concept on which you and possible others have been working, towards being a proposition which can be promoted and discussed with third parties. Here are different ways in which the identity of the opportunity can be expressed:

- name of the business venture – for example, company name
- name of the product, service or experience to be provided
- online: website domain name, URL, twitter hashtag and e-mail address
- brand identity which can include all of these.

Identifying, securing the rights to use the identity and exploiting it are important steps, already referred to in the section on intellectual property in Chapter 4. Here are guidelines for establishing the identity for the opportunity. The identity should:

- communicate the opportunity and its benefits to the target customers
- be distinctive, preferably unique, and memorable
- not be easily confused with similar offerings
- be hard to copy or to 'pass off' imitations.

The concept of branding and identity is well established, so none of this is new, meaning that creating and protecting new brand identities has become much harder. Many of the readily available names and words in the English language have been registered as trademarks or Internet domain names. The identity has symbolic and linguistic importance and being memorable is essential. There is a section on using design effectively in the business start-up process in Chapter 6; it may be worth finding a creative consultancy which specialises in business identity to help develop your ideas.

Example: The Hive

Nottingham Trent University was developing a new facility to support graduate business innovation projects and start-up business ventures. They had located a site and sources of funding, and needed an identity which would appeal to the target market – entrepreneurial students and graduates. The project team came up with 'The Hive' as a name, choosing this because it was short, memorable and expressed ideas of busy-as-bees, hive-of-activity and honey = money. Even though the project team included a designer, they brought in an external design agency to create a vibrant visual identity as a brand, with co-ordinated marketing materials and website, ensuring that these brand values were carried through into the décor of the building. The ideal domain name was not available but they chose the closest available: http://www.ntu.ac.uk/hive/.

The Hive has become highly successful in stimulating university enterprise, and the identity has been an integral aspect of its appeal. Since it opened in 2001, over 250 new businesses have been created and more than 75% of these have remained in business, with a three-year survival rate of more than 85%. The Hive is recognised at European level for the success and rigour of its support programmes for graduate entrepreneurs.

Protecting The Hive's identity has been less successful, and a number of other business centres and networks have adopted similar names, demonstrating the need to protect the identity of a venture at the outset.

Activity

- Do you have an identity for your opportunity?
- If not, start to collect ideas, words and images which could be used. Aim to come up with a range of possible ideas, not just one. While a 'brainstorming' session can be helpful in coming up with ideas, it is just one stage in the process.
- Spend time putting possible combinations of words and images together, associating ideas in new ways which could appeal to the target customer. If there is a project team, everyone can be involved in this activity. Try to come up with as many combinations as you can.
- Try some limited consumer research – ask people in the target group which of the available combinations 'speaks to them' with most positive impact.
- Check the results on a web domain name site to see which brand names and website URLs are taken and which combinations are available.
- Aim to find one which meets the guidelines provided earlier, as far as possible – and which you think will have the maximum customer appeal. Decide which ones to register.
- Once you have chosen the identity, protect it by registering the website domain name (and different combinations of these). Consider a trademark if you think this could be of potential value. Refer to the guidance on intellectual property in Chapter 4.

■ Creating a business model

The basics of a business model were outlined in Chapter 4. The business model demonstrates as clearly and simply as possible how the opportunity will create, deliver and capture value from its operations. This is at the heart of the opportunity plan and needs to show who is doing what; for whom they are doing it; and the financial assumptions and results on which the plan is based.

A business model shows how the opportunity will work on 'day 1'. It does not require planning for a time period of up to a year but captures a moment in time when the business is operating as intended. This can be analysed to show problems, weaknesses and ways of improving it. If you can show how 'a day in the life of the business' will work, then this model can be scaled up to cover longer time periods. It may cover just one product, project or location, for example, but the scope can be extended if it is effective in one instance.

Here are some deceptively simple questions we ask people with ideas for new business ventures. It builds on activities in Chapters 3-4. Try your answers to these questions.

Activity

- Who are your target customers?
- What value will you create for them? (remember: there are multiple forms of value)
- Why will they buy from you?
- How is this superior to competitors?
- How will the business capture value: generate cash flow through sales?
- How will the business generate profits?
- What financial investment does the business require?
- Can you draw a simple diagram to show the business model?

Business models have been addressed in depth by Alex Osterwalder in *Business Model Generation* (Osterwalder and Pigneur, 2010) which offers nine building blocks for a business model:

1. Customer segments
2. Value propositions for customers
3. Communication, distribution and sales channels
4. Customer relationships
5. Revenue streams
6. Key resources
7. Key activities
8. Key partnerships
9. Cost structure

These can be brought together onto a 'canvas' which shows the integrated model (http://alexosterwalder.com/).

One format for a simple business model is shown in Figure 5.3. This is a finance-based model which includes basic financial measures. If you are not familiar with these, they are explained in the financial toolkit. The business model includes:

- the target customer group, the intended product or service and customer benefits
- sales targets and revenue
- variable costs (costs attributable to each customer)
- fixed costs (costs which apply at any level of sales)
- total costs, gross and net profit before tax
- gross and net profit margins and break-even sales figures
- projected sales growth in years two and three.

Evaluating a business model

A business model can be completed and presented to give a readily understandable one-page or one-screen overview of how the opportunity will generate and capture value. Initially this is for the people creating the venture to work on, and it can then be refined to show to potential partners, investors and lenders. It can be revised easily to account for different scenarios. It is important to be aware of the criteria which potential investors and other decision-makers may use in evaluating a business model:

- Are the assumptions and information on which the model is based realistic and reliable? Or are your expectations of the rate of customer acquisition and sales growth over-optimistic?

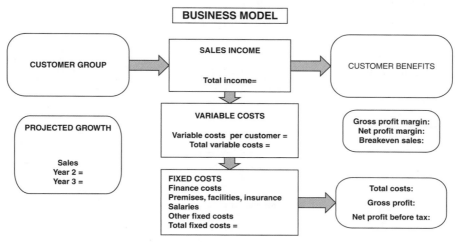

Figure 5.3 Business model template

- Are fixed costs kept as low as possible (e.g., avoiding unnecessary expenditure – hire or lease rather than buy)? Are costs controlled overall?
- At what point are break-even sales reached?
- Are the levels of gross and especially net profit both realistic and attractive?

Activity

An example of a simple business model using this format is shown in Figure 5.4. This is for a pizza takeaway and delivery service aimed at students. Assume this is a first attempt which can be improved.

- Review the business model using the four evaluation criteria in the previous section:
  - Are the assumptions valid?
  - Are costs controlled?
  - Break-even point?
  - Profit margins?
- What problems or weaknesses can you identify in the business model?
- What suggestions would you make for improving it?

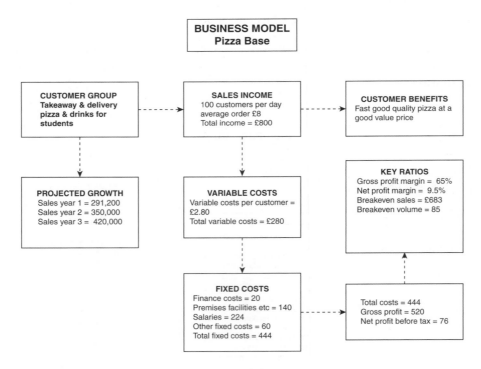

Figure 5.4 Example of a simple business model

What problems did you identify? Check your answer against these points.

Assumptions:

What is the business offering which is different from many other fast food and pizza takeaways: why will customers choose this one if there is nothing special about it?

The 100 customers per day may be an average but much busier days at weekends and possibly quieter days (e.g., during vacations) will affect this so using 'high' and 'low' scenarios would be better.

Is the £8 average order value in line with customer spending? Can it be increased (e.g., by special promotions such as 'meal deals'?)

Cost control:

Can the variable costs per order (food, drink, packaging) be reduced by better procurement deals without reducing quality?

Salaries are the biggest item in costs – are there too many staff? Staffing needs to be adequate to cover the busiest times or orders will be lost but lean at quiet times.

Break-even point: Break-even is 85% by customer volume and sales. Can this be reduced by taking the steps above?

Profit: Net profit is less than 10%.

The power of 1%

By using the '1%' principle, of making small changes which increase customer orders and prices by just 1%, and reducing fixed and variable costs by the same amount, there is a noticeable impact on the profit:

- 101 customers @ £8.08 order value = £816 revenue
- Variable costs reduced to £277 = £539 gross profit, margin of 66%
- Fixed costs reduced to £439 = £100 net profit, margin of 12.25%
- Break-even volume is 85, value is £665, or just over 81%

Bigger improvements may well be possible but this shows the combined effects of making very small changes in price and cost structure which together increase net profit by over 30%. These will be scaled up over a full year. This is the 'power of 1%' which can be applied to any business, whether a new venture or existing firm.

Clearly this is a very basic business model, which by posing some quite basic questions on the initial assumptions can be significantly revised and improved. This holds true for almost any business model at the planning stage. However too many businesses are started using poor business models which have often never been written down and do not work as well as they could or are uncompetitive. This can lead to the failure of the business, so it makes sense to chart, evaluate and improve the business model as a starting point.

Activity

- Develop a business model for your opportunity. You can use the template in the toolkit.
- Evaluate your business model using the criteria listed above.
- What weaknesses can you identify?
- Revise the model to correct these.

■ Building the venture plan

This section covers the development of the venture plan in which the business model is an integral part. This activity will use the work you have done in Chapters 3 and 4 on exploring the opportunity and the work from earlier in this chapter on story-boarding and business modelling. By now you should be familiar with the use of mind-maps for key concepts and we will work on the venture plan in the same way. Figure 5.5 shows an overview of a venture plan, and a template is included in the toolkit. It is suggested that you work on the venture plan using flipchart paper on the wall, a white board, or a laptop or tablet PC as you prefer. The advantage of working on the venture plan in this way is that you can start from the 'vision' of what you aim to achieve through the venture in the centre, and then work on each of the other boxes, starting with the opportunity, then the strategy, and the plans for marketing and sales, operations, finance and people. The final step is the action plan which

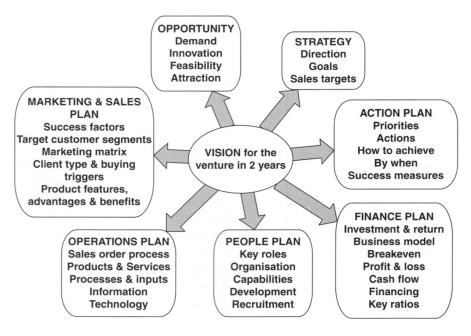

Figure 5.5 Map of venture plan

summarises the priority actions which need to be completed. Additional information under each of the headings can be pasted up and the venture planning map can become a 'header' or summary of the information in the plan. Notes on what to include in each section of the plan follow in the next section.

Table 5.1 builds on the map of a venture plan by showing the headings and sub-headings of a typical venture plan as they might be used on the contents page, with links to where the information can be obtained from activities in this and preceding chapters. This will help you as you develop your venture plan in the next section. Guidelines on completing the other parts of the venture plan are given in the next section.

Executive summary

This section needs to 'sell' the overall business concept effectively. Without giving too much detail, summarise what the opportunity is; how the business will address this as the concept; what investment is required; and the anticipated return, or proposition.

Opportunity

Explain the opportunity in detail: what is the demand, innovation, feasibility and attractiveness? Use detail from market research to demonstrate that the opportunity exists, its

Table 5.1 Venture plan structure and contents

Section	Source of material
1. Executive summary: Opportunity, business concept, investment proposition, anticipated return	This chapter
2. Opportunity Demand, innovation, feasibility, attraction SWOT analysis in relation to competitors, key differentiators	Opportunity evaluation, Chapter 4
3. Strategy: Vision, direction, goals, sales targets	This chapter
4. Marketing plan Target market and customer segments The product/service concept – features and benefits Marketing matrix Promotion, distribution, pricing Sales plan	Market research, Chapter 4 and this chapter
5. Operations plan How the business will operate: capabilities, resources, people, processes	This chapter
6. People plan People: who will run the business, track records	Capabilities assessment, Chapter 2 and toolkit This chapter
7. Financial plan The business model or process Financials: investment and working capital requirements, break-even, pricing, gross and net margins, cash flow, return on investment	This chapter and toolkit
8. Business action planner	This chapter and toolkit

scale and value. Analyse existing competitors and alternatives, using a SWOT analysis to compare the opportunity with these and explain the key differentiators

Strategy

Explain the vision for the enterprise: what will it achieve? What direction will be taken to launch, consolidate and grow the business. Include goals and targets such as annual sales and profit targets.

Marketing and sales plan: key questions to address

- What are the vital success factors which you have to get right? These factors will differentiate the venture from competitors. They may include superior technology, service, choice or other benefits to the customer. Beware of claiming to offer lower cost unless the business model really provides a lower cost structure.
- Who are the target customer segments? Use the information you generated in Chapter 4 to explain these.
- Marketing matrix: the marketing matrix is a simple concept which can be used in different ways to plan and analyse the relationship between customer segments and product types. It relates customer segments to specific product or service offerings and is useful if there are two or more segments or product/service combinations (see Table 5.2).

The example shows that some customer segments form a strong core market for certain products and services, but make few purchases of other offers from the same business. The marketing matrix can be used for the following applications:

- matching products and services to customer segments
- identifying client types and the 'triggers' which cause them to buy a product/service
- showing gaps – why do some customer groups not buy certain products?
- matching product features and benefits to each client type
- forecasting the sales value from each customer/product combination
- forecasting the profitability of each combination
- identifying the marketing activity needed to connect with each customer segment
- analysing strength of competitive position.

Activity

Complete a marketing matrix for your opportunity to show the relationships between customer segments and product service types: which customer groups do you envisage will buy which types of products? Even if you only plan to offer one product initially, you can project which types of customer you expect to buy it.

Table 5.2 Marketing matrix of product sales distribution to customer groups (in %)

Customer segments Product/ service types	Customer group 1	Customer group 2	Customer group 3	Customer group 4
Product A	60	30	10	0
Product B	20	30	40	10
Service A	55	40	5	0
Service B	10	10	10	70

Operations plan: key questions to address

Here we plan how the venture will provide its product or service to the customers.

The business needs to be designed effectively so that it can meet the customer requirements effectively whilst exploiting the opportunity. It can be designed in the same way that a product, a building or a website is designed for effective use, so that it operates effectively and efficiently, enabling it to adapt and grow. Design thinking is covered in more depth in Chapter 6. Here are guidelines for designing a new business venture effectively.

- Form follows function – so make it easy for the customer to find, interact with and buy from the organisation through well-designed selling processes.
- Processes are kept simple, flexible and robust.
- Responsibilities and functions are defined clearly to avoid overlap.
- The organisation is lean and flat, avoiding unnecessary hierarchies.
- The effectiveness of each aspect of the business can be measured using simple, useful metrics.

The key to operations planning is to use simple, step-by-step processes, for example, through process mapping or flowcharting. The aim of a business process is to make it simple to follow for both the customer and worker within the business, to minimise the scope for it going wrong or for introducing variability which affects quality, and to make it as efficient as possible so that costs can be controlled. The most important process for a new venture is probably the sales order process: what are the steps in taking and fulfilling a customer order? The sales order process for a website design consultancy is shown in Table 5.3 and is typical of a generic process in a small service business in which much of the process can be automated.

As part of planning the process, consider what information is generated and retained. This could be as simple as a computer-based customer record, with an invoice being generated. This basic process will be developed using the 'business resource process' technique. There are relationships between the business process, information and people's skills and capabilities which are needed to manage the service or product delivery. Questions for the people plan are considered in the next section.

Table 5.3 Example of sales order process

Step	Time taken (minutes)	Information record
Customer logs enquiry via website	5	Customer log & enquiry record set up
Assess customer requirement	20	Enquiry record
Prepare and send quotation and terms of business	40	Quote
Check acceptance by customer	15	Customer log
Plan job into work schedule	5	Work schedule
Initial design work	420	Design file
Check approval by customer	30	Customer log
Make modifications	60	Design file
Check final approval by customer	30	Customer log
Commission website	120	Design file
Invoice customer	20	Customer log
Follow-up to check customer satisfaction, payment and assess further requirements	20	Customer log

Activity

- Design the sales order process for your venture.
- Map out what you think the key stages will be from enquiry to completion and payment.
- What are the critical check-points in this process?
- What information would be generated and retained at each stage?
- What variations would you expect there to be in the process?

If the business depends on supplier, subcontractor, distributor or reseller relationships, then these need to be identified in the operations planning:

- Which business partners, or suppliers, subcontractors, distributors and resellers does the business depend on?
- Is the business entirely dependent on any of these or do alternatives exist?
- How reliable are they known to be?
- What are the contractual relationships with them for delivery and payment?
- Which types of new suppliers etc. will be required, and how will these be selected?

A new venture often depends on establishing a reputation for high quality and customer service. It is hard to grow a new business if it gains a reputation for low quality and poor service! Quality and service standards do not happen by accident and need to be planned. Simple service standards may include maximum response times to customer enquiries, time intervals between order and delivery, and targets for customer satisfaction.

- What standards of product and service quality will customers expect? If these vary between segments or product types, use a marketing matrix to chart them.
- How do these compare with competitors' standards for quality and service?
- How can the consistency of quality and service be maintained, for example, by minimising variable or inconsistent standards?
- What measures or records of quality and service need to be maintained (some may be contractual requirements)?

Activity

How will the business ensure consistent quality and service for its customers?
Use the questions in the sections on suppliers, quality and service to plan how the business will ensure consistent quality and service, both from third parties such as suppliers and within its own operations.

People plan: key questions to address

It is important to demonstrate that the venture has the people with the skills, expertise and experience to start and manage the business successfully and to provide the service expected by customers. The experience of the venture team and especially the chief executive or lead entrepreneur is an essential aspect of this.

- Who are the key people in the business?
- What are their track records relevant to the venture? This can be important in reassuring investors and reducing the perception of risk.
- What are their roles? For example, who will be responsible for: general management (chief executive); marketing and sales; operations; finance; information; people?
  - The business is unlikely to have one person responsible for each of these, and an owner-managed business may start with one person responsible for all of them. How can responsibilities be shared most effectively within the team?
- What are the key skills, capabilities and expertise required by the venture? Which need to be employed within the venture and which can be bought-in when needed?
- Which people have these, and what training and development is needed (e.g., to meet external requirements for qualified staff)?
- What recruitment of staff is likely to be needed as the business grows, to fill gaps in skill or capacity??

> ## Activity
>
> Use the questions in the people planning section earlier to develop a simple people plan for the venture.

Financial plan: key questions

The financial plan is a vital part of the venture plan and will be scrutinised closely by potential investors and lenders. It needs to demonstrate that the business is viable, that it will show a satisfactory return on the investment to be made in it and that the financial projections are realistic, being based on valid costings and data. It may well be written to meet investors or lenders requirements, as outlined later in this chapter.

These principles are not significantly different for social and 'not for profit' enterprises except that, for these, non-financial values, economic impact, wider sustainability and re-investment of returns will be of major importance. Also, there are sources of investment available to social enterprise projects which can show a strong business case and social impact, and which are not available to private businesses.

The key financial aspects normally included in the plan are:

- Business model: include the business model prepared earlier.
- Sales, pricing and income projections for a minimum of 1 year, extrapolated to show targets for the next 2 or 3 years.
- Investment: what investment is required in the business?
- When is this required (at what points and over what timescale)?
- How this will be spent, for example:
  - in fixed capital assets
  - start-up capital to cover launch expenses
  - working capital to finance cash flow and trading.
- What combination of equity investment and loan finance is required?
- What investment are the venture team making and what percentage of share ownership do they intend to retain?
- Who is expected to provide the investment/finance required?
- What is the projected repayment of loan finance?
- What is the projected return on equity investment? (For example, an investor would require a share in the equity of the business with an anticipated exit strategy through sale of the shares and a capital gain, or a share in the profit stream through dividends on shares, or both.)
- Cash flow: show a cash flow projection for at least 12 months, or until the business reaches positive cash flow (cash income exceeds expenditure) if this is longer than 12 months.
- Profit and loss: show a profit and loss projection for the first 12 months.

- Balance sheet: include a projected balance sheet if investment is required.
- Key ratios: include anticipated:
  - break-even sales figure
  - gross and net profit margins
  - gearing and other ratios.

Activity

The activity is to prepare a financial plan for the venture plan. This may involve significant work so it is suggested that you read through the financial planner in the toolkit. Identify any terms which are unfamiliar to you and check that you understand them. Then gather the financial information on the venture which you have already prepared, as listed in Table 5.1. Identify what additional information you require and gather this, by research, to collect costing or pricing data. Once you have the information then prepare the financial plan.

If you have not prepared a financial plan before, the recommended starting point is:

- Start with your business model.
- Prepare a cash flow forecast for months 1–12.
- Identify what start-up capital is needed to launch the venture.
- Identify what working capital is needed to finance operations when trading.
- What level of sales is required to achieve this?
- These will show the funding required for the first year.
- Profit and loss, balance sheet and key ratios can be worked out from this.

Rather than being considered in detail here, these highly important components of the financial plan are included in the finance planner section of the toolkit. Further reading of financial planning texts at an appropriate level for your knowledge and confidence is also recommended in the resources section.

An important consideration in financing a new venture is the point at which break-even and financial viability is reached. Any venture which involves either innovation (new product, service or process development) or market development is almost certain to have a period in which funds need to be invested prior to trading, and even once trading has started, further working capital will be needed to finance operations. Entrepreneurs are usually optimistic at the planning stage and often do not realise that there are three golden rules governing this period of innovation or market development and early trading:

- Development costs are higher than you expected.
- Development takes longer than you expected.
- If you have under-estimated the investment needed at the planning stage, you will find it much harder to raise second-round funding part-way through this process.

This is known as the 'death valley curve' and is shown in Figure 5.6.

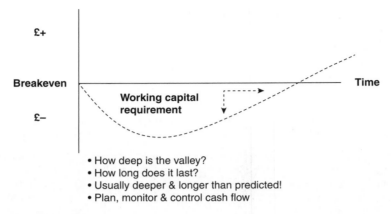

- How deep is the valley?
- How long does it last?
- Usually deeper & longer than predicted!
- Plan, monitor & control cash flow

Figure 5.6 Death valley curve

Action plan

The action plan pulls together the business goals, sales targets, immediate priorities, actions and responsibilities (Figure 5.7). This can be in the form of a project plan (e.g., a Gantt chart) or of the template in the business action planner section of the toolkit.

- The action at this stage is to bring the various parts of the draft plan together and to review them. Are they integrated to support each other?
- Confirm the business goals – is everyone in agreement?
- Decide on the priorities which must be achieved to start the venture.
- What actions must take place, by when, and who will be responsible for each?

■ Establishing and accessing resources

The venture planning process is likely to identify that a range of resources are required to enact the opportunity. Some of these may already be available, but unless you are very fortunate or are planning a venture of quite limited scale, other resources will be required. The types of resources were outlined in Chapter 3, and the networks through which they can be attracted or captured were considered in Chapter 4. Resources may come, for example, from corporate organisations; public sector organisations, research institutes; including universities; and investors, including business angels and venture capital funds. It makes sense to invest capital only in purchasing assets which are known to be of long-term and appreciating value to the business, and to aim to gain the use of other assets at least cost, for example, by renting, leasing or borrowing. Large organisations, including corporates, public sector bodies and the military, often buy and then do not fully utilise capital assets, which

Business Action Planning

Business Goals

Strategic options
Strategic
Direction & goals

Future
Trends & scenarios?

Marketing
Website optimisation
Understanding customers
New business pipeline

Capabilities & resources
Strengths & vulnerable areas

Opportunities
Current & future

Business model
Value creation

Financial plan
Cash flow forecast
Profit & breakeven
1% improvements
Working capital

Your Business
Action Plan

Figure 5.7 Business action planning

may then be targeted by entrepreneurs to use on a 'pay as you go' basis. These can include premises, printing, payroll, manufacturing and distribution facilities.

The types of resources required may include, for example:

- *Knowledge*: specialist knowledge, expertise or information not held by the venture team which needs to be researched or bought-in.
- *Human resources*: skills, expertise and capability required in the venture, including essential social contacts.
- *Finance*: investment or lending for capital asset purchase or working capital.
- *Technology*: product or process technology which needs to be bought-in or licensed.
- *Intellectual property*: permissions or licences which need to be negotiated to provide the rights to use them.
- *Physical resources*: equipment, plant, buildings or land which the business needs to access or control.
- *Capacity*: facilities which need to be bought-in, for example, subcontracting manufacture, packaging, despatch or call-centre operations.
- *Networks*: for access and distribution to customers or resellers.
- And any other specialist resources not included in the aforementioned categories.

Activity

- Review the resources which have been identified as being required in the sections of the venture plan prepared so far.
- Use the resource identification grid in Table 5.4 to identify which resources are already available to the venture. Or draw a resource map (Chapter 3)
- Which resources will be required, but are not currently available to the venture?
- For each of these, identify the options available for obtaining this resource, for example:
  - ○ Which organisation/person has this resource, and could it be borrowed at no/minimal cost? (These may include existing organisations including public and corporate organisations, which often have under-used assets)
  - ○ Can it be bought-in or rented on a flexible pay-as-you-go basis?
  - ○ Cost of purchase?
  - ○ What alternative options are available if the resource cannot be obtained, for example, substitutes or effect on the venture of the resource not being available?

■ Planning as a dialogue

Venture planning need not be a solitary exercise, but can be a way of connecting the venture team promoting the opportunity with the network of investors, resource providers, customers and others. This can explore how their needs can be met through the venture, to the mutual benefit of all parties. Increasingly, value is co-created by producers and consumers interacting, and venture planning can reflect this co-operative process of the negotiated enterprise, as outlined in the entrepreneurial learning model in Chapter 3. It therefore includes conversations and negotiations, both informal and formal, with the network of interested parties around the venture whom we can term stakeholders. Key stakeholders connected with the venture are likely to include:

- the venture team
- investors and lenders

Table 5.4 Resource identification grid

Factor	Resources available	Resources required	Potential sources
Knowledge			
Human resources			
Finance			
Technology			
Intellectual property			
Physical resources			
Capacity			
Networks			
Other			

- technology and other partners
- suppliers, sub-contractors, distributors and resellers (as appropriate)
- customers of potential significance (e.g., corporate clients)
- public sector, grant providing and regulatory organisations.

The venture planning stage is often a good point to contact, seek out and consult people and organisations to get their input into the plan. However they will expect you to be able to 'pitch' an outline of the plan to enable them to understand the nature of the opportunity, so as a minimum you should have completed the business model and a one-page outline of the venture plan, as shown in Figure 5.4.

In addition, expert business and professional advisers, such as lawyers, accountants, technical and intellectual property specialists may be involved where their expertise and advice can benefit the venture. But beware, there are sharks out there who feed on little businesses, so select advisers with care and take up references on them from other entrepreneurs.

Activity

- Look back to your network of industry and related contacts from the activities on networking in Chapter 4.
- Identify the most useful contacts who could guide the venture towards resources or other networks such as potential customers.
- Shortlist these contacts.
- Consider how you could contact them to successfully engage their interest in the venture.

■ Presenting the plan: pitching the idea

The venture plan is 'the sales document for the business'. As well as the venture team requiring a plan, it is needed to convince potential investors, partners, supporters and clients that the venture is credible and able to meet their requirements. This involves strategies and skills of presentation, communication and influencing.

The venture plan is a slim-line, easily revised document which communicates all the necessary information about the venture, as outlined in this chapter. It can also be termed a 'business proposal'. A useful analogy is that the venture plan or business proposal is rather like the 'trailer' for a film at the cinema – it is designed to excite attention and provide as much information as necessary to stimulate the target viewer to want more. For those who do want more, then the full business plan becomes the 'main picture'. Table 5.5 shows the characteristics of an effective venture plan.

The venture plan may be all that is needed for an opportunity where the client does not require more information. However some organisations, including some in the public sector, corporate and institutional sectors, equate the thickness and weight of a business plan with its value and ability to minimise risk. If one of these organisations requires a more detailed plan and you require their support, then it is important to obtain specific information from them about their detailed requirements so that you can follow this.

In presenting the plan or 'pitching' to potential investors, partners or customers, preparation and planning are the key. You need to 'know your audience', having researched their interests, track record and likely goals. You need to anticipate their questions, and particularly those related to areas of weakness, such as customer demand, product readiness, financing and venture team capability, which will be probed remorselessly. So you need to 'put yourself in their shoes' to prepare convincing responses which use factual data rather than excessive confidence. If you are seeking financial or other investment such as technology, prepare your negotiating position: what do you want, and what are you prepared to offer in return.

Key questions in 'pitching' or selling the idea

- Who is the plan written for?
- What do you aim to achieve from presenting the plan? What are you prepared to exchange to gain what you need?
- What are their needs and expectations? (For example, are they looking for investment or lending opportunities, technology or distribution partnerships?)
- How can you fine-tune your presentation of the plan to meet their needs?
- Do you know your audience? What is their investment history, in which types of ventures? What are their investment objectives or lending criteria?
- How can you reassure them of your credibility and capability to make it happen?

Table 5.5 Characteristics of an effective venture plan

Here are 12 features of an effective venture plan:

1. It demonstrates a clear opportunity which has not yet been exploited.
2. It displays strong customer attraction and differentiation from competitors.
3. There is significant, quantified growth potential in identified markets.
    There is a credible strategy and plan to exploit the opportunity, stating success factors with
4. risks identified and minimised.
5. It deploys innovation which can be shown to work effectively.
6. It can succeed both in the online and physical business markets
7. It has unique aspects which can be prevented from being copied (e.g., control of IPR)
8. Investment required is shown with realistic return on investment.
9. Timescale to break-even and anticipated profit stream are realistic.
10. Financial planning is accurately costed and realistic.
11. Potential exit routes and timescales for investors are shown.
12. The venture team demonstrate capability and motivation.

Activity

- Prepare your venture plan and a short presentation of no more than 15 minutes.
- Review your plan against the 12 features of an effective venture plan shown in Table 5.5.
- Rehearse this. If possible video it and view the feedback to enable you to correct mannerisms, hesitation, repetition or over-confidence.
- Invite a small group of your contacts from the previous exercise, preferably including at least one third party such as an entrepreneur, investor or business banker.
- Present the venture plan and invite their feedback on how you could improve the venture plan and your presentation; give them the list of features and ask them to review the plan against this.
- Use their feedback to revise and improve your venture plan and presentation.

■ Critical questions to consider from this chapter

This final section highlights key questions on venture planning to consolidate your learning in this important area. Venture planning is a critical skill-set which you are highly likely to use a number of times during your career, so it is worth reflecting on what you have learned so far.

- What do you think are the objectives of venture planning?
- Do you think it is necessary to have a plan for an opportunity?
- How will you go about preparing a venture plan: what are the main stages?
- What are the key components of a venture plan?
- What are the main factors which make for an effective venture plan?
- What are the key skills you have developed and learning points you can use in planning opportunities and venturing?

Developing the Opportunity

Chapter

6

Chapter Contents

- Using learning networks for opportunity development
- Social innovation
- Divergent and convergent thinking
- Innovation as a creative learning process
- Using tools for innovation
- Applying design thinking
- e-marketing and using online tools to develop and promote the venture
- Raising finance
- Critical questions to consider from this chapter

This chapter builds on the venture planning approaches in Chapter 5 by adding ideas, practical techniques and examples which show how the opportunity can be developed from the planning stage, prior to launching the venture. The focus of the chapter is on developing the opportunity by applying innovation approaches and tools. Innovation is a socially connected, networked process in which the opportunity can be tested out in real situations, with feedback, suggestions and critique from users, experts and peers to inform its development.

The development of any opportunity, in order to translate the concept into reality, depends both on access to a range of resources, and the application of multiple sets of capabilities. No two opportunities have the same needs or characteristics, but these topics which are commonly applied to developing opportunities are explored in this chapter. These include:

- using learning networks for opportunity development

- social innovation
- innovation as a creative learning process
- tools for innovation
- applying design thinking
- e-marketing and using online tools to develop and promote the venture
- raising finance.

The chapter includes short guest contributions from expert practitioners in several of these important topics. These provide practical suggestions you can use and examples of how these can work.

As a result of reading and working through the activities in this chapter, you can increase your awareness and develop your practice in how an opportunity can be developed and refined from the planning stage through using networked innovation and design processes; how online marketing can be used to raise awareness; and approaches to attracting resources and raising finance.

Chapter 3 introduced creative thinking to generate innovation, and Chapter 4 showed how to assess innovative solutions as business opportunities. Being innovative, generating new ways of doing things, new services, approaches and products, is essential for entrepreneurship. However, the nature of innovation itself is continually changing. Innovation was traditionally seen as synonymous with 'new product and service development' but now has to be considered on a much broader basis. It is both an approach to working (innovating) as well as describing the results of the process. Increasingly this process is a human-social organising process which mediates between and connects:

- demands (problems and opportunities);
- resources (tangible, such as technology and intangible, such as information and finance);
- approaches and methods;
- applications and solutions.

Just as social enterprise has altered the concept of 'mainstream' entrepreneurship, a similar shift is occurring in innovation. The rise of social innovation is seeing new ways of working and types of innovation emerge in response to social needs and opportunities which did not take place in a conventional market-based economy. Arguably, social innovation has become one of the fastest-developing and most radical forms of innovation, and will be further explored in this chapter.

■ Using learning networks for opportunity development

This section explores the role of networks and learning in developing opportunities. The entrepreneurial economy operates in a highly social, networked way, with 'social capital' (who you know, and the groups you are a member of) being increasingly important. Entrepreneurs and firms often participate intensely in different kinds of social activity, including buying and selling, collaborating, competing and even copying. But to the pre-start entrepreneur or enterprising student, for example, these networks may not be known, or may seem to be impenetrable clubs of the already-successful; why would they admit *me*?

Industry clusters, for example, are often based on groups of companies in a single industry being closely co-located and operating interdependently, and often competing, co-existing and collaborating simultaneously. In the process they develop a skilled workforce, attracting specialist suppliers and a social and support network, so that particular regions become known as centres of expertise or 'the place to go' for a particular service or technology. Long-standing examples include the high-technology area of 'silicon valley' close to Stanford, California; the biotech industry around the University of Cambridge, United Kingdom; and the software industry in Bangalore, India. This connects with the concept of the negotiated enterprise and the role of industry networks, which were explored in Chapter 2.

Example: Inner East London – Silicon Roundabout to Tech City?

From the late 1990s, creative digital technology firms were starting up around Shoreditch on the margin of the City of London. Unnoticed by most, young technology innovators were developing new firms with digital applications and new business models. London has the majority of digital technology and telecommunication jobs in the United Kingdom, and this economy both fuelled and benefitted from these firms. By the time the story 'broke cover' with an article about 'Silicon Roundabout' on Old Street in 2008, the growth of an organic techno-cluster was well under way. Mapped by DEMOS in 2012, they found over 3,200 firms and 48,000 jobs in a corridor of high-tech activity across inner East London, with a 'hot zone' centred on Clerkenwell and Hoxton. Within this area, some firms had established international reputations, such as MindCandy, Unruly Media, Songkick and Last.fm. Google Campus opened a technology hub in 2012 and corporate organisations were increasingly attracted to the opportunities represented by the innovations, people and business ideas. Most of the firms were started by highly educated white British men in their thirties. The firms were mainly micro-businesses with fewer than ten employees and less than five years old, but over a third had some form of international structure, often tapping into expertise and supply chains globally. Many fitted the 'digital creative descriptor': rather than developing new technology, they were applying it in ingenious ways to develop new services and business models.

Why East London? Office space is relatively cheap for London. The local cafes, bars and amenities offer social space which makes working and hanging-out with like-minded people attractive, providing a highly localised social and creative network and ecosystem. Men tend to find the urban, 'edgy' environment more attractive than women, reinforcing the 'techno geek' stereotype in an area with few normal retail facilities. The labelling of the area as 'Tech City' by a government keen to align with and support one of the few areas of economic growth in the United Kingdom and extend eastwards to the Olympic Park was viewed with some suspicion by many. The main lesson from East London is to recognise an entrepreneurial network as an organic, self-supporting ecosystem which grows in the right conditions rather than by responding to official strategic planning (Nathan et al., 2012).

The notion of clusters was based in part on the theory of 'industrial districts' first developed by the economist Alfred Marshall, describing an intense concentration of firms in specific and related industrial trades. For example, in the Black Country of the UK West Midlands, each town once specialised in a particular metalworking product: Willenhall in locks, Tipton in chains, Walsall in leather aprons for the metalworkers. The industrial district concept has progressed and been updated beyond being simply geographical, with a particular emphasis on the role of social networks and the connections between networks and innovation (Pittaway et al., 2004). Lave and Wenger (1991), in writing about 'communities of practice', described these types of social networks as communities where participation, the creation of social identity, and social learning are important processes. Learning, exchanging of information and ideas, and innovating can all occur more rapidly as 'spillover effects' in such clusters because of the improved availability of information through social connections which bring firms together (agglomeration), when compared with firms working in isolation.

These ideas are highly relevant to the exploration of opportunity. The traditional stereotype of the 'the entrepreneur' as the 'lone wolf' – the individualistic, solitary achiever who builds a business independent of society or social connection is a myth, neither valid nor effective in building a business, since entrepreneurship is an intensely social and networked activity which depends for its existence on social networking. Industry clusters attract intermediaries, such as investors and financiers, specialist experts, technologists and consultants, legal and accounting professionals, as well as building up a social capital of experienced and well-connected company owners and managers. It has been found that the same people can be involved in forming and investing in a succession of businesses over a long period, and this 'genealogy' factor can be traced in clusters such as Cambridge, United Kingdom.

The cluster and its social network can be seen as a spawning-ground and hatchery for business opportunities. The concentration of related firms creates new opportunities, attracting customers and stimulating interaction between innovations and the resources needed to develop them. The social connections mean that people work with, find, talk to and develop ideas with other, like-minded or compatible people. This socialisation process means that people get acquainted, form human bonds of friendship and trust (as well as rivalry, dislike and distrust) and the formation of new business ventures occurs. So clusters and networks can be seen as 'hotspots' for finding opportunities, resources and the human, social and financial capital for entrepreneurship. It is easier to start a digital media business where there is already a cluster of similar people and firms, and easier to attract staff and customers, than when starting in 'virgin territory'.

Some clusters and industrial districts are more supportive to entrepreneurship than others. The clusters of hi-tech companies around Boston and San Francisco in the United States, for example, resulted from such factors as the presence of research-intensive universities, including MIT and Stanford, with a high rate of producing industry-disrupting innovations and spin-out companies, and attracting investors and venture capital funds. Major customers such as defence industries and film studios stimulated cluster growth and these areas have become intensive and self-sustaining centres of innovation, entrepreneurship and business growth.

The concentration of a particular industry in a district does not necessarily lead to such activity. Many industrial districts in developed countries in Europe and North America declined and shrank or died, including centres of coalmining, steel making, shipbuilding, textile production, heavy engineering and so on. These became uncompetitive in cost and productivity, primary resources ran out, they failed to innovate, renew or migrate into new technologies and market needs changed faster than the industries. State ownership or regulation often played a part in their decline.

For the new venture, assessing the 'entrepreneurial ecosystem' of opportunities, resource and support available in a cluster is important. Among the indicators to look for are:

- the numbers of new-firm starts,
- the survival rate of longer established firms,
- the attraction of new clients and investors,
- the productivity of innovation (e.g., number of patents registered),
- the presence of entrepreneur networks and social connections,
- enterprise-friendly universities, research and enterprise development agencies.

Example: Membertou First Nation – a Canadian case of community entrepreneurship

Sydney in Cape Breton, Nova Scotia, was an industrial centre of coal and steel production which brought prosperity and economic development from the nineteenth to the mid-twentieth century. The decline of these heavy industries left a void which many similar communities struggle to fill. But one group, which had never been allowed to share in its prosperity was the First Nation Mi'kmaq tribe, who for generations had been excluded from mainstream opportunities and deprived of their Reserve lands. They occupied the Membertou district at the edge of the city, named after Grand Chief Henri Membertou. Small-scale entrepreneurship, in traditional crafts, then retailing and services, became part of their way of life.

Their chief, Terry Paul, had been exposed to economic development ideas in the early days of the Harvard Project on American Indian Economic Development, while he was living in Boston. He started to apply those principles from the 1990s to create business activity and employment for the Membertou community. After a few false starts an approach, developed through experience, was to create a 'First Nations Progression Model' of initial capacity-building to develop leadership, management and systems for financial accountability and governance, whilst being based on principles of conservation, sustainability, innovation and success. This enabled preparation for strategic planning, resource allocation and investment in business opportunities. The result was economic development through partnerships, agreements and new ventures, creating income streams and employment. Over 20 years, a series of businesses have been established, increasingly based on the Membertou Reserve, including a Trade and Convention Centre, a major hotel, a restaurant, a Gaming Commission, a Business Centre and other businesses including seafoods, retailing and a Corporate Division which develops services such as geomatics, data management and insurance broking to address corporate client needs.

Scott (2004) attributed the success of Membertou's business growth to its leadership and human capital development, 'using a business approach to achieve social objectives'. Chief Paul developed a management team which has expanded to run a range of service divisions and businesses. Long-term commitment to education and human capital development is enabling young people to progress into Higher Education and then into responsible roles in the organisation. The community continues to expand its land ownership, its population, its business activities and rate of employment. The total revenue has grown to $110 million, with over 530 employees.

By 2013, Membertou was one of the two fastest-growing parts of the Cape Breton economy, the other being the First Nation of Eskasoni, now earning enough from its fishing company to have paid off decades of debt. This success demonstrates that a community-led, collective approach to strategic entrepreneurial development can inspire the regeneration of the wider and still struggling regional economy. This was recognised in 2014 when Membertou Development Corporation won the Canadian Aboriginal Economic Development Corporation's inaugural award for excellence in aboriginal economic development. Chief Terry Paul, re-elected for his 16th consecutive term as chief, commented: 'We must envision the future for all Aboriginal communities, a future of self-governance, self-determination and economic independence' (http://www.membertou.ca/; Scott, 2004).

It is much harder to work on an opportunity in isolation than when support, ideas and resources can be gained from participating in a relevant industry or social network. New entrepreneurs often fear they may lose their business ideas by networking, but generally there is much more to be gained by locating and participating in such activity. Previous experience and relationships in an industry can be of great assistance, and this is where the student or 'newbie' with less experience is at a disadvantage and therefore needs to work harder to develop a base of contacts.

This aspect of opportunity exploration is concerned with the social network and industry cluster dimensions of the opportunity. These networks and clusters are zones where ideas, opportunities, resources and social contacts are available more intensely than elsewhere. Even though there will inevitably be competition, participating in these networks will enable you to learn more quickly, for example, what different people and organisations are doing, what ideas and technologies are 'hot' and what resources are available. You can meet people with complementary skills, interests and experience who are likely to 'speak the same language' as you and explore possibilities for collaborating. You can also start to develop ideas of how you can make a distinctive contribution to groups you may want, or find it useful, to become part of. Ideas and innovations will develop much more rapidly and creatively in an intensively networked environment than elsewhere. There are likely to be needs and opportunities within the group where your interests, skills, expertise and experience can be of use to others, which can be a good way of becoming accepted by them as a participant.

We can simplify entrepreneurial networks by thinking about the categories they occur in, even though these often overlap.

Informal, personal networks may include:

- family, education, community and neighbourhood
- hobby, interest or sports based
- spiritual, faith or charitable

Formal and business networks:

- professional institutions (e.g., Institute of Directors)
- industry/trade associations (e.g., Guild of Master Craftsmen)
- regional or local business groups (e.g., Chambers of Commerce)
- entrepreneur networks (e.g., Federation of Small Businesses)

Online social media networks

- LinkedIn groups
- facebook communities
- media-based groups (e.g., Guardian Small Business Network)
- twitter threads

Increasingly these converge, so that personal as well as business networking take place both online and face to face. It can often be easier and more efficient to find and connect with new people online first and then develop a face-face relationship, similar to online dating.

One approach to developing your entrepreneurial networks is to draw an opportunity map of them, and to use this to explore how developing your networking connections can also develop the social domain for the business opportunity (Figure 6.1).

Activity

- Draw a simple mind-map of your networks of contacts. Use the headings of personal and business or career to start with and develop branches of these.
- Use online research to find out the formal groups which are associated with the type of opportunity you are exploring. For example, they may be related to industry clusters, technology or geographic areas. Search engines and the social media apps mentioned can help with this.
- Which informal groups and social networks did you find?
- Which ones look interesting and possibly of value to you and your opportunity?
- How can you identify any members and find a way into these networks? For example, do you already know anyone who participates in any of these networks, and can you use these contacts to become involved?
- Can you identify any groups of innovative companies, where new opportunities are being worked on and new ventures are being formed?
- Seek out people: who could you contact to find out more about these networks?

■ Social innovation

Social innovation is a rapidly growing and relatively new movement which focuses on developing and applying innovative approaches for societal benefit. It draws on collective knowledge and capabilities from networks of concerned people. NESTA (2012) defines social innovation as

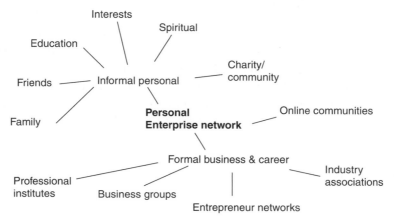

Figure 6.1 Opportunity map of personal enterprise networks

'innovations that are both social in their ends and in their means'. In other words, it covers new ideas (products, services and models) that simultaneously meet socially recognised social needs (more effectively than alternatives) and create new social relationships or collaborations that are both good for society and enhance society's capability to act.

As Murray et al. (2010) commented,

> Two sometimes clashing, sometimes coinciding, themes give transformative innovation it its distinctive character. One comes from technology: the spread of networks and global infrastructures for information and social networking tools. The other comes from culture and values: the growing emphasis on the human dimension, on putting people first, giving democratic voice and starting with the individual and relationships rather than systems and structures. (2)

Social innovation is based on the idea of a social economy in which active citizenship, collaborative action to bring about change and the applications of changing technology can be used to address societal challenges which would otherwise be unresolved by conventional approaches.

There are many overlaps and connections between social innovation, social entrepreneurship and social enterprise. Social innovation takes a more radical and longer-term stance to changing the dynamics of how societies and economies work by connecting the market, social, household and public economies, whilst social entrepreneurship is more concerned with initiating activities to address specific needs and opportunities within this context.

Example: Hill Holt Wood – a case of social enterprise and innovation

The story of Hill Holt Wood began with the ambition of Nigel Lowthrop, a biologist, to own and bring into active use an area of ancient woodland. Nigel saw that many small and old woods were neglected and unproductive, being too small for commercial forestry, yet having the potential to become community assets. Aided by his wife, Karen, he found and in 1995 purchased Hill Holt Wood, a 14-hectare envelope of mixed woodland between Lincoln and Newark in the East Midlands of the United Kingdom. He recognised that by putting the wood to active use, it could become a resource for social enterprise and community development. Guided by three key interdependent principles of social, economic and environmental sustainability, an organisation was established to include an education and training charity and a community-based subsidiary trading arm.

The woodland itself is managed actively whilst being conserved and maintained for public use, and promoting environmental sustainability. Young people experience it as a learning environment in which they can develop skills and realise their potential, and as an enterprise it provides useful products and services for the community. The educational arm provides an alternative curriculum for young people who are often at risk and excluded from mainstream education. The woodland management service has expanded to provide ranger and countryside management across a wide area of over 500 acres of other woodland, employing about 40 rangers. The therapeutic environment has enabled eco-therapy woodland activities for adults with mental distress to improve their well-being. An events and café business have developed as commercial services. Weddings take place in the hall, trees planted to celebrate births and green burials provide income to support Hill Holt Health.

Creating buildings within the woodland required a mix of new and old skills to be developed. This led to the formation of a design team for sustainable buildings, whilst providing work experience for architecture students. This specialises in creating sustainable buildings using traditional methods and natural materials including timber framing, rammed earth, straw bales and limecrete. Many projects have been created, including the spectacular Woodland Community Hall in the wood itself. Hill Holt Wood has won many awards, but also has growing recognition from not only policy-makers but a wide range of community groups, environmentalists and social enterprises for its contribution to developing innovative approaches to tackle social and environmental problems by using the principles of sustainable, environmental and local action in economically viable ways, by creating jobs, providing valued services and maintaining woodland as a community asset.

Hill Holt Wood's founder, Nigel Lowthrop, commented:

If you have vision, viable ideas and leadership skills, then lead or it probably will not happen. Following on from this, develop communication skills to ensure that you can explain your vision, inspire and enthuse communities to support the development and not be seen as imposing your model but providing solutions to multiple problems.

For local community enterprises, adding value is key to success and survival. (http://www.hillholtwood.com/)

■ Divergent and convergent thinking

The relationship between creativity and innovation is shown in Figure 6.2.

Creative thinking is divergent, often intuitive and unstructured, opening up new ideas, connections and possibilities. Innovative working is convergent, focusing on combining a

Divergent thinking:
• identifying the opportunity
• making creative connections
• exploring new information
• researching & analysing information

Convergent thinking:
• deciding possible solutions
• planning what to do
• developing & implementing the innovation
• communicating the idea
• monitoring progress & results.

Figure 6.2 Divergent and convergent thinking

limited number of ideas on a workable application or solution to a problem. Think of pouring water into a funnel: the mouth is broad and contains splashes and turbulence, but the spout is narrow and produces an easily directed and consistent flow of water.

Divergent thinking is valuable in generating ideas for an opportunity or project. It includes these activities:

- identifying and defining the opportunity, need or problem
- making creative connections
- exploring – open-ended quest for new information
- researching – gathering and analysing information
- investigating – focused search for specific information.

Convergent thinking focuses on moving from many ideas and rich data to concluding, developing and implementing an opportunity or project. Convergent activities are structured and focused on completion – making decisions and choices, taking action, getting results and 'making things happen':

- deciding the possible solutions
- planning what to do
- developing and implementing the innovation (e.g., a product or service)
- communicating the idea to stimulate demand
- monitoring progress, measuring and reviewing the results.

Creativity involves imagining a new reality, but innovation is required to make it work. Innovation develops ideas into applications and solutions, and introduces new products, methods or technologies through convergent thinking, by moving from opening-up many options to selecting between alternatives. Innovation integrates knowledge to solve problems and meet needs in new ways, by applying ideas, technology and resources to create new solutions. Innovation is an iterative process, driven by the search for 'what works'. It is assessed by the utilitarian criteria of meeting a need successfully, and producing applications which work and are economically viable.

Innovation is integral to the entrepreneurial process. New ideas are of little value without the ability to apply and harness them as value-creating products, services or processes. It includes research and new product development, and applying science, knowledge or technology in new ways to create new methods, processes, and applications. It can take many forms, from technology, science or engineering-based activities to simple forms of 'doing something new'. However it is best considered as a logical process, often iterative, going back repeatedly, by trial and error, to find the best approach.

The ability to innovate can provide vital advantages for an entrepreneurial organisation. Being able to think creatively and identify new applications and markets for ideas, products and technologies and working quickly and flexibly are essential. Innovative companies have higher rates of new or improved product introduction, and are faster or first to market compared with competitors. They are more flexible, better able to attract external finance and experience more positive impact on company performance, turnover, profitability and return on investment than the norm. However innovation is inherently uncertain because it involves risk and is resource-hungry, so effective project management is vital for successful innovation. Moving effectively between divergent and convergent activity is one means of achieving this.

■ Innovation as a creative learning process

These are common features of innovative practices:

- Iterative – a 'try-it to see if it works' experimental approach; innovations are tested out with users, adapted and tried again repeatedly
- Failure is inevitable at stages in this process; unsuccessful innovations are rejected but learning should occur at every stage
- Risk and uncertainty is inevitable because it is not known at the outset what will work; innovation takes longer than and usually costs more than you anticipate
- Successful innovations are copied, failures are forgotten; protect the successful innovation and the intellectual property (Chapter 3).

The process of developing and implementing innovation was described as a journey in Chapter 4 rather than a conceptual model because, as on a journey, there are different starting and finishing points, you may well go backwards as well as forwards, and diverge to explore interesting avenues, possibly becoming lost or side-tracked at times. That is what the innovation experience is like in practice, because it involves trial and error, experimentation and even luck. Innovation, like entrepreneurship, is a creative and discovery-centred learning process, in which review and reflection of what does or does not work from past work as well as direct experience is essential. An innovation which is unsuccessful in one situation may be capable of being transferred effectively into a different one.

Innovation requires a balance between creativity and control which can be explained in terms of divergent and convergent thinking. There are many models of innovation, often linear and complex, but it is unlikely any one model can be universally applicable. Here we introduce a simple framework for innovation which can be used for creativity, action, learning, evaluation, planning and application of new knowledge in the innovation process. It includes four modes of working, each of which is necessary for innovation. These are shown in Figure 6.3. They are not in a fixed or linear sequence, but an innovation is likely to move through each mode a number of times.

- Generative: recognising needs and problems, creative thinking, formulating opportunities, forming and connecting ideas.
- Reflective: reviewing what is known and what works, gathering and shaping existing knowledge and practices, evaluating experiments, analysing data, drawing conclusions to inform the innovation and critically evaluating what does and does not work, conceptualising what has been learned and how this can be used.
- Prospective: future-oriented thinking, project planning how to test out the innovation, designing, developing proposals and business models, strategy formulation.

Generative

Problem & opportunity recognition
Creative thinking & association
Curiosity & discovery
Idea development

Active

Organising & controlling experiments
Engaging users
Project management
Gathering data
Practical application of what works

Reflective

Reviewing knowledge & practice
Analysis & assimilation of data
Conceptualisation
Critical evaluation & concluding

Prospective

Future-thinking
Designing how innovations will look & function
Project planning & business modelling
Developing forward strategy

Figure 6.3 Innovation: four modes of working

- Active: experimenting and testing, project management, doing the innovation work in a structured way, involving users, controlling the experiment, measuring and gathering data.

An innovation could start with idea generation, and then move clockwise through the modes. But it might equally start with a review and reflection on current knowledge, leading into prospective thinking and then active experimentation, which generates new ideas and leads back into reflection. There is not a single sequence, and several of the modes (if not all) will be used more than once in developing the innovation.

Innovation generally requires a more formal approach than simply 'trying things out to see if they work' which can be wasteful, unproductive and risky. Specific skills and tools, some of which have already been explored, are used in the innovation process. Using research to establish what is already known, drawing conclusions and learning from this will provide a much better platform than uninformed fresh experimentation, and may even show that new innovation is not required because a transferable solution already exists.

Activity

- Look at the four modes of innovative working:
  - □ Generative
  - □ Reflective
  - □ Prospective
  - □ Active
- Which of these have you used in developing your opportunity so far?
- Which have been:
  - □ More effective?
  - □ Less effective?
- Which modes do you prefer to work in?
- How can you gain more experience and confidence of working in the other modes?

Innovation should be planned to reduce variable or unintended outcomes and to make best use of resources. Using formal methods, such as mathematical 'design of experiments' (e.g., Bailey, 2008) during the iterative process can add rigour and reliability, with observation, measurement and review processes being critical. Reviewing and conceptualising what has been learned, how this can be used and protected will capture and reinforce the value of the innovation. This structured approach may seem antithetical to creativity, but the ability to balance creativity and control with learning and doing is at the heart of successful innovation.

Innovation vanguard firms show the way to beating the downturn

Robert Tucker (2008) studied 'vanguard' corporate organisations in many industries which created the conditions for stimulating innovations through 'idea factories' in *Driving Growth through Innovation*. He suggested seven strategies for generating new ideas and creating value through innovation-led growth:

- Invite everyone to join the quest for new ideas.
- Involve customers in the process of generating ideas.
- Involve their customers in new ways.
- Focus on the needs that customers don't express.
- Seek ideas from new customer groups.
- Involve suppliers in product innovation.
- Benchmark idea-creation methods (www.innovationresource.com).

One feature of this approach is that it reflects the inclusive and socially networked approach to innovation; involving customers leads to co-creating value, with ideas and solutions being originated and developed through users interacting with creators and producers.

Innovation in action – creating work opportunities

One of the major concerns many people have is their ability to find work opportunities, mainly paid but also unpaid to gain experience. This is especially the case with young people trying to gain entry to the job market, people returning to work and older people. There are a number of examples of social innovation which aim to help older people to extend their active lives, including self-employment and finding work.

Figure 6.4 shows the four modes of innovation focused on the problem of creating work opportunities for people in these groups who are often at the margins of formal job markets and need to gain experience to enhance their employability. One important point here is not to assume that a 'solution' always lies in doing something new, but rather finding out and reflecting on what already exists, and how far some of these initiatives and resources can be worked with and adapted to provide what is needed.

The innovators were a group of three students who had themselves experienced difficulty in gaining experience and who recognised that this was a general problem they could try to do something about. To begin with they used the four modes to develop a map of the situation as a possible starting point.

■ Using tools for innovation

In this section a set of tools which can be used for developing innovative solutions as opportunities are introduced. These can be used within the framework of the four innovation modes and they are illustrated by an example. They use both divergent and convergent thinking in each mode of the innovation process.

- Innovation function analysis – prospective innovation mode

Generative

Ideas for:
Business start & self-employment
Community based & social enterprises
Apprenticeships in small & microfirms
Jobsharing, mentoring
Web directory of job sites
Using technology to access work
Register of experienced experts
Micropayments system

Active

Work with existing organisations
Promote network & self-help groups
Co-operative self-employment groups
Apply technology to access & do work
Reclaim underused assets for community ventures
Aim to grow the market for new services

Reflective

What already exists?
What research is out there?
Public services-Jobcentre+
Online job sites & agencies
Policy initiatives
Legal frameworks
Online & career networks

Prospective

What does 'future of work look like?
Longer, more flexible careers
'Design your own career'
Increasing needs & demand in 50+ economy
Define & bridge the gap: people who need work but
lack social networks to find it
Designing a mediating/connecting service

Figure 6.4 Applying innovation modes to new work opportunities

- Idea space – generative and prospective innovation modes
- Innovation solution development – prospective and active innovation modes

In this section we follow the development of an initiative to help people seeking entry to the job market as an example of an innovation design project. The team identified that there was an unmet need to connect potential workers, including students, with small businesses and social enterprise organisations who could provide short, often informal, work experience opportunities for them. They then used more structured approaches to engage potential users to identify what they needed to do, and then to design the innovation using the 'Idea Space' technique detailed later in this section.

Innovation function analysis

The purpose of using innovation function analysis is to assess the detailed requirements for what an innovation has to provide, by establishing the design and performance parameters which it needs to achieve. This is a semi-structured enquiry process with sets of questions about the users (who), purpose and value (why), success criteria (what) and approach (how) of the proposed innovation. It works best by involving groups of users fully and collaboratively in the enquiry process. The language may seem formal but it is necessary to move from what can be quite fluid and ambiguous thinking in the generative mode, to become much more specific and 'grounded' in developing a clear brief for what the innovation will actually do. It can be used for a more detailed investigation once the existence or potential of an opportunity has been identified, and helps the innovation journey to move from 'idea' to 'opportunity'.

The method is to identify, analyse and specify systematically the job, task or function which has to be performed. This can be applied to any situation, from a personal service or product, such as a digital entertainment device, to new business models, websites, industrial and service applications. The technique is to identify customers, users or 'performers' of the function, and gather information by information-gathering methods, such as online surveys, interviews and observations in order to analyse the function. The aim is to specify the task the innovation must perform by collecting as much of the following information as is applicable:

- What is the job, task or function which has to be completed?
- What is the value produced as an outcome or result of this function?
- What are the success criteria of this function for the user?
- What are the success criteria for the customer of the end result (if different)? These success criteria should include:
  - value-added
  - cost/value for money
  - speed
  - consistency of performance
  - how the quality of the outcome is assessed.
  - What inputs are used to complete the task (materials, information, human effort, energy, money)?
- What is the cost of these each time the function is performed?
- How is this task or function performed at present? What is the process?
- What problems, deficiencies or frustrations arise at present (e.g., what costs, time, effort, inconsistent performance or quality occur)?
- What desire or scope for improvement can the user or customer suggest?
- As well as the function being specified in this way, the scale of adoption of the task also needs to be assessed or estimated as far as is feasible:
  - How many users of this function can be identified? Are they increasing or decreasing in number?
  - What is the cost of this activity (number of users x frequency of use x cost per use)?
  - Which products and organisations benefit from the function being performed at present?
  - What would be the costs to the user of changing to a new system?

Once the function and its scale has been specified in this way, it can be assessed whether this is a 'problem worth solving'. If it is a widespread task in which users experience variable performance and frustration, and if there may be scope for enhancing quality of outcome and performance, or reducing cost, then further investigation is worthwhile. If so, the specification which has resulted from the function analysis is the starting point for creative thinking and problem solving to develop an innovation which is capable of meeting it.

Figure 6.5 shows the innovation function analysis the team completed for the work experience project. This format can also be used as a problem map to gather the information.

Activity
- How can you apply innovation function analysis to your opportunity?
- Try using it to understand users' requirements for your innovation
- Work through the questions, answer the questions you can
- Present the results in a mind-map or alternative format

Designing innovations and solutions

This moves from defining the need for the innovation to thinking creatively and developing ideas for potential solutions. Just defining the problem may have started to trigger ideas. Start to write these down, either on Post-it notes or on a piece of paper. Rather than using a checklist, which may not be helpful to creative thinking, some of the following questions can be used to stimulate analysis of the problem. You can do this by developing further the innovation function analysis map, as described earlier, to generate ideas of how to work on the opportunity:

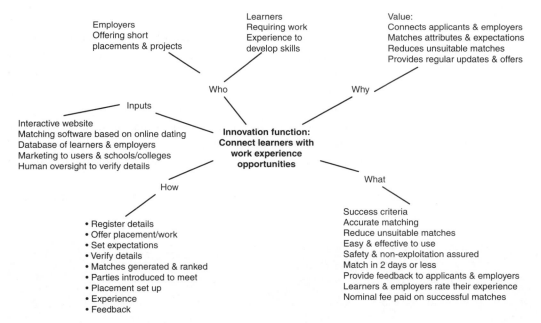

Figure 6.5 Innovation function analysis

- Consider each of the branches and how it relates to the problem.
- What are the causes, and how could these be prevented or minimised?
- What would people affected by the problem see as the ideal solution?
- What factors need to change for the problem to be solved? These may include:
  - changing people's *behaviour* (e.g., that of people who cause the problem)
  - changing or introducing a *system* as a formal way of doing things
  - changing or introducing *technology*
  - changing *awareness* by educating or making information available
  - changing or influencing *environmental* factors.
- What resources are available? How can you combine these resources in new ways to solve the problem?
- Resources could include:
  - information
  - skills and know-how
  - technology
  - social, supplier and distributor networks
  - capacity, land, finance.
- How have similar problems been solved by others? What can be learned from them?

Once you have identified one or two possible ideas to work on, start to develop these to show how these might work. The Idea Space is a technique which can help you to do this.

Idea Space

The Idea space is a design technique for developing ideas spatially, in relation to four sets of criteria, to establish its attributes as part of the innovation process (Figure 6.6). Once we have an idea for something new, how do we define what it looks like, what it does and how it works, so that it can be realised? The Idea Space is a simple way of making this information explicit and then connecting this information in new ways to develop new ideas and explore how they can be operationalised. Associating or combining information in new ways can help us to imagine new possibilities by shifting our perceptions of reality, even if no practical use or innovation results from the creative insights. If we 'flip-flop' by looking at different perspectives, such as seeing a problem through the customer's eyes rather than an organisation's, or starting from the end of a process rather than the beginning, and working back, creative insights begin to emerge.

Activity

Creative thinking using the 'Idea Space'

The purpose of this activity is to introduce a method for stimulating creative thinking by associating ideas, to show how this can assist innovation.

Resources & capabilities
Eg Product
Technology
Material
Artefact
Process or method

Attributes   **Environment**
Purpose   People
Shape/structure   User experience
Colour, texture, feel   **Idea space**   Place
Emotional dimension   Technology
Physical/virtual   Close or remote
Aroma/taste

Information
Knowledge
Opportunity or problem
Demand
What works/does not work

Figure 6.6 Idea Space

   The Idea Space has four boxes (see Figure 6.6) headed 'resource', 'information', 'attributes' and 'environment', which all feed into the Idea Space. All the factors listed in these boxes can be changed, depending on the specific details of the idea you are working on.
1. Select a 'resource'; this may be a product, technology, material or process which is easily available to you.
2. Select from the list of 'attributes', those which apply to this resource, for example, purpose, shape, colour, structure, texture.
3. Select the 'information' which is available from the list of resources, for example, knowledge of a problem, opportunity, demand, 'what works' or does not work, 'what-if' idea for improvement.
4. Select the 'environment' factors which affect the conditions in which the resource is used, for example, people, place, posture, language, close or remote.
5. How can the resource, attributes, information and environment factors be combined in new ways? Experiment with making different connections.
6. Think of how each of the attributes can be changed in turn to see what ideas this produces.
7. List the new combinations from stages 5 and 6 in the Idea Space in the centre.
8. Harvest the best, most feasible or interesting ideas from the list.

The work experience placement website idea was developed using the Idea space technique.

■ Applying design thinking

Design involves thinking about all aspects of the customer or user's interaction with the opportunity – not only what it looks like, but the physical and emotional experiences they have with it. We are used to a website or product being designed, but design thinking can be

Resources & capabilities
Ability to generate employer contacts
via social media & networks
Provide small-scale work opportunities of mutual benefit
Web-based service, register to use

Attributes
Enable users to explore & make new connections
Explore & develop multiple connections
Post questions, problems & opportunities
Share learning experiences
Prioritised matches using online dating functionality
Ratings & feedback generated by users

Idea Space

Environment
Online experience
Browsing via phone, tablet, PC
Provides regular updates to promote use
Enjoyable & interesting to use

Information
Work experience project & placement opportunities
Connecting with
Learners with motivation to gain experience
Verifies information to safeguard users

Figure 6.7 Idea Space example

applied to all aspects of realising an opportunity. What messages and cues does it give out about its identity? Is the user's experience formal or enjoyable?

Some initial ideas about the role of design were covered in Chapter 5. Design affects our experience of everything we interact with, and successful innovation relies on good design. You may not have been trained as a designer, but you could work with a design student on your opportunity, or develop your own thinking and skills in this area.

Applications of design thinking to realising an opportunity

- Creating a visual image and identity, for example, branding and signage
- Website and app design
- Marketing, advertising, communications and promotional material
- Business card, letterhead and stationery
- Product design
- Service design
- Premises – office, shop interior and exterior
- Event or promotional stand
- Processes used by customers such as making an enquiry or placing an order.

Any project or business venture is certain to require some of these at some stage, probably quite early on. Good design works, by attracting people and making their interactions with the enterprise rewarding. Bad design, or non-design, where no one has given any thought to the experience, is both bad for business and surprisingly common. Increasingly, services and

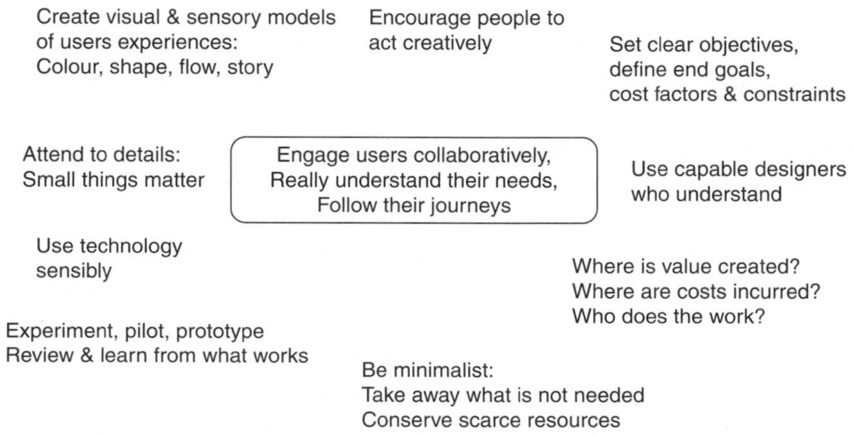

Create visual & sensory models
of users experiences:
Colour, shape, flow, story

Encourage people to
act creatively

Set clear objectives,
define end goals,
cost factors & constraints

Attend to details:
Small things matter

Engage users collaboratively,
Really understand their needs,
Follow their journeys

Use capable designers
who understand

Use technology
sensibly

Where is value created?
Where are costs incurred?
Who does the work?

Experiment, pilot, prototype
Review & learn from what works

Be minimalist:
Take away what is not needed
Conserve scarce resources

Figure 6.8 Principles of service design

processes are consciously designed and Figure 6.8 illustrates some general principles which are applicable to service businesses as well as more generally.

An important idea in service design is that the customer's experience is co-created between the enterprise and the user, in just the same way in which value is co-created. That is, the enterprise is not simply doing it for them but they are doing it together. That applies to anything from sending twitter messages to assembling flat-pack furniture. So we need to think about how design can enhance and support the co-creation of value with the customer, to make it easy and rewarding.

Activity

- Imagine yourself as a customer or user of your enterprise. From the first contact, what would you want their experience to be? What would they see, how would they be treated, what would they do, how would they feel?
- Create a storyboard or draw a picture to express the customer's interactions with the enterprise.
- How can you use design to create and realise the opportunity effectively?
- What functions will need to be designed in your business?

The next section develops this by including guest contributions from two practitioners, firstly in design and then in using online technologies for business.

Design essentials for new businesses

By Alison Branagan
Creative Consultant and Associate Lecturer, Central Saint Martins College of Art and Design and author of The Essential Guide to Business for Artists and Designers (www.alisonbranagan.com)

In business, design goes far beyond traditional associations with the creation of marketing materials. Design is as much about the way we think; it is a cognitive process of visualisation which can be applied to (for example) planning, strategy, systems and the environment. Intelligent design application can save a business time, money and resources in the long term.

When starting out, you may be a sole practitioner or team enterprise. If you desire growth it is often obtained by hiring or employing other professionals, crafts, trades, manufacturers, agencies and trainees. It is wise when you start any venture to think through how best to communicate with other individuals, companies or organisations. This will help in designing the flow of communications.

All communication channels have to be approached individually. Try not to become reliant on e-mailing and texting when conducting business. Being remote will hinder your ability to build rapport and engage clients in real-time conversation. Make it easy for people to find the information they require – especially the customer.

Suppliers will require information in different ways. A new assistant may be working remotely but will need guidance in task administration, and to be able to find information and resources. Your accountant will request financial data entered in spread sheets. A manufacturer will wish to view a working prototype and detailed specifications. Social media fans will want to see amusing posts, photographs and exclusive deals.

An important application of design is business branding (logos), design format and font choice. It is vital, if you are not an illustrator, graphic or interface designer, that you find talented professionals who you can commission to create your print and online marketing materials.

A common mistake people make in setting up their business is in trying to be their own designer. It is possible to use various cheap template web kits and budget logo web portals and bodge together a brand identity. But if you wish to build a reputable, impressive and stylish business, then you need to hire professional designers, illustrators and photographers. Poorly designed websites using boring stock photography will not attract the clients you seek.

Numerous websites can offer sophisticated yet affordable management solutions to all sizes of businesses from sole traders to international corporations. One example is the availability of efficient digital payment systems, which are supplied by banks and online payment merchants such as PayPal. Several smartphone apps can also turn your mobile into your own credit card terminal. Another well-designed service is Eventbrite, an online booking service which reserves seats, issues tickets and takes payments for all types of events. Dropbox is a mostly free cloud storage and digital file transfer system. Many of these online providers now make global operations possible from iPads, tablets and laptops.

In the beginning you don't need to spend tens of thousands of pounds on design, but you should be prepared to budget for website/blog, brand design, stationery, business cards and other marketing materials. When going into business you have to be realistic about what design services cost – good design will always pay for itself in the longer term.

Good design can make the difference between an ordinary and outstanding innovation. The principles of design can be applied to any innovation, from a physical product such as a mobile digital device, an Internet application or a service such as a travel tour organiser. Good design makes the customer's experience 'natural' and enjoyable, whilst also being functional, robust and economical and conveying the distinctive identity of the product. Finally, the innovation must function effectively and provide the benefits the customer expects. This means that all aspects from design, production, delivery, customer information and support must be provided and managed effectively. All these aspects contribute to the creative process of originating the innovation.

■ e-marketing and using online tools to develop and promote the venture

Use of online technology platforms, digital media and cloud computing applications have become essential aspects of entrepreneurship and no longer confined to tech-savvy innovators or e-entrepreneurs. Rather, online technologies have become a democratic way of enabling people to have much wider access to a huge range of applications, information, market opportunities and scope for development and innovation.

From 2009 we found that student business teams taking our Entrepreneurship module and using the Opportunity-Centred approach were starting to use free proprietary online tools to research, model and develop simulated, beta-version and 'pop-up' enterprises. The students found the applications they wanted to use, found out how to use them and often achieved impressive results. Most students were using netbooks or tablet devices so access was easy. In 2011 we started running an accelerated entrepreneurship programme in six weeks for international master's students, and asked every group to make some use of online tools to help them in researching, developing or demonstrating the business concept. Everyone uses it, and it works.

The field is developing rapidly and a book is likely to be outdated in the time between being written and published. However, it is essential for aspiring entrepreneurs to gain an understanding of how to use online tools to develop business opportunities and then to learn by experimenting and using these. This section includes a guest feature by a practitioner who is at the cutting edge of using online applications for entrepreneurial development.

Online technology platforms: the technology through which the entrepreneur and user access the software applications; conventionally a desktop or laptop PC, but increasingly via smartphones, iPad and tablet handheld devices, and heading towards wearable devices such as Google glass.

Digital media: the wide range of software applications by which the user interacts online with the enterprise. Based on the web browser, these include online search engines, survey tools, price comparison and aggregator sites. Social media applications have become the norm in interacting in real time with large numbers of users.

Cloud computing applications: cloud computing is a broad term, but it enables an enterprise to conduct all its operations through web-based tools and to have all data stored on remote servers. It means a business can be scaled up very quickly to enable rapid growth.

Building an online business

By Paul Parkinson
E-entrepreneur (www.paulparky.com/)

The internet has brought commerce directly into our homes. We can research products and services, compare prices and product attributes and buy these products from anywhere in the world using a tablet from home or whilst travelling.

The Internet provides the same opportunity to any UK-based entrepreneur or small business owner who wants to tap into the ever-growing e-commerce marketplace. The Internet has created a new economy, which by its explosive growth and sheer size has forever changed our perception of the 'traditional' way of doing business. With digital commerce in the United Kingdom estimated at over £121 billion a year all businesses should be looking at how to take advantage of this online opportunity. The majority of businesses in the United Kingdom are doing business online and do have a website to facilitate this. However, it is estimated that there are at least 1.5 million businesses in the United Kingdom that don't yet have a website (*Source*: Pearson Business Services & Google www.gbbo.co.uk/).

As over 41 million people in the United Kingdom use the Internet to research and make online purchases, there are great opportunities online and every business needs an online presence.

Many entrepreneurs and small businesses still hesitate to stake a claim on 'online real estate' but doing business on the Internet has a number of advantages and benefits that include

- Savings in set-up and operational costs – you don't need to rent high street premises, pay shop assistants or answer a lot of pre-sales queries.
- Reductions in order processing costs – customer orders can automatically come straight into your orders database from the website.
- Increased reach – access to a global audience, thereby increasing sales opportunities.
- Enhanced ability to compete with larger businesses – competing by being open 24 hours a day, 7 days a week.

- Better cash flows – by receiving payment more quickly from online transactions.
- Access to potentially more customers – by attracting customers who would not normally have investigated your type of high street outlet.
- Improving offerings through data management – through effective use of data gathered by tracking customer purchases and the use of other analytical tools.

You don't have to be a Google, Amazon or ebay in order to be successful on the Internet. In fact, thousands of small and mid-size companies have managed to develop profitable online businesses. Studies show these small companies will be the main growth force of e-commerce in coming years. Gartner Research recently stated that 30% of small businesses with a web presence and fewer than 20 employees now generate more than 25% of their revenue online.

This should convince you to take your business online.

Planning your website

To make a success of an online business, most of the same factors apply as in an offline business. You will need a well-developed idea, a business action plan, an excellent value proposition and of course personal belief in the idea and in your ability to deliver it.

In addition, with an online business you will need a website. The key to the success of any website is in the planning. The main considerations in planning your website are as follows:

- What are your business objectives?
  - Do you have a specific turnover target?
  - Do you want to build a reputation for quality, error-free products and services?
  - Do you wish to build a solid customer base that grows by X amount per quarter?
- What are your marketing objectives?
  - Will you be promoting a single product, a whole range or a specific offer?
  - Where and how will you market?
- What are the objectives of the website?
  - Do you wish to sell or do you simply wish to inform and/or educate?
- What do your clients require?
  - Put yourself in their shoes. Are they getting what they want from your site?
  - Can they find what they want on your site?
- How are you going to design it?
  - Make it look professional
  - Images on your site are accurate and show products in their best light
  - Well-defined products and services
  - Easy to navigate and user friendly
  - Making ordering procedures straightforward and quick

- What functions are you going to have?
  - One-click purchasing?
  - Confirm orders immediately by e-mail
  - Providing a way for customers to track down the progress and availability of their order
- Where is the content coming from?
  - You and your team
  - Outside experts and copywriters
- How will clients use it?
  - To be informed?
  - To purchase something?
  - Both of the above?
- How will it help convert hits into sales?
  - By ensuring all of the above is tailored to your site visitor's needs should go a long way to ensuring that convert hits into sales.

Note: You can use the above points to prepare a one-page action plan outline.

Products and services that sell well online

Online selling will work best if you have well-defined products or services that can be sold without human involvement in the sales process. In addition, fixed prices for all types of potential customers work well on the Internet as do products or services that can be delivered within a predictable lead time.

The bestselling products on the Internet are gadgets (electronic) clothes and books. In addition to these, 'information products' have exploded on the Internet as they are easy to produce, and selling is made simple via downloading directly to the buyer's computer.

An information product is 'a piece of valuable and saleable knowledge' that has been recorded in some way, either in print, audio or perhaps video format, so it is easy to deliver by downloading. Some of the most popular products are:

- print books and e-books
- booklets and special reports
- manuals and workbooks
- MP3 downloads or other downloadable audio files.

Social media

We have all surely heard of social media? Wikipedia defines social media as 'web- and mobile-based technologies which are used to turn communication into interactive dialogue among organizations, communities, and individuals'.

Social media takes many different forms including Internet forums, weblogs, social blogs, micro-blogs, wikis, social networks and podcasts. The most popular of them and some of the well-known ones include twitter, facebook and YouTube.

These social networks and networking sites allow individuals to interact with one another and build relationships. When products or companies join those sites, people can interact with the product or company. That interaction feels personal to users because of their previous experiences with social networking site interactions. They quickly become cool, popular and the content goes viral.

The two main business benefits they provide are: audience interaction and proactive branding.

Audience interaction

Think about how much effort had to go into interacting with your audience before social media came around. Company events and trade shows required a tremendous amount of resource to get started. Audience interaction is very important in today's online marketing space because it ultimately instills confidence in your audience, allowing them to look at you in a whole new light.

Proactive branding

Social media, when done correctly, also allows your online brand to grow, not just your rankings. Website branding is as important as website rankings and with branding comes much deeper market penetration in front of your audience.

So I hope you can see that by doing business online you can start to build a global business. You don't have to invest large sums of money to make this happen, and there are literally thousands of vertical and horizontal e-marketplaces available to you online.

According to AMR Research more than $1.3 trillion worth of goods and services currently flow through global online B2B marketplaces. What entrepreneur and small business owner would not want a piece of this valuable action?

Go...get online now!

■ Raising finance

The period since the banking crisis in 2008, which included first a 'credit crunch' as banks stopped lending to each other, and then a prolonged recession lasting until 2013, was the most difficult period for new and small businesses to gain finance since the 'great crash' of the 1920s. Within the United Kingdom, for example, we saw:

● major clearing banks focus on rebuilding their own balance sheets and profitability;

- a decline in bank lending to new and small firms, with steep rises in charges for lending;
- disappearance of most public grants and state support for small business;
- few new models of small business finance to replace these.

The question of 'market failure' in bank lending to small firms had previously been much researched, with few conclusive results, but in this period there is no question that the mainstream financial system did not meet the funding requirements of most new and small firms effectively, and government intervention had little effect in changing this, despite having refinanced and gained control of several large banks. From the entrepreneur's perspective, the question remains 'how do I raise the money I need to start, run and grow my business?' rather than one of public policy.

What options are there for the new business to gain funding? Increasingly, with the relative decline in bank lending to enterprises, there are market opportunities for new forms of venture finance. Also, the people most likely to make astute decisions about investing in a business will be those who have run and made money in business, and are looking for investment opportunities. Yet innovative approaches to providing finance for enterprises are emerging, if more slowly than is necessary to enable new firms to start and grow without encountering real hardship in finding finance.

Types of finance

Equity: A limited company sells a number of its shares to an investor at an agreed price. The investor expects either an increase in the capital value of the shares over time; a share in the profits via dividend yield; or both. Investors are likely to be individuals, or specialist funds such as venture capital trusts. UK banks generally do not take equity investments in small firms.

Lending: A lender makes a loan, normally for a fixed period of time, at a fixed or variable rate of interest to the business. This may be a bank, fund or individual.

Credit: A supplier, customer or other party advances goods, money or other commodity to the business in advance of payment. For example, customers pre-pay in advance of delivery, or employees work in advance of payment.

New approaches to gaining finance include:

- Short-run high-cost unsecured loans. For example, www.wongabusiness.com used its experience of the UK personal convenience finance market to develop short loan facilities for businesses; this can be regarded as 'distress funding', normally best avoided as premium rates of interest are charged.
- Peer-to-peer lending. This developed initially in the retail market, where ZOPA (see example later) launched as an intermediary service between private lenders and borrowers. This concept has transferred to the business lending market via Funding Circle who created an online market in 2010 for investors to offer loans against applications by businesses.

ODI (2013) estimated that £550 million had been lent by P2P between 2009 and 2013 to businesses and consumers.

- Crowdsourcing. This developed in the United States as a way of stimulating small investments from relatively large numbers of people in the creative enterprise field via social media, rewarding investors with a token such as a piece of artwork or a designer T-shirt. PledgeMusic 'hands on, direct to fan' has become an established model for rock music acts to raise funding from fans for new recording and film projects, for example.

- Credit unions and co-operative financing. Credit unions are small savings and loans providers owned and administered by their members, so you need to save with one before borrowing. There are about 500 in the United Kingdom and although their prime focus is on small amounts of personal finance, some are now able to lend small amounts for business start-up as well as loans to community organisations who become members. There is an Enterprise Business Credit Union and this form of financing seems likely to continue to grow.

- Microfinance. Comparable with Credit Unions, this developed as a way of providing financial services to poor people in developing countries excluded from conventional banking, most notably by Mohammed Yunus through the Grameen Bank, which lends to over seven million women in Bangladesh. Microfinance has grown steadily in developing economies but has not kept pace with demand, operating where the transaction costs and risks are too high for conventional banks. Interest rates tend to be high to reflect this and there is a steady critique of microfinance (Dichter and Harper, 2007).

- Funding for social enterprise. Social enterprises have started to be able to gain access to finance through different channels not open to conventional businesses. Examples in the United Kingdom include Big Society Capital, the Social Investment Business administers a range of funds, community development and local investment funding may be available; Big Issue Invest runs a Social Investment Loan Fund. So there is diversity and growth in the range of funding available for social and community enterprises, but they tend to change frequently where they draw on government funding, for example. Also, funds may be targeted to achieving specific types of social impact, and applications will need to be presented as professionally as business lending proposals to be successful.

Ways of financing your opportunity

Options depend on the type of opportunity, and its attractiveness to investors can be assessed using the Opportunity Assessment (pentagon) in the toolbox. Investment requirements can be identified using the venture planner in Chapter 5.

'Bootstrapping' or starting and growing the business through self-funding is the oldest and most frequently used means of financing a start-up venture. Investing personal savings and then using revenues to finance working capital and growth means there is little reliance on external funding, but it is likely to constrain opportunities to expand the business and puts personal finances under strain.

Investments and loans from family members are often used to finance start-ups, but tolerance of risk is needed in case the business fails.

Customers may be asked to pre-pay for services or products to finance bringing them to market. This has become an established method of funding in the creative industries including film, music, events and publishing, for example. Trust is essential to reward loyalty.

Example: ZOPA.com

ZOPA was established in the United Kingdom in 2005 as the first online 'peer-to-peer' lending marketplace, as an intermediary between personal lenders and borrowers. It is one of the few successful financial innovations in recent years which has truly benefited savers and lenders as well as the business owners and investors.

Peer-to-peer lending works because it recognised and addressed two problems:

- bank lending both to individuals and small firms was inefficient, with banks reluctant to lend and applying high interest rates and fees
- savers received low rates of interest on deposits, meaning there was a large pool of available finance looking for better returns

Rather than using a bank, the ZOPA model enables lenders to choose their risk profile and lend to borrowers scored A*, A or B, spread across a loanbook in small chunks of £10 each to minimise risk. The ZOPA is the 'Zone of Possible Agreement' which enables lenders to match their interest rate, time and borrower risk profiles. Borrowers are charged an initial fee and lenders 1% annually. ZOPA has grown to lend over £256 million since its launch, and the model has been copied by over 35 other peer-to-peer lenders. Giles Andrews, CEO of Zopa, anticipated peer-to-peer lending would double in 2013 and could increase from 1% to 10% of the personal loan market in the next few years. Lenders have received an average of 5.3% return after charges and borrowers pay on average 6.7% in 2012; the spread or differential between these rates is far lower for ZOPA than with conventional banks, making ZOPA more attractive to both groups. ZOPA uses in-depth screening to minimise bad debt and fraud.

ZOPA received £10 million from the UK government to match with private lending to lend to small businesses as part of a £100 million investment through the Business Finance Partnership. This was an important development as it signalled that previous government initiatives to increase small business lending via major banks had failed. Funding Circle developed a similar business model for lending to enterprises, and have also been supported by government.

ZOPA has won a series of awards for personal finance and business innovation, but their success will be measured by their continuing growth and move from personal to business banking. As their website states, 'peer-to-peer lending is a financial category of genuine and increasing importance'. The ODI (2013) report on 'Opening up big data in finance' powerfully illustrates the growth of P2P lending for businesses and consumers (http://uk.zopa.com/).

■ Critical questions to consider from this chapter

1. In practical terms, how is creativity different from innovation?
2. How would you go about developing an innovation from an idea you had identified?
3. What tools and techniques can be used to develop an innovation effectively?
4. What is social innovation, and why is it becoming so influential?
5. In terms of financing a new business venture, what are the potential options open to an entrepreneur?

In this section we...

Critical questions to consider from this chapter

1.
2.
3.
4.

Part IV
Acting on Opportunities

This is the fourth and final section of the book. Chapter 7 covers the final quadrant of the Opportunity-Centred Entrepreneurship map: acting on opportunities to make them happen. It includes frameworks, techniques and examples of approaches used in enacting opportunities. Chapter 8 completes the text of the book by encouraging you to think and to plan how you can use opportunity-centred approaches for your personal and career development.

Enactment: Making Opportunities Happen

Chapter Contents

- Introduction
- Acting on opportunities: going beyond the venture plan
- Six essential activities in the early-stage venture
- Generating responses to opportunities: evaluating, learning and responding
- Success and failure in early-stage ventures
- Making sense of what works in entrepreneurship
- Managing the enterprise
- Finding what works: practical theories for the venture
- Entrepreneurial management in the new and growing venture
- Entrepreneurial management capabilities
- Strategy and business growth
- Critical questions to consider from this chapter

■ Introduction

The purpose of this chapter is to show how to act on opportunities and to make them happen in a range of situations. The chapter includes, for example:

- creating an launching a new business venture or social enterprise
- launching a new product or service
- starting a new project.

The scope goes beyond this to include the management and growth of an early stage enterprise, and the execution of opportunities within an existing business venture.

This includes implementing a venture plan and applying skills of entrepreneurial management and strategic thinking. The chapter builds on the previous sections which have emphasised planning and preparation. It recognises that, however thorough the planning and preparation might be, the reality experienced in enacting, or making the opportunity happen, will always be different.

So the approach in this chapter is on learning through discovery and experience 'what works' for the opportunity and developing the techniques, skills and understanding which are needed in the particular context of the opportunity to achieve success. For whilst there are useful general principles and frameworks which can be applied, much learning is specific to the opportunity in its market, social and technical context. However, knowledge of critical success factors and ways to avoid the common causes of failure can be applied in early-stage business ventures.

This chapter covers the final quadrant of the Opportunity-Centred Entrepreneurship map: acting on opportunities to make them happen, as shown in Figure 7.1.

The learning goals of this chapter are to enable you to:

- act on the opportunity by selecting appropriate methods
- implement the venture plan and review its effectiveness
- develop practical theories of 'what works', in relation to the venture management and personally
  - identify what can be learned from critical success factors and causes of failure in early-stage ventures
  - develop, implement and review strategies for the new venture
  - assess, review and learn from the impact of actions and feedback
  - analyse and reflect on entrepreneurial and management capabilities for personal development and venture management.

The outcome of this chapter will be to help you to assess and enhance your awareness and ability to translate ideas and intentions for opportunities into effective action.

You will gain most from this chapter by being ready to act on an opportunity you have been developing during the early chapters in this book. Even if the action is small-scale, such as test-marketing or an online pilot, you will learn much more by doing and practical action than by simply reading about the topic.

Entrepreneurship theory has limitations in relation to acting on business plans. The chapter proposes that enacting the opportunity involves a process of real-time, dynamic action learning and sensemaking in conditions of constant change and uncertainty, in which the models, tools and ideas from previous chapters are applied in making the venture happen. Enacting opportunities involves going beyond venture planning, since plans are rapidly overtaken by events, responding to new opportunities, and handling setbacks and failure.

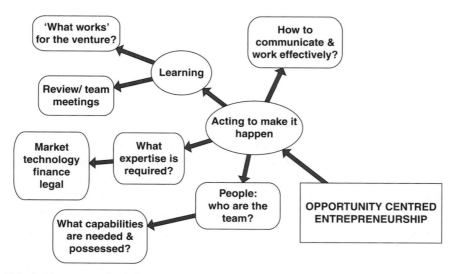

Figure 7.1 Acting to make it happen

Essential activities in an early-stage business and reasons for success and failure of businesses are considered. The practical theory approach is applied to establish both 'what works' in businesses and what happens when it doesn't work. Assessing, learning from and responding to failures are explored as essential habits, and the chapter demonstrates how these can contribute to developing venture strategies and sustainability.

The development of entrepreneurial management as a means of connecting entrepreneurial and managerial skills with a strategic focus is explored. Strategic decision-making, types of entrepreneurial strategy and methods of reviewing the effectiveness of strategy are explored. The final exercise prompts experiential learning, through problem solving, reflecting, using experience and moving forward both personally and organisationally.

■ Acting on opportunities: going beyond the venture plan

Rationally, you might expect that the actions required to implement a venture plan would simply be to implement what had been planned, and that a well-researched plan, well executed, would be successful. As discussed in Chapter 5, future planning is a necessary aspect of entrepreneurial working but any plan is likely to change when the reality of implementing is likely to be both considerably more complex and – crucially – different from what had been expected. Alan Gibb (1996) talks about the 'lifeworld' of the entrepreneur, a lifeworld characterised by uncertainty, complexity, independence yet interdependence with stakeholders, control and ownership.

In this lifeworld, planning is a continuous activity which interplays between planning and acting, and which is more important and useful than slavishly implementing a plan which may quickly be superseded by events and environmental change. What happens is always different from what was planned, and what you actually do is more important than what you intend. Being able to act effectively in the moment, as explored in Chapter 3, is often crucial.

Learning to make it happen

In Figure 7.1, the map of acting to make it happen, the most important word is 'learning', because it is the speed and effectiveness of real-world learning which often makes the difference between the success or failure of a venture. This is related to 'action learning', originally developed by Revans (1980), which is the exploration of problems or questions that arise in everyday practice and which do not have evident solutions. Action learning investigates the causes, effects and possible actions through investigative and problem-solving skills, and is generally a group-based activity. In a new venture, the quest is to find 'what works' as quickly as possible, and this is explored further in the section on practical theories. The connections between decision-making, problem solving and learning in launching and managing a new business venture or an innovation project in an existing enterprise are vital (Figure 7.2).

Implementing the plan and making it happen can be usefully seen as a process of real-time learning by discovery. The entrepreneur discovers which aspects of the plan are effective and useful, and which were founded on incorrect, partial or outdated assumptions. For example, it makes sense to conduct market research to test out demand and consumer reaction to a new product. But the mere fact that this shows a positive result, with potential customers saying they would buy the product, does not guarantee that this will in fact occur. Many students organising events such as club nights and trips to sports or entertainment have conducted surveys of their friends who always *said* they would buy tickets – the reality was often different.

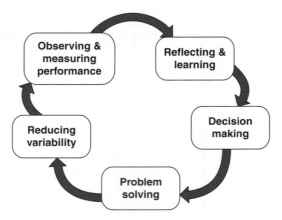

Figure 7.2 Problem solving, decision-making and learning

Example: Pip and Maria's pop-up café

Chapter 3 included the example of pop-up businesses. Pip and Maria launched a small café based in a shop, with a menu they had market-tested of light meals and snacks, and a dining area with tables and chairs on the pavement outside. They opened for business, expecting their trade to build up as they had planned. What actually happened was that existing food outlets increased their sales promotion and special offers to attract more customers, and their café struggled to gain customers. They realized they had not considered their proactive marketing with sufficient care. They made time to talk to the customers who visited them, as well as studying the patrons of the existing outlets. They found that whilst they had focused on retail customers, there was a market segment of office and other workers in the area who were time-limited and not as well served by these outlets. They promoted their café to local businesses, offering a book-ahead service for lunches and take-away sandwiches with a simple web-based app, and a simple loyalty card to incentivise repeat business. They found that this created a level of business which enabled them to break even, so that retaining these regular customers and attracting retail customers on top became their strategy.

This simple example shows that factors such as competitor actions, flaws in the research and planning, new information from customers and competitors, and other considerations mean that starting a business or actioning an opportunity are much more complex and dynamic than simply acting on a plan.

Activity

- Identify the opportunity you are going to act on. This may be starting a business venture, introducing a new product or service or something else.
- Review the planning you have done and establish what steps you are going to take to launch it.
- Think through each of these, imagining what you will do to make each of them happen successfully.
- Then go and put the very first one into action. Do it now!
- Continue reading once you have started.

Review exercise

- Think back over the actions you took in the previous activity.
- Did you do what you intended?
- What happened?
- Was this what you expected, or was the result different?
- If different, why was this?
- How do you feel about the outcome: satisfied or disappointed?

- Review: what have you learned from this action?
- Get into the habit of systematically reviewing the effectiveness and what you can learn from your actions to enact an opportunity.

■ Six essential activities in the early-stage venture

This short section sets out six key activities which are essential in the early stages of most new ventures. Whilst these are necessarily general, they contain practical steps to assist in relating them to the specific nature of each opportunity, and are summarised in Table 7.1.

Managing holistically: see the whole picture

The art of managing a new business venture successfully is first to realise that you, as the manager or part of the venture management team, are responsible – there is no one to delegate to, blame or pass on the unwelcome tasks to. You cannot simply concentrate on your 'comfort zone' of tasks you enjoy and are good at, but must take holistic responsibility for the whole business. This means connecting all the different aspects covered in the venture plan, of marketing, sales, finance, operations and people management, to make sure that they happen. Self-organisation is essential in order to plan, to prioritise and allocate time for all the essential activities, and to work sustainably. It may feel necessary to work 80-hour weeks just to get through everything which needs to be done, but after a few weeks or months it will become clear that this is not sustainable, efficient or very enjoyable. So managing personal time and energy is vital.

Communicating effectively to build up the customer base

The customer is the reason the business exists. The first rule of business is never to rely on other people to find your customers for you. You, and everyone in a new business, have to be a sales representative, able and confident to call up, go out, meet and get to know potential customers. Selling requires confidence, communication skills and interpersonal skills or 'likeability'. So a confident approach to finding prospective clients, opening a dialogue with them to find out what they require, how and when they want it, building rapport, listening and learning from them and developing effective selling skills is vital. Marketing and selling are means of attracting and communicating with customers and satisfying their needs.

Behind this business process there are real human relationships, and the early life of a business is a vital and sometimes scary period of talking to some people you already know – and, it is recommended, to many you do not – to establish their needs, interest them in your selling proposition and in some cases to start a business relationship with them. The business will depend on developing a positive reputation for quality and delivery among customers, so it is essential to get to know your prospective and actual customers by valuing

Table 7.1 Six essential activities in the early-stage venture: action points

Activity	Action points
Managing holistically: see the whole picture	Set realistic but stretching targets for the business: sales, finance, innovation and development Collect and use information to monitor results against targets (see operations) Review performance and adjust business targets Ensure you assess business performance from all aspects
Communicating effectively to build up the customer base	Talk to customers to build close customer relations, aim to appreciate the business from the customer's experience Use social media and direct contact to collect customer comment, feedback and ideas Use these to create new sales opportunities Build the brand through consistent and effective communication Use public relations and media to get your news stories out Attract people to visit your website and social media
Build a fan club around the business by working effectively with people	Attract, select and manage a fan base around the business Carefully select employees and associates who have the passion, values and skills you need and who can grow with the business Make them feel part of the business by sharing rewards and success stories with them Develop your staff so you can delegate essential tasks to them
Widen the talent pool, accessing and using expertise	Identify critical areas where knowledge and expertise will be needed Identify and contact people and organisations who can provide this Develop a network of trusted advisors
Managing business operations	Define the basic business process Identify what information will be produced on sales, customers, operations, people, suppliers and finance Plan how this will be analysed to monitor business performance Ensure business data are secured and backed up Aim to minimise dependence on any single element: customers, staff, suppliers, product, technology, computer server
Managing financial resources effectively	Plan and control cash flow to maintain a positive cash position Control costs, especially fixed costs, by growing the business on a variable cost basis Ensure customers pay promptly and debt is collected Assess and monitor the break-even position to establish profit or loss of the business, of each activity and major customer Maintain personal supervision of business finance Employ a competent and trustworthy person to maintain the business accounts using a standard accounting package

and appreciating their business. Not only do these habits make running a business more enjoyable, they develop social capital and make it easier to find new customers, to develop more business from existing clients, to deal with problems and complaints and to get paid reliably.

Build a fan club around the business by working effectively with people

Running a business is a social activity, and in this negotiated enterprise you achieve results through and with other people. Therefore finding, selecting and working effectively with people both inside and outside the business are essential. The capabilities of interpersonal interaction, leading and managing people, are vital ones to develop. Some entrepreneurs adopt a 'hard', instrumental approach to working relationships, in which they use people for their own ends, but this is usually not the way to get the best from them. Others have adopted a more social approach of 'building up credit in the favours bank' and 'giving without expectation of return', which can be more productive. Again the concept of developing social capital within networks is helpful. The aim should be to create a network of 'recommenders' based on staff, customers, suppliers and other contacts: people who will advertise the business to others.

Widen the talent pool, accessing and using expertise

This leads into the fourth activity. Building up the business will present problems, opportunities, decisions and issues which you have not met before. Frequently, these will not have 'textbook' answers and you cannot know the answer to every question, but you need to be able to find out the options quickly. However it is certain that similar situations have occurred many times before, and the collective expertise to deal with them exists out there. There are many situations, from dealing with large bad debts and negotiating with potential investors to defending your intellectual property, which you would face for the first time and possibly not handle in the best way. It is in your interests to develop a network of experienced and expert advisers whom you can trust and learn from. Some of these should be professional advisers such as a lawyer, accountant and possibly technical expert, whilst others can be experienced and battle-hardened business owners. As the business grows there may be merit in having one or two trusted advisors as non-executive directors.

Managing business operations

Small businesses have a habit of growing organically, adding activities and products in response to opportunities. It is easy to lose focus in this way. The basic business process needs to be planned, organised and managed efficiently to ensure customer requirements are progressed quickly and efficiently, whilst people and resources are working productively.

The business resource process included in Table 5.3 in Chapter 5 is a technique for planning, organising and measuring the business process from sales enquiry to fulfilment. This analyses the relationship between the business process, information and people's skills and capabilities which are needed to manage the process efficiently and effectively.

Managing financial resources effectively

Managing finance effectively has never been as critical as in today's business environment, since it is often extremely hard to raise money. In an early-stage venture, effective financial management is crucial in five respects:

- First, by planning and controlling cash flow you can achieve and maintain a positive cash position and minimise unplanned (and expensive) borrowing requirements, whilst keeping in contact with lenders or investors.
- Second, it is needed to control costs, especially fixed costs, and grow the business on a variable cost basis, except where committing fixed costs is essential and makes business sense.
- Third, it helps ensure customers pay promptly (preferably in advance) and debt is chased and collected.
- Fourth, it is vital to assess and monitor the break-even position to establish profit or loss of the business, of each activity and major customer.
- Fifth, maintaining personal supervision of business finance keeps you aware of the risk of theft or fraud, although employing a competent and trustworthy person to maintain the business accounts and using a standard accounting package are recommended.

Activity

- Review the list of six essential activities for the early-stage business.
- How relevant is each of these for your opportunity?
- What steps can you take to incorporate the most relevant ones into your business intentions?

■ Generating responses to opportunities: evaluating, learning and responding

Starting and running an enterprise is a real-time learning process, and one of the major differentiators between businesses which survive, adapt and are able to grow and those which do not is the ability to learn rapidly and to use this learning to change or improve what the business does. This section explores methods of doing this.

Activity

- You have initiated a new opportunity.
- How will you gather information to assess its success?
- What information will you look for? From what sources?
- How will you assess and review this?

Types of information which early-stage entrepreneurs often use relate to business plan targets and frequently include the factors shown in Table 7.2.

Were these in your list, and what other sources did you have?

The advent of online businesses and social media greatly accelerated the pace at which businesses can offer new opportunities, the intensity of competition and their ability to assess their effectiveness. Using even basic statistics to track customer acquisition, conversions from interest to placing order, customer value and other aspects specific to the business is essential. Reviewing the key indicators at least weekly (many large businesses, such as retailers, will do this daily) means that decisions can be made quickly to respond to emerging trends.

■ Success and failure in early-stage ventures

Why do new ventures succeed or fail? There are of course many reasons for this. However if the new venture can recognise the reasons for failure and their possible causes this can help in planning, managing the venture and solving problems. Similarly, and more positively, if the characteristics and behaviours of successful businesses can be identified these can act as positive exemplars to learn from.

It is important to note that in the United Kingdom, for example, a high proportion of new businesses – as much as 36% – do not survive until their third anniversaries. In December 2008, 90,000 firms closed, many attributed to the sudden onset of financial crisis and recession, followed by a further 500,000 firms in 2009, shrinking the business stock by 4.6%, although this started to recover in 2010 (Duedil.com, 2012). Not all of these businesses

Table 7.2 Measuring business performance

Qualitative	Financial
Missed sales opportunities and declined orders	Number of customers attracted
Customer satisfaction, feedback and complaints	Sales revenue
Customer recommendations (e.g., via social media)	Average customer order value
Comparison with competitor performance	Achieving breakeven
	Gross and net profit

failed; some closed voluntarily, as a result of lifestyle changes, the founders finding alternative employment, or for other reasons.

Reasons for business closure

Common reasons for failure and early closure include the following:

Financial

- cash flow shortage/exhaustion
- inability to obtain or renew financial loan or investment
- bad debt incurred by customer
- insufficient sales revenue
- costs of running the business higher than expected in relation to income.

Competition, marketing and selling

- failure to secure sufficient customers
- size of market too small to sustain business
- action by competitors or lack of competitive advantage
- loss of customers
- over-pricing or under-pricing and lack of viability.

Operational

- failure to satisfy customer quality or delivery requirements
- high rates of complaints, rejects or re-work
- unreliable suppliers, subcontractors or distributors
- inability to obtain essential items or services
- essential data or information lost or unavailable.

Legal

- failure to protect intellectual property
- costs of defending or losing legal action
- costs or difficulty of complying with legislation or regulation.

Human

- insufficient skills and expertise to manage the business
- inability to find or retain employees with necessary skills or experience
- disagreement or incompatibility between people in the business

- ill health or death in the business.

Environmental

- economic downturn or recession
- loss or unavailability of premises
- fire, flooding, weather damage or effect on seasonal business.

These 25 reasons for business failure illustrate the diversity of events and problems which can disrupt a business and result in failure or closure. Some can never be predicted. During 2010–2011 there was a series of 'wildcard' events, including the eruption of a volcano in Iceland which disrupted air travel in the Northern hemisphere for several weeks, followed by 'freak' weather conditions including flooding and heavy snow in the United Kingdom. These affected many businesses, some so seriously they were forced to close. Most others traded through. However many business failures result from incorrect or over-optimistic assumptions or decisions made by the founders, or from lack of skills and readiness to address problems at an early stage.

Many such problems can be prevented by better planning and research, or are capable of being managed to enable the business to survive. Resilience in the face of unplanned events is crucial. Having contingency plans to deal with setbacks, whatever they may be, which result in business disruption, is essential. These include loss of key customers and suppliers, staff, data, energy and financial loss, for example. It is not possible to anticipate every contingency, but planning should enable most of the financial, marketing, operational and human problems to be prevented or identified early enough to be resolved, so long as the business is being run in a competent way. Therefore, management skills are critical in reducing the exposure of the business to normal events and contingencies. They are addressed in more detail in the section on entrepreneurial management skills.

Reasons for business success

The National Business Awards celebrated ten years of rewarding business success in the United Kingdom during 2011. Alex Evans, editor of the National Business Awards, drew ten observations from judging the 2011 awards to account for the success of the shortlisted firms and winners.

1. The corporate pride instilled by ethical practice creates brand value.
2. Award-winning businesses know the value of their people – and invest.
3. The most innovative organisations have an open and collaborative culture.
4. Entrepreneurs win by taking calculated risks and making it happen.
5. Humility and emotional resilience are key characteristics of transformational leaders.
6. Social media has revolutionised business through customer insight and feedback.
7. There's a big difference between transformation and just getting better.
8. E-commerce is booming because it is designed around customer experience.

9. Successful enterprises combine family values with autonomous, entrepreneurial management teams.

10. Some truly innovative business ideas are being tested in charities. (www.nationalbusinessawards.co.uk)

Activity

Business success and failure

Consider the opportunity you are exploring in relation to the reasons for business success and failure.

- Which reasons for business closure and failure do you think your business could be most exposed to? What steps could you take to reduce the risk or impact of these?
- Which of the characteristics of business success do you think will be most important to your business? How could you develop these characteristics as distinctive strengths for your business?
- How could you use the six essential activities for early-stage businesses to help you in managing the launch and early trading of the venture?
- Overall, which of these factors do you think are most critical to the success or failure of a new business venture?

Example: business failures

During 2012, retail business failures peaked in the United Kingdom and a number of high-profile UK retail businesses closed; they included electrical retailer Comet, photography store Jessops, JJB Sports, entertainment media chains HMV and Blockbuster, as well as other less well-known brands in clothing, furniture and hardware. Most of these firms had been experiencing problems for some time and their difficulties were well known, and there had been attempts to refinance them. A few, such as HMV, continued to trade with new owners. What can be learned from these failures? Information from the Centre for Retail Research offers useful information:

- Consumer confidence and spending was depressed, with a downturn on the High St;
- People were increasingly shopping online in search of more choices and lower prices;
- The business models used by these retailers were uncompetitive and obsolete in comparison with the most advanced online retailers and some supermarkets;
- Their costs were too high, partly due to automatic increases in rents and high business rates;
- Their retail offer failed to offer enough customers a new, distinctive proposition.

Overall, they had failed to respond and reposition themselves to trends which had been apparent for some years, making failure inevitable (http://www.retailresearch.org).

■ Making sense of what works in entrepreneurship

The vital task of entrepreneurship is to make opportunities happen. Yet it is often difficult to apply the general theories and principles in the literature on the subject to the specific nature of real situations. Textbooks and journal articles refer to 'implementation' of the business plan or the 'exploitation' phase of an opportunity but making opportunities happen is a practical, real-world activity rather than a theoretical domain. So we need to develop approaches which enable us to develop skills of discovery learning and practical action in opportunity exploitation and enterprise management.

Karl Weick, in *Sensemaking in Organizations* (1995), described sensemaking as a way of making sense of complex and changing environments, which explained unexpected surprises, and individual and social behaviour. Sensemaking is how we continuously interpret the world around us and create new meaning through our interaction with it. This has become even more important as levels of volatile change, risk and uncertainty have increased in the business environment. Weick's theory is generic and not limited to entrepreneurship, although it is increasingly connected with entrepreneurial opportunity recognition (Gartner et al., 2003). Entrepreneurs construct opportunities based on their 'readings' of their environment and their abilities and resources to act effectively within it. The opportunity may not be apparent to other people at the time, and the approaches used to act on it are ones which are reasonable and practical to the entrepreneur, even if they do not appear logical to others. Yet they have to be communicated to other people as strategies, in ways which make sense, through narratives, symbols and other devices.

Sensemaking, Weick (1995) proposed, is a process with seven characteristics. It is:

- grounded in identity construction
- retrospective
- enactive of sensible environments
- social
- ongoing
- focused on and by extracted cues
- driven by plausibility rather than accuracy.

What does this mean, and how does it help in understanding how to act on entrepreneurial opportunities? The seven properties of sensemaking are outlined in Table 7.3, with possible applications in entrepreneurship listed in relation to each of them.

Using sensemaking in entrepreneurship

The sensemaking framework is useful in entrepreneurship, not only in textbooks but in the reality of businesses. We all use the skills and properties of sensemaking without necessarily being aware of them. Having a heightened awareness means that our skills in assessing and

Table 7.3 Sensemaking in entrepreneurship

Sensemaking property	Entrepreneurial application
Grounded in identity construction: the discovery of who I am through how and what I think, in relation to others	Becoming and behaving as an entrepreneur in society – personal and social emergence, Chapter 2; career development, Chapter 8
Retrospective: creation of meaning from reflection and conceptualisation of meaningful lived experience	Reflecting on learning to work effectively – 'what works for me' as an entrepreneur, the concepts of 'practical theory' and the entrepreneurial learning model, Chapters 2 and 7
Enactive of sensible environments: constructing reality and order from creating, acting and relating; producing part of the environment we face	Recognising opportunities and innovating to create new products, services, ways of working and organisations within an existing environment which impact on that environment, Chapters 3–4
Social: contingent on conduct and interaction with others in shared learning, meaning construction and negotiated or joint action	Working with others through the concept of the 'negotiated enterprise' and entrepreneurial teams, Chapter 2
Ongoing: 'in process' and emergent, in-flow but subject to interruption and emotionality	The real-life process of making things happen and making decisions in unpredictable environments, Chapter 7
Focused on and by extracted cues: selective structuring of experience and meaning, dependent on context	It is important to pay attention to clues and to what we have learned , such as market signals, opportunities, competitor behaviour – contextual learning, Chapter 3
Driven by plausibility rather than accuracy: coherence, reasonableness and emotional appeal are important in producing socially acceptable accounts or 'good stories'	The message or story, for example, of the business plan or marketing presentation, must be plausible to be accepted, Chapter 5

working on opportunities can be enhanced. The concept of enactment, or 'going and doing it', which this chapter strongly encourages you to do, is especially useful here. Through enactment we generate interpretations of the changing world and act in ways which cause further change. By acting, we create new reality and change the environment; however this environment can constrain further action.

■ Managing the enterprise

At this point in the chapter, the focus moves from the individual or group who is working on an opportunity, towards the opportunity being located within an organization we shall term 'the enterprise'. This may well be a start-up business, but it could equally be a social enterprise, an existing business or other form of organization. The important point is that to develop, enact and take full advantage of the opportunity, at some stage the identity, resources and backing of an organization, as distinct from individual action, will be needed.

There is a very large knowledge base on organisations in relation to entrepreneurship: for example, on new, small and growing firms and their strategies; social enterprises; corporate venturing and entrepreneurship; and other related categories. Some of these will be referred to but they are each a topic for study in their own right. The next sections deal with the topics of:

- Finding 'what works' for the venture
- Entrepreneurial management in the new and growing venture
- Strategies for the new and growing venture

■ Finding what works: practical theories for the venture

The key factors of strategy, skills, business model and product-market fit which can result in success are an individual combination for each entrepreneur. Every business is in a quest to find out 'what works' in its specific circumstances. This section addresses how to generate practical theories of 'what works' for a business using the practical theory model shown in Figure 7.3 and detailed in Table 7.4.

Entrepreneurs can produce practical theories in their own words from their experiences of their own practice, together with observation and social exchanges with other practitioners. Shotter (1995), described 'practical theories of action' as analytical tools which enable the manager as a 'practical author' to develop 'knowledge in practice' as 'special, contextualized forms of knowing', enabling them to see connections and create meaning between aspects of their lives and practices.

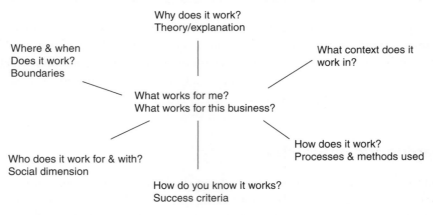

Figure 7.3 Practical theory

Table 7.4 Framework for practical theory

Question	Explanation
What works? (or 'what happens ?')	What practices generally 'work' or occur and are effective? In what application?
Why does this work? (why does it happen?)	What is the logical explanation? What are the theories, factors or variables which explain it and which cause or define its effectiveness?
How does it work? (how does it happen?)	What are the activities, processes or conditions
How do we know it works?	which are necessary for it to occur? How can we measure or observe that it works?
Who does it work for? With whom?	What are the social conditions and relationships within which it occurs?
What are the boundaries within which it works?	When, where etc. is it known to occur or not to occur?

Source: Rae, 2004.

Practice is simply 'what we do', and entrepreneurs as effective practitioners discover 'what works for me', reflecting and making sense of their experiences to develop these 'practical theories' to explain or *account for* 'what works' and why it works. These theories govern such issues as decision-making, dealing with recurrent situations, problem solving and the routines of managing relationships with others.

This knowledge can be used to develop an enhanced understanding of entrepreneurial practice. Through trial, error and reflecting on action, people discover and adopt the practices, rules and routines which they describe as 'what works', often described as 'gut-feeling'. This is intuitive and tacit 'know-how', 'know-what' and 'know-who'. This social knowledge and acquired wisdom is practical, contextual, experiential, yet hard to analyse or test, and is formed and shared through social interaction, for example, through the 'war stories' entrepreneurs often share.

Practical theories can be derived from interpreting entrepreneurs' practical theories at a more general level above the level of the individual case. These not only provides an understanding of 'what works', or what happens, but go beyond this to explain why it works or occurs, how it works, with and for whom it works and the conditions or boundaries within which it works.

Practical theories especially relevant to entrepreneurship can be identified in the following areas:

- personal learning and development
- transition from pre-entrepreneurial to entrepreneurial action
- opportunity recognition and selection
- creating and starting business ventures

- decision-making
- risk spreading and minimisation
- developing entrepreneurial managers and management teams
- employee attraction and retention
- market and customer relationship development
- innovation development
- managing growing businesses.

Here is an example of a practical theory illustrating the concept of negotiated enterprise which was introduced in Chapter 3.

Practical theory: negotiated enterprise

What works?

The creation of value in media businesses involves a negotiated exchange between paid-for information and content by advertisers or content providers with media producers who can show, in measurable ways, they are gaining their required exposure by attracting targeted groups of non-paying customers.

Why does it work?

The media enterprise meets the needs of the advertiser to gain exposure and of the customer to have information or entertainment in ways which create cultural value.

How does this work?

The media enterprise provides a media channel which attracts both advertisers and their target groups of customers in a culturally distinctive way through the mix of programming, style and services.

Who does it work with?

With advertisers or content providers who are prepared to invest consistently in gaining exposure for their message among target groups they wish to attract, and who are receptive and culturally attuned to their messages.

What are the boundaries within which it works?

Independent commercial media including print, radio, TV and Internet online media.

Activity

- Identify a business or organisation which you are familiar with, for example, as a customer, and which is successful or effective in what it does.
- Apply the practical theory framework to it and use this to identify:
- What works for them? How does it work, and why? Who does it work for and with? What are the boundaries within which it works?
- Is this practical theory transferable to other organisations?

Generating strategy from practical theory

Having a base of defined and understood practical theory gives important business advantages. These include being able to grow, by being able to recruit managers and employees to work, and being able to train people in ways which are known to work. The practical theory may be used to franchise or license the business model, or to sell the business as an effective going concern. Practical theory is therefore an aid to developing options for growth strategies, as well as being a means of reducing risk; you would not be likely to invest in a business which did not know 'what worked' for it. This will be developed further in the section on strategy for new and growing business.

■ Entrepreneurial management in the new and growing venture

One of the criticisms often made about business education is that it assumes that 'what works' in large, complex corporate organisations can be applied successfully to new, small and growing firms; it is not often so. For whilst some of the organizational skills and sense of strategic ambition may be transferable, small organisations are socially and qualitatively different to most large firms. Why is this so? Reasons may include:

- The small enterprise is a social group, often likened to a family, and in a family business is an extension of the family
- The purpose, culture and ways of working are shaped by the founder(s) and owners, often with informal, personalised approaches
- There is often a sense of shared responsibility, ownership (even if in a legal sense this is limited), teamwork and co-operation.

The 'family values', coherence and teamwork of an effective small firm are often seen as a great strength, which corporate organisations can seek to emulate but which are often lost if a small firm is absorbed; as shown in the case of Autonomy later in this chapter.

Entrepreneurial management is a distinctive approach to managing organisations, which connects both entrepreneurial and managerial skills to enact opportunities in the context of the enterprise. Both sets of skills are required to start, and more importantly, to grow and sustain an organisation over time. This builds on the model of entrepreneurial and managerial skills introduced in Chapter 2 (and available in the toolkit) which we will return to in this section.

The academic literature on entrepreneurship started to connect with strategic management during the 1980s, for example, through Kanter (1983), Drucker (1985) and Burgelman (1983). These proposed that established corporate organisations could rejuvenate their fortunes by systemising entrepreneurial behaviour and innovation, as conceptualised in Guth and Ginsberg's (1990) integrative model. The related concepts of corporate entrepreneurship and corporate venturing were developed partly to meet the needs of large corporations, but this literature reflected a tension between the qualities of corporate strategic management and of entrepreneurship which was written mainly in the context of North American corporations. Aiming to reconcile this, Stevenson and Jarillo (1990) advanced propositions for corporate entrepreneurship, focusing on the pursuit of opportunity regardless of resources controlled; the orientation of employees towards detecting and exploiting opportunities; connecting resource networks to opportunities; and organisational risk-taking. Kanter (1983) proposed a dynamic model of innovation within a networked organisational context as a framework for corporate entrepreneurship, advocating cross-functional working within very small business units.

These were principally North American perspectives on the transformation of corporate organisations through adopting entrepreneurial approaches, but more recently there have been British and European perspectives on corporate entrepreneurship including Burns (2013) and Tunstall (2011). There is of course a large body of knowledge on the development of owner-managers, and leadership and management in the smaller and growing firm, going back several decades. Allan Gibb (2000 and subsequently) has long advocated the virtue of 'smallness' in organisational thinking to stimulate entrepreneurial behaviour, arguing that large organisations are agglomerations of small ones. In enacting the 'entrepreneurial lifeworld' concept, he proposes the need for autonomy in strategy making, ownership, linking responsibility with reward, holistic management and networked, trust-based, rather than hierarchical relationships.

In the practical setting of the new or smaller firm, the people trying to run them often have not gained formal management skills or qualifications. Yet we have found from extensive experience in running development programmes with group of entrepreneurs and small firm managers that so long as they are open to learning, they are able to develop themselves and their businesses considerably. This section explores the idea of entrepreneurial management and its application in the smaller firm, from the new start to the more established, often growth-oriented business.

A simple conceptual framework for entrepreneurial management is shown in Figure 7.4. Entrepreneurial management is not a fixed or permanent state, because it requires a balance to be maintained between managerial control and organization, with entrepreneurial creativity and opportunity-seeking. This is a dynamic relationship, but it is one in which both entrepreneurial and managerial modes can work in synergy within an organisation to

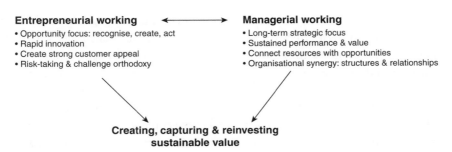

Figure 7.4 Entrepreneurial management

create and sustain new value by stimulating and meeting customer demand in new ways. The two modes can be successfully integrated, enabling the organisation to grow through an entrepreneurial focus on customer attractiveness and rapid innovation in response to new opportunities, whilst managing the direction, processes, relationships and resources of the business organisation.

Entrepreneurial working

In this model the business has a strong *opportunity focus*, constantly searching to anticipate and identify potential opportunities by being close to its chosen market. It *innovates rapidly* to create and implement new business models, products and services, which are presented as attractive buying propositions to stimulate the customer demand. The business behaves dynamically in the market, *challenging orthodox* business models, being prepared to take risks, being first to introduce change or responding swiftly and energetically to competitive or environmental threats. It uses new and existing ideas and technologies to engage the customer in new ways, to reduce costs and continually improve efficiency or service, while approaches which do not work are quickly rejected.

The business creates a strong *customer appeal*, using its own images, myths and stories to personalise the brand identity and using public media effectively to attract customers and to meld an affinity with its customer base, knowing that their loyalty can be fickle and quickly lost.

Managerial working

The business is managed with a strong, long-term *strategic focus* through which the mission, strategic goals and business values are tightly focused, interdependent, mutually consistent and communicated effectively.

There is a focus on sustained performance through creating and capturing value, enabling decisions to be taken to achieve market power in the interests of both competitive short-term and longer-term success of the business.

There is *organisational synergy*, co-ordinating and communicating effectively between all parts of the business through effective, lean structures to ensure customer satisfaction and successful completion of innovation and new business development projects, for example. Hierarchy is minimal and people are empowered to make operational decisions, with self-managing teams and a culture of dealing with problems quickly as they arise. Attention is paid to *managing relationships* effectively both within the organisation and externally, with groups such as investors, suppliers, customers and government agencies.

There is active and effective management to ensure that financial and other resources, especially talent, are available and allocated to capitalise on the most promising opportunities, to grow the business and to meet customer demand. At the core of the business there is a robust economic model of *systematic value management*, which optimises demand, resources and profit through making pricing and cost control decisions which enable the business to operate more efficiently in the market place than its competitors whilst offering 'best value' to the customer. Operational processes are robust, simple and designed to achieve maximum efficiency at least cost.

Creating, capturing and reinvesting value

The result of entrepreneurial management is a sustained approach to creating new value, capturing and reinvesting value back into the business for growth. This can take multiple forms, including:

- developing new market opportunities and channels to market
- growing market share and presence
- introducing product, service or process innovations
- growing sales revenue and profit stream
- creating new business models
- increasing asset value and share value of the business
- increasing demand for employees and supply chain businesses

Sustaining a culture of entrepreneurial management is challenging as there are inevitable tensions between the implicit values and practices of each mode. At the most basic level, most people involved in running smaller businesses tend to be either more entrepreneurial or more managerial in their outlook and preferred approach to working; very few people are equally adept at both, and similarly, few organisations are able to sustain entrepreneurial management for a prolonged period unless they consciously set out to renew themselves. So organisations which were described as exponents of entrepreneurial management in the early 2000s have, in almost all cases, become established corporations and are no longer especially entrepreneurial in their approaches; examples include Virgin, Tesco, EasyJet, Microsoft and Dell. It is difficult for large organisations to maintain a culture of entrepreneurial management as the business grows, the founder or entrepreneurial leader moves on and ownership may change, such as through flotation or acquisition. An exceptional example is Ryanair, where Michael O'Leary has been chief executive since 1990 and led it to a position of dominance over the European short-haul budget airline market, seeing off all competitors. O'Leary's high profile persona and the remorseless pursuit of competition and cost reduction enabled Ryanair to maintain a highly entrepreneurial approach to date, through being frequently controversial and unpopular.

Activity: Entrepreneurial management

- Can you identify any organisations which you think demonstrate entrepreneurial management? These could be organisations of any type or size.
- What are their entrepreneurial attributes and characteristics?
- In what ways are they effectively managed?
- How well do you think they have combined entrepreneurial and managerial working effectively? How are they sustaining this?

Example: Mike Lynch and Autonomy Corporation

Mike Lynch is a brilliant mathematician and Cambridge technologist with research expertise in signal processing and adaptive pattern recognition. Having started two earlier businesses, he formed Autonomy Corporation in 1996 to apply adaptive pattern recognition to develop computer search and knowledge management tools to understand and manipulate many forms of unstructured information. This ability to perform highly complex data analytics coincided with the rapid growth of web-based business applications. Autonomy floated through an IPO in 1998 and grew rapidly by developing innovative applications and by acquisition until May 2011. Autonomy had a lean, highly entrepreneurial, rapidly innovative and risk-taking culture. Lynch became celebrated as one of the United Kingdom's most capable technology entrepreneurs and leaders, winning many business awards, and it seemed he could do no wrong.

Hewlett Packard purchased Autonomy in an agreed sale finalised in October 2011, which valued the business at £7.8 billion ($11.7 billion). The departing HP chief executive Leo Apotheker had aimed to use Autonomy to revitalise the struggling US corporation. There were strong allegations at the time that HP had paid too much but were unable to cancel the deal; Oracle later alleged that they were offered Autonomy too, but turned it down, as the firm's market valuation at the time was $6 billion. Senior managers in Autonomy responsible for finance, marketing and sales departed soon after, reporting that the HP culture was bureaucratic and could not integrate Autonomy. Lynch left in May 2012 after HP declared disappointing results and accused Lynch and his team of failing to deliver on revenue targets. It seemed that the cultural fit between Lynch's entrepreneurial management of Autonomy and the established corporate world of HP, which itself had been a fast-growing and innovative technology start-up, did not work, being subject to very different dynamics. The senior management team at Autonomy was largely replaced to integrate it into HP.

In November 2012, HP very publicly accused Lynch and the former Autonomy management team of 'accounting improprieties, misrepresentations and disclosure failures to inflate the underlying financial metrics of the company'. HP wrote down £5.4 billion of the value of Autonomy, wiping out its own profits, and announcing an investigation by the US Department of Justice into alleged fraud. These serious accusations were robustly denied by Lynch, who challenged HP to substantiate them. As the case unfolded, it laid bare the tensions between the rapid entrepreneurial growth of Autonomy as an independently led public company, and the ability of HP as a corporate to assess its true value and to manage the acquisition effectively (http://autonomyaccounts.org/).

Activity

- Read the background history on the Autonomy case; more is available on business news websites such as FT.COM and Bloomberg.com.
- The Autonomy–HP acquisition ended in acrimony; why do you think this happened?
- What conclusions do you draw on the strategic management of Autonomy from the narratives provided by Mike Lynch and by HP?
- Which do you think are more convincing?
- Are there any wider lessons which entrepreneurial managers can draw from the Autonomy case? If so, what do you think these are?

■ Entrepreneurial management capabilities

Entrepreneurial management capabilities are essential for the effective development and management of the entrepreneurial venture over time, and as the scale of the business grows, the level of management capabilities required will become more advanced and sophisticated. The type of strategy pursued, as shown in the next section, will affect the balance of capabilities required, but both entrepreneurial and managerial skills are needed. However few people could justifiably claim to be equally capable in both these forms of working, and there is the need for venture teams to include a combination of both. Figure 7.5 illustrates the set of entrepreneurial and managerial capabilities. These are detailed in the toolbox (Appendix 1) which you are encouraged to use to self-assess your capabilities. This can be used in preparing your career plan in Chapter 8.

Figure 7.5 Entrepreneurial and managerial capabilities

Activity

- Use Appendix 1 in the toolkit to assess your entrepreneurial and management capabilities.
- Compare the results.
- How does your self-assessment of entrepreneurial and managerial capabilities compare? Which are stronger?
- How could this preference be explained? In what ways could it affect your career choices?
- What roles would you be most capable of adopting in a venture management team?

■ Strategy and business growth

In acting on an opportunity, the decisions and actions required to pursue a strategic direction are vitally important. In the exploring and planning phases of the opportunity, many decisions will be taken regarding the market segment, product or service combination, the fit between the product/service offer and the market opportunity, the differentiation from competitors, pricing, the business model and other issues. These are all strategic decisions, even if they did not appear to be so at the time they were taken. It is surprisingly easy in starting new ventures to make what seem to be 'natural' or 'obvious' choices without realising the strategic implications these can have later on.

Entrepreneurial action is often based on opportunistic and quite short-term factors, without too much thought about how an opportunity can be developed and sustained in the longer term; of course, it may be primarily a short-term occurrence, which is enacted in the 'now' and without too much thought being given to longer-term factors. This chapter has encouraged this form of activist approach as an approach to business start-up.

Strategy is concerned with the future direction and optimisation of the opportunity. There is extensive writing about strategy for entrepreneurship, small and growing businesses, but within this knowledge base there are some critical questions which the entrepreneur needs to ask in planning and developing the opportunity beyond the immediate present.

Questions for entrepreneurial strategy

1. What works:
   a. For you as an entrepreneur?
   b. For the business?
   c. For your target customer segment?
   This question refers back to the section on 'practical theory'

2. How can you build on and extend what you know works:
   a. By doing more in the same customer segment?
   b. For a related customer segment(s)?
   c. For a new customer segment?

3. What are the most attractive wider market opportunities for what works?
   a. Where there is least competition but good demand and profit margins?
   b. Where there is greatest potential growth?

4. What is the anticipated lifetime of the opportunity? How can this be extended?

5. What is your personal ambition, longer term?
   a. What is your ambition for the business?

6. What is your orientation to risk? Tolerance towards downside and losses?

7. What is your orientation to control? Growth tends to diffuse ownership and control through shared equity ownership and collaboration.

These are not definitive questions but they aim to help you think through market, business and personal aspects which all affect strategic decision-making. It is clearly essential to have developed a concept which works effectively in a given market to be able to consider strategic development, since without this, there is nothing proven on which to build a business. Then the wider potential of this business opportunity in the current, related and other markets can be considered. Current competition and growth potential in possible markets need to be evaluated. Next, the lifetime of the opportunity, how this may be extended and potentially replaced or moved beyond can be considered. The final three sets of questions are personal rather than business-centred, because your own level of ambition, and orientation towards risk and control of the business are relevant factors in decision-making. It is often these psychological and attitudinal factors which determine strategic decisions and actions in small firms (and can be the reason for staying small and not pursuing growth opportunities) rather than the extrinsic, business-centred factors.

Activity

Consider the seven entrepreneurial strategy questions. Answer them as far as you are able in relation to your opportunity. If you do not have an opportunity or a concept for which you can say 'I know what works', then consider the personal questions 5–7.

Strategy tends to be a combination of what a business says it is going to do, often through a plan; what it sets out to do, which may be related to but not necessarily the same as it declares; and what it actually does, often in response to other pressures and events. Argyris (1970) referred to this situation as theories (rather than strategies) being espoused or in use. There is a tension between intending, declaring and doing, which is reflected in the fact that most plans and strategies are only ever enacted in part, and often not at all. For this reason, we treat strategy on the same basis as learning; that is, strategy is what people in businesses do (strategy in use) rather than what they say they are going to do (espoused strategy). Minimising the gap between what you intend and what you actually do is essential.

Chapter 5 covered venture planning and referred to business goals. By definition these are strategic statements. The strategic goals or objectives, and the methods used to achieve them, are the intended strategy. They reflect the founders' ambition and the business need to achieve, at the very least, sustainable trading and preferably a point of strategic advantage over competitors. This can be expressed in targets for customer acquisition, sales revenue, and market share, for example.

It is important for a business to be able to evaluate how effective its strategic decisions and action have been in practice, and to confirm, modify or re-think the business strategy. You may remember that two of the features of successful companies identified earlier in this chapter were their readiness to reinvent themselves together with courage to change. It makes sense to review the effectiveness of the business strategy regularly, and the framework in Table 7.5 provides a means of doing this.

Strategic framework

A regular review using the strategic framework should inform and evaluate the business strategy. The scope of key items from the review can be determined by the characteristics of the business and many will review the operational issues of sales and financial performance weekly. It may not be necessary to review the vision every month, for example, but the effectiveness of strategies in achieving the vision should be reviewed. This applies even in the smallest business where it is normal for the founders to be so enmeshed in the tactical day-to-day issues that they feel unable to 'work on the business rather than in it'. Yet it is essential to do so regularly. Perceptions from customers, employees, community (such as social media) and intelligence on competitor behaviour all need to be reviewed because no business can afford to be isolated from these stakeholders, and it is an important input to organizational learning.

Table 7.5 Framework for strategic review

Scope of review	Information available	Review process
Vision	Quantitative measures of progress against performance targets or indicators (e.g., sales targets, market share percentage, cash flow, profit)	Is progress as planned?
Purpose or mission		What has and has not been implemented?
Strategic direction		What has changed?
Goals or objectives		If different is this better or worse?
Actions to achieve these		
Business model	Qualitative information or feedback (e.g., customer and community feedback – compliments and complaints, staff suggestions, intelligence on competitor behaviour)	What are the reasons for variation?
Sales targets		What decisions or changes are required?
Financial targets		
Key decisions		What options for action are available?
Market segments		
Product/service development		Which will be most effective?
Customer perceptions		How will this be measured?
Competitor strategy		
Employee feedback		
Community feedback		

The information gathered to review should include both quantitative data and qualitative information. The former enables achievement of targets to be measured, while the latter is likely to include suggestions, feedback and ideas from customers, employees and community. It is a mistake either to run a business by purely 'managing by numbers' or to ignore quantitative data, because vital trends will only be apparent through this analysis. The risk is either of managing minutiae or of paying attention to the bigger picture and missing crucial detail.

The vital factor lies in how the information is used in the review process. The starting point should be to compare progress with the projections in the venture plan, and to identify whether this is as planned or has changed. The reasons for variation, whether 'better' or 'worse', need to be established as clearly as possible, since these could reveal either assumptions which have turned out to be incorrect or changes which have taken place. The decisions which need to be taken, the options available and the actions which need to be taken should be established. Both creative and rational approaches are needed – creative thinking to turn problems into opportunities or open up new possibilities, and rational thinking to ensure that implementation and implications are considered. It is important that tactical decisions which seem right at the time do not exclude or 'lock off' future options and that they are congruent with the strategic direction of the business. The most effective options should be selected and success measures, responsibility and timescale decided for review at the next meeting.

This activity of reviewing the strategy is a learning process which every business will undertake differently, but which is vital in order to check the effectiveness of decision-making and implementation. It needs to be as factual, objective and emotionally neutral as possible because egos, personal pride and vulnerability will fog analysis and decision-making. So the key factor is always: 'What do we know now that we did not know before, and how can we use this knowledge?'

Here the owner of a media business describes how he reviews business strategy for a group of radio stations as well as monitoring key information in three vital areas of the business – costs, income and audience figures:

> I sit down with all the senior managers responsible for programming, sales, finance, administration and human resources once a week besides company board meetings. At that meeting we review sales and expenditure, we talk about the overall strategy. I had previously been involved in meetings with individual stations, but now I've stepped back to focus on strategy.
>
> I still see the sales figures for each station and every sales executive every single day; it only takes me two minutes to look at them. I sign all but a very small number of invoices, I do look at them carefully so I still know exactly what we're spending. Our currency is audience, and I still deal directly with all the audience research for each radio station. So although I've stepped back from the individual man-management, I am still managing our three principle things: audience, revenue, expenditure.

It is often situational factors, either externally or within a business, which provoke strategic changes. The effects of the recessionary period in 2008–12 affected many businesses, and whilst the immediate effects were often negative, for some the 'crisis' enabled them to rethink what the business was about and to focus on more attractive areas of opportunity and more effective strategies and business models.

Example: Flying Power

Flying Power was set up as a plant and equipment hire company in 2001.

Owner and director Lesley described how major changes in the business after the 2008–2009 recession led her to restructure the business. This happened to coincide with her participating in an entrepreneurial leadership programme, Business Inspiration.

> We specialise in generators and lighting tower hire. We started by doing plant hire – diggers and dumpers. But construction was badly hit during the recession, we suffered as a result and over 3 months we had major bad debts from construction companies of almost half our turnover. We had 22 dumpers, and we went down to two. We just couldn't compete against the national contractors and were making no profit in each item we hired.
>
> We moved the business over to portable electricity generators, acting purely on gut feeling. It was a very logical decision in one way, but based on a gut feeling of what could work, because we knew that if we didn't the business wouldn't survive. We

now have 60 generator units and expect to make £0.5 million profit this year, and we've had a 50 fold increase in profit.

We had made the move to generators before the programme came along, but I went to an event with a female entrepreneur as a speaker and I was really inspired. She was so honest about what had happened in her business when it failed, and how she was able to come out of the other side. I thought our business could fail, and we really were starting to worry about it. I'd gone back to the hospital to work as a nurse to support the business The course came at just the right time so I signed up for it.

We came out of the course with an ability to run the business much better. We looked at the finances, market place, making sure we have the right product for the right market place, and developing the website. It all focused my mind.

I really enjoyed looking at our future strategy. It's so interesting talking about different ways to look at the future, and how by doing that can you change the future. I also enjoyed how to market, and learning about the route to market. We learned that we should tier the marketing, with some quick wins, and longer-term goals to get people secured into contracts.

It made me aware that you need to go out and meet people if you're going to sell your product. We now just market our generators, we don't market plant hire at all. We also have sophisticated telemetry systems, lighting and tower hire, and can offer a fully integrated package. This has enabled us to win contracts for major outdoor events and really fuelled the growth of the business in the past few years.

We have gained contracts for major music festivals, agricultural shows, air displays, County shows, retailers, antiques fairs and University balls. All our crew are fully trained, we provide the distribution gear and run the whole package. It is more expensive than just hiring a generator, but the clients are much more likely to want to pay for the complete package and know that everything will work and it will be completely safe, no matter what the weather throws at it. They are much better customers than we had on the plant hire side.

Financially, my horizons were broadened on the different ways to finance things. It's quite complicated for us as we have a lot of capital equipment on HP and depreciation to consider, so we're more specialised than most companies. We have an accountant but I can now look at our accounts and understand what I need to. We have 60 generator units now and expect to make about £0.5 million profit this year.

The main benefit has been access to people who know more than you do. It's like there's a knowledge pool there of people who know how to guide you. I felt so much better working on my business knowing there's so much support there. It took me out of my comfort zone. I realised there were big cracks in our company, but also big strengths that we're not using.

I know now what works for me and our business is planning very thoroughly, and having all the systems and checks in place to ensure everything always works safely and reliably for all our customers.

An entrepreneurial business needs to seek opportunities for strategic business growth, based on offering product/service/technology innovation, based on 'what works' into emerging and future markets. There is a very wide literature on business strategy but this section selects just one model to illustrate how entrepreneurial strategy often differs from conventional business strategy, and introduces the concept of resource-based, opportunity-based and relational strategy. As shown in Table 7.6, resource-based strategy is used when an organisation decides its forward strategy on the basis of how to allocate its resources to opportunities most efficiently. Opportunity-based strategy is different: it identifies and selects the most promising opportunities first, and locates the resources required to exploit them; these may be within the organization, or located externally, for example, through partners. A relational strategy seeks to match resources and opportunities in optimal ways. Both entrepreneurial and managerial capabilities are required, for example, an opportunity-based strategy will require enhanced capabilities of investigating opportunities, whilst a resource-based strategy will require rather more operational and organisational management capabilities.

This model suggests that, for many organisations, their priority will be to make the optimum use of the capital-intensive resources they already own. So companies in industries such as processing and manufacturing will allocate the existing resources they own to opportunities which they can accommodate in the most efficient way possible. Their potential is limited by the need to manage resources economically and to 'fill the factory'. Their scope for entrepreneurial strategy is constrained by resource optimisation, although the addition of new resources to add value by complementing existing ones is one strategic approach. They need to create new opportunities by innovating and finding new combinations and applications for both existing and new resources. Whilst the targeted customer segments may be either existing ones or extensions of existing markets, they may need to develop new market opportunities in which they can exploit their products and capacity, as in the case of automotive manufacturers selling mature vehicle model types into developing-world economies.

An example of resource-based strategy is a government agency which has to work with delivery organisations to provide the most economic services for its community, by allocating its limited managerial and financial resources to meet ever-growing needs, apparently leaving little scope for entrepreneurial innovation. Yet even in these cases, the move towards

Table 7.6 Opportunity, resource and relational strategy

Strategy mode	Resource-based strategy	Relational strategy	Opportunity-based strategy
Organisational priority	Efficient allocation of existing resources to opportunities	Profitable matching of short-term opportunities and resources	Identifying future opportunities and finding resources to exploit them
Activities	Capacity planning Cost control Addition of new resources Innovation	Market and capacity planning Sourcing decisions Innovation	Customer segment development Strategic innovation Partner acquisition
Examples of types of business	Capital-intensive manufacturing, health, process and utility industries	Consumer electronics manufacturing, air travel, hotels, financial services, trading, retail fashion	Next generation technology Design and media Knowledge-based business

a commissioning rather than in-house service provision model is leading to change and developing new income streams.

The opportunity-based strategy is more creative in identifying potential and emerging opportunities in line with the strategy, and finding resources required to exploit them, which will very often not be owned or controlled by the organisation. This approach lends itself to the nimble and fleet-of-foot business which is adept at finding and deal-making with partner organisations who control the productive, knowledge or other resources required. Ownership of capital-intensive resources restricts this, and there are surprisingly few organisations able to pursue a purely entrepreneurial strategy. For a business which has a significant resource base to adopt an entrepreneurial strategy, it must be prepared to see that base simply as a potential resource, which in future may either not be fully used or even not required at all and be divested.

It is often easier for individual entrepreneurs to pursue serial entrepreneurial strategies than it is for entire businesses. There are many examples in fashion and retail, one being Gok Wan, who appeared in a number of successful TV 'makeover' series, and this enabled him to establish a designer apparel label and to supply Sainsbury's with female fashion. Most organisations find themselves in a relational strategy of trying to match opportunities with resource allocation in the most profitable way, and of shifting internal resources and buying in external capability in 'make or buy' decisions. Major brands such as IBM and Rolls-Royce have moved away from ownership of manufacturing capacity to focus their resources on the customer relationship and technology innovation, buying in hardware and services they require. Relational strategy may seem a sensible middle way, and even inevitable for many businesses, but the disadvantage is that it can become a series of short-term compromises, consuming a significant amount of management time, which is therefore not invested in opportunity development. One way of countering this is to have a director and team within the business that are responsible for identifying and developing new market opportunities, and to separate this from the part of the organisation that manages current business operations. Innovation can result from converging internal capabilities with external opportunities.

Example: Lumus Lighting

Lumus Lighting is an independently owned business in the United Kingdom which designs, manufactures and installs exterior lighting systems for sports, industry and retail sites. The lighting sales, design, manufacturing and installation business units are managed efficiently and profitably, using a resource-based approach. However for 30 years the business had been active internationally, and pursued a relational strategy of finding clients and identifying suppliers of lighting components outside the United Kingdom with whom it could form partnerships to broaden its product base and differentiate its service from competitors. The potential of the Asian market was identified and a joint venture set up in China to manufacture lighting equipment for the rapidly growing Pacific market, and to import this into the United Kingdom where the domestic factory was not price-competitive on commodity products.

Activity

Can you identify examples of organisations pursuing:

- resource-based strategies?
- relational strategies?
- opportunity-based strategies?

Alternatively, if you cannot think of any organisations which fit neatly into each category, then look for organisations which are moving between resource-based and relational, and relational and opportunity-based strategies.
What do you think are the advantages and limitations of such strategies for these organisations?

■ Critical questions to consider from this chapter

- What do you consider to be the most important activities in enacting opportunities?
- In creating a new business venture, what factors would you pay most attention to?

- What lessons do the reasons for success and failure of early-stage business ventures provide for entrepreneurs?
- How can the concept and principles of sensemaking help you in enacting an opportunity?
- How would you establish 'what works' in a business venture?
- What approach would you take to strategic decision-making and reviewing the effectiveness of the strategy?
- How would you achieve balance between entrepreneurial and managerial effectiveness in the organisation?

Putting It into Practice: Where Do We Go from Here?

8

Chapter Contents

- Introduction
- Opportunity-Centred Entrepreneurship in context
- Continuing the journey: emerging and future challenges in entrepreneurship

- Developing your entrepreneurial career
- So what are you going to do?
- Critical questions to consider from this chapter

■ Introduction

The purpose of this final chapter is to explore the future of entrepreneurship, at a conceptual and also personal level. It aims to develop conceptual ideas and practical approaches from academic, practical and personal perspectives, and to stimulate you to think about the opportunities and implications these raise. It moves from a general understanding to a personalised approach, with the aim of enabling you to think about how you can develop your entrepreneurial future.

It proposes ways for you to continue the journey, personally, practically and academically, through developing ideas and strategies for personal career planning in the context of the future development of entrepreneurship. There is a section which explores entrepreneurial career options at different life stages, and activities intended to assist in personal career planning. The chapter closes with a challenge to the reader: what are you going to do to create your entrepreneurial future?

A number of significant themes are proposed as for the future development of entrepreneurial research, learning, policy and practice. These suggest possible topics for further study, including independent studies and dissertation projects. The themes include

- distributed innovation
- inclusive entrepreneurship
- internationalism
- economically and environmentally sustainable enterprise
- diversity and multiculturalism
- women's enterprise
- beyond legal capitalism to the informal and criminal economy
- education and learning.

The learning goals of the chapter are to enable you to:

- reflect on your learning from the book through reading and applying the opportunity-centred approach
- assess the emerging issues in entrepreneurship and the implications for you, in personal, career and academic dimensions
- review your career goals and develop an entrepreneurial career plan.

The outcome from the chapter is to help you in planning your entrepreneurial future and career by reviewing and using the key learning points and tools from the book. It closes with a challenge: what are you going to do to create your own entrepreneurial future?

■ Opportunity-Centred Entrepreneurship in context

This is a reflection on Opportunity-Centred Entrepreneurship and its contribution to entrepreneurial theory, learning and practice,

This book aims to increase your awareness, skills and readiness to act in entrepreneurial ways. It puts the human experience of entrepreneurship at its heart, by focusing on it as a real-world learning process. This section encourages you to develop your own views on how useful this has been for you, and how you might apply it. So the approach concentrates on personal and social development, in the wider context of family, community, work and life experience. It emphasises that entrepreneurship is a path open to everyone, because the skills and approaches are capable of being learned. It offers a focus, a way of working, questions to ask and tools to use. It is a joined-up approach to entrepreneurship.

Enterprising behaviour is a normal and everyday aspect of human life. People are inherently curious about problems, opportunities and possibilities. We like playing, whether this is playing with people, with ideas, with tangible objects and technology, or with pictures and music. Just as everyone is inherently creative, everyone has the latent capacity for enterprise. The need for an entrepreneurial mindset is continually growing as the global economy becomes less predictable and the role of governments and major corporations less supportive to the individual.

However, to develop and apply this, we have to recognise that people have powerful and sometimes disempowering formative experiences in society. Families, communities, educational and government systems and employers have very strong formative influences which can encourage or discourage creativity and enterprise, sometimes by exercising repressive control. So whilst individuals have choices and are responsible for taking or not taking enterprising choices, the social worlds within which we live influence and enable or constrain these choices in many ways. Therefore there is much more to becoming an enterprising or opportunity society than simply encouraging individual enterprise. The concepts behind Opportunity-Centred Entrepreneurship need to be adopted above the level of the individual, by educational institutions, business support and government agencies. These issues will be addressed in the next section.

It is significant that major movements in management thinking and practice have often been accompanied by the development of accompanying tools, language and defined practices. If we think of such movements as total quality and the related Kaizen movement, strategic management, business process re-engineering and knowledge management, they have been implemented and enacted with the help of defined or 'best practice' methods. Whether we agree that the movements themselves and the tools used have been effective is another matter, but there is a body of knowledge and practice available for use. Entrepreneurship and entrepreneurial management have been different, often lacking an acknowledged base of knowledge and practice. If you read the leading texts on the subject you will find a rich assortment of theory, many case studies, rational decision-making frameworks derived from marketing, strategy or financial origins, and one recurring tool – the business plan. Surely there is more to entrepreneurial practice than the business plan? There has been extensive critique of the value of this, and there are movements towards more person-centred approaches, for example, though effectuation theory (Sarasvathy, 2001).

One important contribution that Opportunity-Centred Entrepreneurship makes is to provide a process and a set of tools. They are not the only tools, but they are a start. The process and tools are not ideal for every situation, but they are flexible and can be added to. Some of the tools, such as the opportunity mapping and sensemaking approaches, have been gathered and adapted from other sources outside entrepreneurial practice. Others, such as the opportunity assessment tool, have been developed and tested over several years. People can use these as a starting point and adapt them for their own needs and situation. The result can be a systemic improvement in the way that entrepreneurial opportunities are developed and implemented because there is a framework and methodology available for our use.

■ Continuing the journey: emerging and future challenges in entrepreneurship

Part of the fascination of entrepreneurship is that it is a dynamic and continually evolving area of practice and study. Increasing numbers of students are conducting research studies and dissertation projects at final year undergraduate, postgraduate and doctoral levels. There are an ever-growing number of research conferences and academic journals dedicated to small business management, entrepreneurship, enterprise education and related issues. The volume of research and scholarship in the field is ever-increasing and it is therefore important that this is directed towards the important, complex and challenging issues faced by entrepreneurs, policymakers, researchers, teachers and others. This next session summarises eight emerging trends which are creating fresh challenges for society as well as presenting emerging business opportunities for entrepreneurs. These are listed in Table 8.1, and can also offer topics for independent study, enabling you to gain in-depth understanding of these emerging issues.

Several of these have arisen within the book so far, and they are included here, both to provide guidance, ideas and suggestions for students considering dissertation research topics related to entrepreneurship, and to indicate the major challenges and sources of opportunities which we face in continuing to develop entrepreneurial activity.

Distributed innovation

Innovation is inseparable from entrepreneurship as a significant driving force in creating new forms of value. There will be a continuing convergence of ideas and technology which anticipate or respond to demand and economic and social forces. The role of science, technology and knowledge in stimulating, enabling and exploiting innovation continues to grow, but in parallel we see new approaches to innovation emerging.

There are major new areas of technological possibility entering the market, including new bio and genetic technologies, aspects of nanotechnology, and many other science and

Table 8.1 Emerging issues in entrepreneurship

Distributed innovation
Inclusive entrepreneurship
Internationalism
Economically and environmentally sustainable enterprise
Diversity and multiculturalism
Women's enterprise
Beyond legal capitalism to the informal and criminal economy
Educational and learning

research-based innovations. There are also increasing convergences of previously separate areas of science and technology, for example, connecting life, materials and computing sciences, which have the potential to create new industries.

The challenge will be to develop and exploit these in ways that both create wealth and meet social needs. There are, as set out in this section, many economic, social and resource-based challenges which require entrepreneurial innovation to develop new technologies, for example, in energy, water, climate change, health, agriculture and transportation. The old approach to innovation was through a 'closed system' of research laboratories in universities and industry feeding large corporations which exploit new products in limited ways to advance their own interests. High-cost industrial economies, such as the United States and EU, are increasingly challenged by the speed and greater efficiency of growing Asian economies in innovation, especially in China and India but also in smaller countries.

New era entrepreneurship is moving towards a much more distributed pattern of innovation, in which people across the world are able to interact, experiment and apply new knowledge, technologies and ways of working outside closed systems. These cannot be controlled easily by corporates or governments, although agile organisations can create the conditions for innovators to produce new approaches, as Apple did in liberating the market for producing iPhone applications within a business model it controlled.

For example, 3D printing is developing from there being few, very high cost machines to being a distributed technology, with mass adoption of low-cost printers. 3D printing is a fusion of 3D design software, with a range of printing technologies from affordable and low-intensity to highly advanced metal spraying devices. A loose network of innovators, producers and users is continually experimenting with new ideas, applications and materials. The applications are virtually limitless, with products being developed in health technologies, engineering and automotive, as well as hobby, modelmaking, fashion and jewellery, for example (http://3dprintingindustry.com/makers/).

In ways like this, the 'clock speed' of innovation is increasing, and accelerating the development of innovation in processes as well as products and services. If one organisation can innovate through close partnerships with a network of suppliers and distributors and enter the market before another which is less well organised, it clearly has a major advantage.

The Internet continually transforms the way we do business, enabling many new business opportunities and models to be created as access, speed and online technologies develop whilst costs of access fall, making all kinds of business opportunities available to worldwide markets. Entrepreneurial working is increasingly challenging the ways in which corporate and public sector organisations in particular function. It is easy for them to stifle innovation, yet they often control the resources which are essential for innovation. The development of new ways of innovating between organisations, for example, in the Indian computer software and applications industry and of 'cloud' technologies around major centres such as Hyderabad and Chennai, is essential for competitive development of new technologies (Joseph, 2012).

Entrepreneurship as economic inclusion

Entrepreneurship in the 'old era' was integrally linked with capitalist economic growth theory. Whilst this link is not broken, in the new era we are seeing a wider range of entrepreneurial approaches, models and cultures both co-existing and in some senses competing. Old-era entrepreneurship was based on the notion of individualistic 'free enterprise' and self-enrichment through the investment of personal. We are moving from this being the norm to its being questioned and different, social and collaborative approaches emerging.

Potentially, entrepreneurship is a popular force which opens up the prospect of business activity, independence and ownership to a wide range of the population, thereby under-pinning democratic participation in developing and post-socialist countries. However there is a need for plurality and inclusivity to be achieved through different types of enterprise being formed and supported. There are more inclusive models of entrepreneurship to be found by studying, for example, such cases as:

- the micro-finance movement pioneered by Mohammed Yunus;
- the family-owned medium-sized *mittelstand* businesses in Germany;
- the collaborative business networks in Emilio-Romagna;
- Canadian First Nations community entrepreneurship (Membertou case, Chapter 6);
- rural village enterprises and new production models in the wine-producing areas of South Africa.

These examples are quite traditional and long-established, based on principles of distributed ownership, collaborative resource use and production, and shared rewards within an economic and social ecology. However new business models are rapidly being developed which also draw on being able to access distributed resources and knowledge. Rather than productive assets being owned by the business, the people who own them make them available when not required. This is similar to the peer-to-peer lending model in Chapter 6.

Example: Airbnb

Airbnb was launched in 2008 as a website which enabled people with property to rent temporarily to visitors looking for short-term accommodation, providing a web-based marketplace, ratings and booking service integrated with social media applications. The service grew rapidly internationally, with over 11 million guests by 2014 and attracting major investment prior to a flotation. The Airbnb model enabled flat renters and property owners to earn from bedspace they did not require, whilst giving travellers the ability to find accommodation outside hotel chains. The traditional hotel and hospitality industry saw it as a threat to their markets, but its rapid growth outstripped most opposition (www.airbnb.com).

Airbnb inspired both imitators and other business models based on making distributed assets available to meet market demands, making the 'sharing economy' or 'collaborative consumption' model a rapidly growing and attractive approach. This has been applied to car sharing, temporary work and other assets.

An innovative approach to creating work opportunities was developed by Student@Home which connects IT students with people and organisations requiring computer support. First developed in the Netherlands, it provides work opportunities for students and improves access to technology for digitally excluded people (www.studentathome.co.uk/).

As the Airbnb example shows, a successful online innovation can be replicated or adapted quickly and offered internationally, which leads to the next issue.

International entrepreneurship

Entrepreneurship is inherently international, and it is no longer sensible to think or practice in entrepreneurship without adopting an international perspective, but this provides challenges as well as opportunities. Customers and market opportunities may be available globally, but so are not only low-cost competitors, but also imitators and fraudsters. The rapidly growing economies of China and India are stimulating and benefiting from the entrepreneurship of their own populations, as well as becoming increasingly attractive to external investors and partners. They are moving up the 'value chain', producing products and services with higher value-added in knowledge and technology which increasingly challenge US and European producers in domestic markets.

The projected increase in the world population of 50% or 3 billion extra people by 2050, primarily in developing economies, will place huge strain on the world economy and on resources to feed, house, employ and support this population. This is both a problem for entrepreneurship, and one that requires entrepreneurial ingenuity to address, to find new approaches and solutions. In principle, the entire population of the world is entitled to develop entrepreneurial skills and opportunities and cannot be denied that right, but this has major implications. The concentration of wealth and resources in developing countries into a tiny super-rich minority, as has happened in several West African states, does not help the wider population to access resources and to work towards entrepreneurial emancipation. Corruption and 'robber baron' capitalism occur in changing economies, such as Nigeria and Russia, but criminality and lack of open legal frameworks make these risky places to set up and do business. For the majority of potential entrepreneurs in the developing world, enterprise will mean moving initially into some form of 'necessity entrepreneurship' as a route out of poverty. This is happening even in previously failed or despotic states such as Myanmar, whilst in others without free markets or support for new businesses or trading activities, such as North Korea or Somalia, the conditions for safe and legal entrepreneurship may not yet exist without a change in government. But for millions of others it is clear that neither state intervention, multinational investment nor other solutions are on hand and entrepreneurship is one of the few options available; therefore the challenge to develop inclusive models of enterprise is imperative.

However, economic growth increases resource use, which can quickly become unsustainable, especially in combination with population growth. This is not only about oil- and carbon-based energy sources, serious though that situation is. The changing world climate, resulting from the carbon-based economy, also increases demand for water as a resource, with the effects being felt worldwide, from Nevada and California to Africa and India. So whilst one strategy to assist in African development is to improve agricultural practices and increase food production, this is impossible without water. There are growing tensions in Northern Africa about access to and use of Nile water, for example, and this competition for natural resources is likely to increase. These are geopolitical questions which cannot be dodged by entrepreneurship researchers and practitioners, for they arise from entrepreneurial activity, and present challenges which entrepreneurs and innovators have the responsibility and opportunity to try to overcome.

Sustainable enterprise

Therefore the next challenge for entrepreneurship is to develop models of entrepreneurial activity which are sustainable: environmentally, ecologically, socially and economically. They cannot be dependent for growth and continuity just on competition for and consumption of scarce and limited resources. Access to resources is vital for entrepreneurs, yet it is essential to move from a 'use it up' to a 'use it again' model for the world economy to be able to support its increasing population. One place for researchers and entrepreneurs to start is to connect with environmentalists. There has been significant progress in environmental awareness, resource conservation and waste recycling, especially in some mainland European countries, since the 1990s. Waste dumping of recyclable resources is reducing and new industries are being created to provide advice and services in energy generation and conservation, ecologically friendly building and waste recycling. It is not the whole solution, but the limits have certainly not been reached.

There is unlimited scope for continuing innovation to achieve sustainable enterprise based on renewable resources, and these forms of enterprise offer significant scope for creating new knowledge, wealth and employment worldwide. There is an urgent need to develop 'lean resource' methods of business which make minimal demands on non-renewable resources, just as companies have been able to develop 'lean production' methods. Distribution and transportation are resource-intensive and often wasteful, offering scope for cost and resource reduction through smarter technologies. Water, energy and material conservation and recycling are clearly areas of rapidly growing importance which we cannot afford to ignore, yet where new value can be created. There is scope for developed societies to learn from the scavenging practices of the acutely poor people in developing economies who eke out a living by finding recyclable resources from waste dumps, including waste exported from the United Kingdom. Innovation is starting to develop more efficient methods of reclaiming recyclable valuable materials by screening waste, for example, Angela Murray, a PhD researcher at Birmingham University, developed a process for separating precious metal products originating from catalytic converters, such as rhodium, platinum and palladium, from road dust. She started her own business, Roads to Riches, to develop the technology.

Diversity and multiculturalism

Diversity and multiculturalism are inevitable outcomes from an international and inclusive approach to entrepreneurship. This must be welcomed as a positive advantage, yet it also brings challenges which need to be resolved. Multiculturalism offers multiple perspectives, the potential for conflict arising out of misunderstanding or competing ideologies, and the need for dialogue, negotiation and shared understanding. The case of Leicester demonstrates the point.

In the 1960s and 1970s, Leicester was an unremarkable British provincial city, dependent on a textile and garment industry which was destined to decline, and with a middle-ranking football team and university. However it became an attractive destination for immigrants from India and East Africa, initially to work in the textile industry. Over the next three decades, Hindu and Moslem communities became established in inner-city Leicester. Tensions with the indigenous English population arose over employment, housing, education and racial issues, which led to urban disturbances in the early 1980s, a period during which the local economy declined.

Since then, the renaissance of Leicester has been increasingly the story of its ethnic enterprises. Both Indian communities have established business networks, with visible retail presences, Belgrave Road developed a national cluster of Indian costume jewellery businesses and Narborough Road became a destination for curry houses and restaurants. Away from the vibrant shopfronts, progress had a lower profile yet arguably has been more significant. An increasing number of businesses are Indian-owned, and as the textile industry declined the proportion of printing, service and professional businesses has increased, with a growing number being higher value-added firms. A group of young women who felt excluded from economic and social opportunity formed their own network, the Peepul Centre, which has become a major force for social and community enterprise and renewal. Increasingly, economic regeneration, cultural activity and enterprise are driven by ethnic entrepreneurs, who have put Leicester on the cultural map.

Leicester is not unique, but the lessons it offers are that ethnic and cultural diversity creates new ideas and possibilities, whilst presenting challenges and possible conflict which need to be defused through tolerance, building trust and mutual understanding. How can entrepreneurship be encouraged in ethnically diverse yet economically deprived areas? Public and government agencies need to be sensitive yet bold in promoting equality of opportunity and seeking participation across the community. Enterprise needs to be seen and supported as a means of engaging people and groups in self and collective expression and improvement. Community support networks need to be recognised as valid and useful, and offered public support where they can reach people who feel excluded from mainstream public and private services. We can conceptualise this as a collective learning experience, in which Leicester became more enterprising by developing inclusive approaches to enterprise which work.

Women's enterprise

The Leicester experience is one in which ethnic minority women play an increasingly important part, and it is recognised in many societies that increasing their contribution to entrepreneurial activity is vital, for women and for society; the question is how. There is growing interest in both theoretical exploration and practical development of female entrepreneurship on a worldwide basis. Historically, women have been less active than men in formal entrepreneurship, if this is measured by the statistics of business ownership or the GEM (2012) report. However, this is changing rapidly as growing numbers of women recognize opportunities to start their own businesses. It also understates the informal roles which women have played in businesses owned by men or in family and village enterprises, and the powerful cultural forces which have discouraged and constrained their participation in business in many societies. Generally these are diminishing, with a few 'hardline' exceptions, such as Saudi Arabia.

How can female entrepreneurship be developed? There are at least three reasons why this is a vital area both for academic study and for practical action. First, entrepreneurship can provide women with independent income, by helping to alleviate poverty or dependence and increasing the lifestyle choices they can make for themselves and their families. The significance of this in developing economies should not be underestimated as a potential contribution to their economic and social empowerment.

Second, as levels of education for women increase, their capabilities, ambitions and expectations of career roles also grow. Levels of female graduates in the United Kingdom and in other developed countries continue to increase. Whilst at present female rates of entrepreneurial participation in most age groups are just over half those for men, these are also increasing. The GEM (2012) report on women entrepreneurs estimated that 126 million women worldwide were starting or running new businesses, and 98 million running established businesses, in 67 countries worldwide. Entrepreneurial activity represents just 1% of the female population in Pakistan, yet 40% in Zambia; Sub-Saharan African countries have the highest participation rates of female entrepreneurship, whilst North African, Middle East and mid-Asian have the lowest. As the availability of jobs to meet women's career aspirations and preferences is not keeping pace with their aspirations in many societies, for an increasing number, self-employment and entrepreneurship are a better career option at certain stages in their careers. For women with family responsibilities, for example, running their own business is an option they may be able to manage more flexibly and with greater reward than a part-time job. However support measures for female entrepreneurship need to be explicitly addressed, especially through education and training for women who are considering or preparing to start business ventures, and through reducing the barriers they face of lack of access to finance, resources and expertise (GEM, 2012).

The types of business created by women are often qualitatively different from those started by men. They see different opportunities, have different ideas and use their skills and social contacts in different ways, contributing to a greater diversity of business activity. The inclusive new business models and approaches to enterprise which are needed are highly likely to originate from female entrepreneurship. The real progress made in social enterprise has resulted in large part from the networking and collective action of enterprising women. An example of this is Banmujer, the Women's Development Bank of Venezuela. This was formed in 1999 by Nora Castaneda and a network of women's groups. They had found that conventional banks were reluctant to lend money to women who wanted to start businesses but had no assets to guarantee the loans. State-funded, all its employees are women and it makes loans to women who work as part of a group who co-operate on business projects. Through its network of field advisors, the bank also provides business, financial, legal and health advice. Examples such as this show how female and social entrepreneurship are moving into the mainstream and changing the nature of mainstream business activity.

Beyond legal capitalism to the informal and criminal economy

Every human activity has a shadow-side, a negative and destructive aspect which is one we usually prefer to ignore. Since entrepreneurship is a natural form of social activity, what is the shadow-side? The answer is criminality, and immoral and unethical behaviour. As Rehn and Taalas (2004) argue, we cannot ignore the role of criminality in entrepreneurship. They proposed that the study of entrepreneurship operates within an 'unconscious legalism' and that we should consider that entrepreneurship, which they define as the enactment of social networks, can operate outside the legal-market nexus. Historically, entrepreneurs have operated at the margins of, or outside, the law at certain times in most societies. To pretend otherwise is to opt for a sanitised and artificially wholesome narrative of entrepreneurial history. In the nineteenth century, British merchants traded in slaves and opium, activities which were legal at the time but which had known moral consequences. These trades are now illegal but human and narcotic trafficking continue to be major activities worldwide. The activities have not changed fundamentally, simply the legal frameworks. Also, we know that certain activities of major banks prior to and during the financial crisis of 2008–2012 were illegal, such as in fixing interest rates. Entrepreneurship was illegal in Eastern bloc socialist societies, yet 'black market' enterprise flourished. When the socialist system collapsed, entrepreneurship was legalised. This strengthens the case for viewing enterprise as a fundamental aspect of human social behaviour, in which the relationship with socially imposed legal frameworks changes over time.

Entrepreneurship is not in itself a moral concept, being neither 'right' nor 'wrong', ethically good nor bad. However it can be argued that entrepreneurs have a moral responsibility to act ethically and within the law; it is too simplistic to say that 'what is legal is entrepreneurial, and what is illegal is criminal and therefore not entrepreneurial'. Accepting that entrepreneurial activity may take place either within or outside the legal framework, there are entrepreneurial activities which will be illegal and hence criminal in some societies at certain times. There are types of entrepreneurial activity of which society approves because they are morally acceptable, and there are other types of activity which are disapproved because they are ethically undesirable, or just plain wrong. This forces us to accept that the slave and drug traders, together with other profit-opportunists operating outside the law, are entrepreneurs of a kind. Entrepreneurs may dislike legal frameworks, seeing them as restrictive, yet they are vital in creating fair and open conditions for trade and commerce. The distinction we have to make is about the entrepreneur's moral responsibility for the choices which he or she makes, and that we have entrepreneurs who choose to behave ethically, in ways which society approves, or unethically, because society proscribes their activity. Therefore the important distinction is between ethical and unethical entrepreneurial behaviour.

In all countries there is a significant amount of economic activity taking place in what is termed the 'informal' or 'grey' economy. Not all of the business activities are illegal; there are legitimate trades being practised such as car sales and repairs, building work and many other activities by 'get-rich-quick merchants', but the people performing them are not registered as businesses or self-employed, and the transactions take place outside the legal and fiscal systems. These are informal and technically illegal, so workers, customers and suppliers have no legal safeguards against fraud or defective goods or services. Beyond the informal sector is the criminal economy, where the activities themselves are illegal, including theft, smuggling, narcotic trading, violence and so on. One problem with this sector of the economy is that the informal and criminal do not simply run in parallel but converge and intermingle.

In societies with poor legal enforcement, or where the legal system is oppressive from a business perspective, informal and criminal enterprise will flourish. The business environment in those countries will be unattractive for legal entrepreneurs, and as a result the formal economy will not grow. Where criminal or political organisations have established networks of illegal businesses, such as in Southern Italy, they tend to intimidate and place legitimate businesses at a disadvantage. The judgement we have to take is that, although people running these organisations are demonstrating entrepreneurial skills (amongst others), the informal and criminal enterprises do not help, but rather undermine, social and economic progress in societies which have sound legal frameworks for enterprise.

Williams (2008) explored 'the hidden enterprise culture' in the United Kingdom in depth and concluded that neither deterrence nor a 'laissez-faire' approach to informal entrepreneurship would work effectively, recommending strategies to enable 'underground' enterprises to start legitimately, and to participate legally in the mainstream economy.

Education and learning

Education and learning for entrepreneurship remains a live issue because all seven of the prior challenges depend on the effectiveness of the entrepreneurial learning process. So education and learning are vital for innovation, socially inclusive entrepreneurship, international and sustainable entrepreneurship, multicultural and female enterprise and movement from informal to formal business activity to progress. Entrepreneurial learning and research are means of facilitating the changes and transformations which are needed. This is increasingly recognized internationally by reports from organisations such as the World Economic Forum (2009), European Commission (2012) and increasing interest from the United Nations (UNCTAD, 2012).

Enterprising learning has an increasing role in school education, throughout the curriculum. It offers a holistic way of developing abilities and habits of independence, self-efficacy, creativity, innovating and organising across and between subject areas. In this way, enterprising learning can enable students to apply knowledge across subject boundaries, embracing sciences, technology, sports, arts and humanities. Students need to 'feel the enterprising experience', and the learning environment, teaching and learning methods and capabilities of teaching staff must all evolve to provide transformative, enabling learning experiences. Technology is becoming used more effectively to facilitate interactive entrepreneurial learning.

The challenge is to make enterprise education a means of achieving social change and empowerment, enabling marginalised groups such as students who have become alienated from formal education, those with learning difficulties or from migrant communities to engage with learning experiences through which they connect practical skills, creativity and self-development into purposeful activity, enabling and inspiring them to see what they can do and who they can become. There are many school, college and community education projects doing this worldwide, but much more still needs to be done.

Enterprising learning must be lifelong; as the section on entrepreneurial careers shows, economic and demographic changes mean it is inevitable that increasing numbers of people will need to become entrepreneurs at different stages in their lives. We can also point to many successful experiences of entrepreneurs becoming involved in the learning process, as guest speakers, role models, coaches and trainers. So there is scope for continued innovation, research and challenge in researching and developing enterprise education.

Generating ideas for entrepreneurship research and student projects

These eight issues are all significant in relation to entrepreneurial practice, in policy at all levels from regional to international and in academic research. They all offer potential for both practical action as real-world opportunities, as well as for independent study, for example, for an entrepreneurial studies research or dissertation project. These options can be combined, with, for example, academic research leading to practical action informed by the results, or as an action-research project. However, either option requires investigation and identification of a specific problem or question. The following activity is intended to help identify this.

Activity

- Which of the eight issues in the previous section interest or affect you most at present?
- How could they affect you in future?
- Select one (or a combination of more than one) of these issues which you find most interesting or relevant to your own situation – for example, 'female and multicultural entrepreneurship'.
- What do you think are the aspects that need to be explored in relation to this issue?
- Try to identify the problems, interesting questions and 'hot topics'.
- What problem or question could you investigate for either a coursework project, such as a dissertation, or an independent investigation to identify possible opportunities?
- What would be the personal, academic and practical benefits from investigating this?

■ Developing your entrepreneurial career

These macro-level trends will affect all of us in different ways, and this section moves from considering these major issues of entrepreneurial future concern and opportunity to the very specific and personal concern of your own entrepreneurial future. The aim is to help you to plan and to start your entrepreneurial career. It brings together the themes of previous chapters and prompts you to reflect on these key questions:

- What goals do you want to achieve, and why?
- How will you accomplish your goals?
- What is your personal value, and how can you increase this?
- What do you need to learn in order to achieve your goals, and how will you gain this learning?

The section aims to encourage you to reflect on your learning from the book, and to help you to create a career plan for yourself which you can then go forward and make happen. If you have already prepared a plan, this section will give you an opportunity to reflect on it with some fresh insights. Here are some reasons why you, as an aspiring entrepreneur or enterprising person, should have a career plan:

- A plan puts you in control; you decide and direct where you want to go.
- You are therefore much more likely to achieve your goals.
- A career plan is your personal business plan; your entrepreneurial career is your core business and a plan will help you to develop and manage it proactively and effectively – you will 'make your own luck' rather than hoping to 'get lucky'.

- Planning enables you to envisage and create new possibilities, and then to think through how you can achieve them.
- You can judge whether opportunities which arise help you to achieve your career goals.
- The plan can help you to increase and maintain your individual value in all senses – personal, business and financial.

A model for entrepreneurial career pathways

Conventionally, careers have been considered as pathways with a series of roles and progressions which include working largely as an employee. However for many people their career routes have included periods of self-employment and entrepreneurship. As working lives become more fragmented and people seek greater self-direction, we need to look at how entrepreneurial options can be chosen at different career stages. Schein (1993) proposed a career model with ten major stages, from childhood to retirement, and eight 'career anchors' or preferred career options, of which five could include aspects of entrepreneurial management: entrepreneurial creativity; autonomy and independence; pure challenge; lifestyle; and general managerial competence.

The demographic profile of the United Kingdom and other developed countries displays an ageing population, in which state spending on each person will be limited, and more people will need to develop their entrepreneurial capability to find new opportunities for economic activity or extending their working lives. This need for lifelong entrepreneurship is increasing as economic changes require an increasing proportion of the existing working population, from a broad social and demographic background, to be able to develop entrepreneurial skills at any stage of their career, and especially whilst they get older and as fewer employment opportunities may be available. Mid-career entrepreneurship can be especially significant in the lives of women, for family as well as career reasons.

The annual GEM global and national reports provide valuable statistics which indicate the scale of entrepreneurship at different career stages. The GEM survey shows that total entrepreneurial activity (TEA) is highest in the 25–44 age groups. This age profile is getting younger; previously, the peak age range for entrepreneurship in the United Kingdom was 35–55, but in the United Kingdom and the United States, 35- to 44-year-olds have the highest level of participation in entrepreneurship. However the cut-off date of 64 will need to change in future, since people are living longer, and increasingly seeing '3rd age entrepreneurship' as a way of extending their active, earning lives.

Entrepreneurial career development

The Opportunity-Centred Approach can be applied as much to developing your career as to creating entrepreneurial ventures: think of your career as your personal enterprise.

How are entrepreneurial careers different from 'normal' career development?

First, the 'normal' career progression route no longer works in the 'new era' economy, which features unpredictable, rapid change and which has not provided the growth, new jobs, revenue streams and profits which used to drive career advancement. Instead, a combination of market forces and global competition, technology advances and political changes can lead to organisations contracting, disappearing or transforming rapidly. Sectors such as banking, retail, professional and business services demonstrate the speed at which they are changing.

Second, entrepreneurial people tend to be optimists who recognise that a recession or flat economy actually creates many potential opportunities. Also, they may believe 'unreasonably' that they can act counter-cyclically to perform better than those who believe the gloomy 'mood music'. Lots of people are successful, increase their wealth and build businesses in these conditions; look at the growth of 'pound stores' in retailing, for example.

Third, success in the New Era economy is based on recognising, seizing and making opportunities work. Increasing numbers of people in all age groups are starting their own business ventures and by doing this creating new career options. The entry costs of 'micro-entrepreneurship', such as eBay trading, creating e-books or online retailing, among many examples, are now universally affordable.

Fourth, being in control of your own business is life-affirming, fun and can be good for you, your family and ultimately your career. Someone who has developed entrepreneurial skills is going to be much more employable in value-creating roles than a cautious procedure-follower.

So we should see entrepreneurship as an attractive, challenging and rewarding career option, for getting started, developing and being successful, and ultimately extending your career on your own terms. An entrepreneurial career is also about creating and asserting your unique identity and value, 'personal branding' being one way of describing this.

Winnie Liu's career story

By Winnie Liu
There I was, one evening in 2008, waiting for the last train in Taipei Metro station – 11:00 pm, again! After a long day's work, I couldn't even remember when the last time I had left work at 5 pm, maybe 10 years before? There was only an empty home waiting for me. I asked myself, 'Is it a real lifestyle I want?' There seemed to be just endless work and overtime, sleepless nights because of stress and complicated workplace politics. I was not happy even though I earned quite a high income, I had worked as Human Resources Manager and reported to the CEO for over eight years, gaining three promotions, yet I was fed up with repetitive HR work in the same company over fifteen years.

I enjoyed my work and was proud of achievements of being promoted from entry level to senior HR Manager in my career. However, I still felt there was something missing, because I knew I could do something different and I had unachieved dreams – to study abroad and to become an interpreter.

So, in 2009, I made the biggest decision in my life; I quit my job and came to England to do my MBA. In the 'Entrepreneurship' course module, I led a team of Chinese women and we developed a travel business concept which boosted my confidence, and I completed the course as one of the two top students. Now I am asked back to share my experiences with the students. At the time, reflecting on my career plan, I realized that I have more than one career option for my future, and that I could do more than working as an HR professional.

Firstly, I listed what opportunities and skills that I possessed, including Certificates of Mandarin Chinese interpretation, translation and teaching which I had obtained whilst in Taiwan. Secondly, I listed my options and prioritized these, based on their feasibility and other criteria. Investigating the possibility of starting my own business, I found that the United Kingdom is a 'self-employed, entrepreneur-friendly environment', easy to register a new business and simple to start working.

I used the methods and skills I had learned on the course to start my own business, which helped me target the opportunities and to have a strategy. In 2011, I started my first interpreting case, working for the immigration service, and I also started my first Mandarin teaching course in a local language school. In 2012, I started doing medical interpreting cases in local hospital departments, as with the increasing Chinese population in the United Kingdom there is growing demand for this service. Medical interpreting was a totally new area for me, as I have no medical background, so I have invested in studying medical terminology and knowledge, finding that these are also very practical in your daily life, and demand for my service is increasing, including cases in immigration, Social Services, law court and civil law cases. I also started teaching managers Mandarin in a large corporate organization this year.

I have purchased www.winnieliu.co.uk as my website to promote my linguistic services. I love to be a freelancer as I enjoy my freedom, I can choose what kinds of case and the customers to take, and you will never know what you will see in the next case. It is never easy but exciting, and I always learn something new every day. I see lots of different life stories which enrich my knowledge and trigger my motivation to learn, to study and to experience the world.

Comparing this with my previous employment as an HR manager, when work occupied most of my life, with no personal life at all, now I have better work-life balance, a partner who loves me and we take care of each other – my home is no longer an empty house, and I have an adorable cat for company. I don't earn as much as before, but my heart is fulfilled. I have learned how to cook and live a life of much better quality. A Chinese old proverb says 'Live to old, learn to old' 'Live and learn'. My ultimate dream as an interpreter has finally come true here in England. Figure 8.1 shows Winnie Liu's career plan.

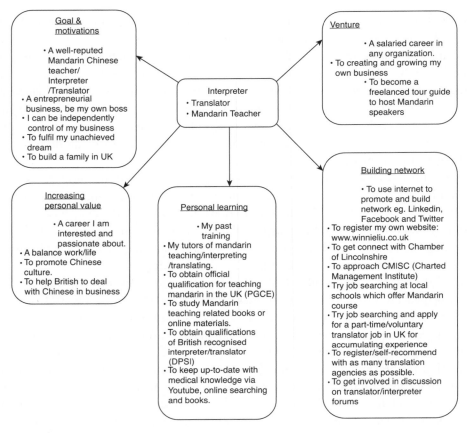

Figure 8.1 Winnie Liu's career plan

Table 8.2 sets out five generic career stages, from education to 'third age' and suggests typical events and entrepreneurial options which may occur in each of these.

Activity

• Which career stage do you think you are in at present?
• Which of the events relate most closely to your own experiences?
• Which of the entrepreneurial questions and options are most relevant or interesting for you, now and in the future?

Table 8.2 Entrepreneurial career stage model

Career stage	Typical events	Entrepreneurial questions and options
Late career/third age Age 55+	Seniority retirement	How to use existing contacts, expertise and resources?
	Develop wider interests	How to extend economic activity?
	Divest from own business or hire succession management	Self-employment, lifestyle business
		Develop portfolio of interests
		Social or community enterprise
		Advisor, coach or non-executive roles
Mid-career Age 35–54	Career advance and responsibility	
		How to achieve successful career transition?
	Marketable skills and expertise	How to identify and develop opportunity based on existing skills and experience?
	Reassess career direction	
	Unachieved aspirations	
	Redundancy	Leave employment to start new business
	Parenting or caring	Return to work or start own business
	Career break/return to work	Consultancy
	Changes in family relationships	Management buy-in or buy-out
		Create spin-out venture
		Join or lead innovation project or venture team
		Grow existing or family business
Early career Age 25–34	Establish career direction	How to choose independence over employment?
	Develop skills and experience in corporate, profession or small business	Learn entrepreneurial capabilities from experienced people
	Professional or technical training/ development	Start own business
		Creative innovation at work
	Expand social and work-related networks – social capital	Team member in innovation project, start-up or spinout venture
	Child rearing	Continue to work full or part time or freelance
	Accumulate personal resource	
Initiation into working life Age: 16–24	Early work experience	How to develop skills, interests and social contacts into enterprising projects?
	Development of social networks	
	Quest for independence	Small-scale ventures with friends
Education and early life Age: 5 up to 21	Exploration and personal growth	Graduate start-up
	Partnering, possible marriage	How to turn interests and needs into earning opportunities?
		Enterprise education
	Vocational, further or higher education/training	Participation in family business
	Academic or vocational choices and specialization	Enterprise in personal interests
	Family influences	

Source: Rae, 2007.

Planning your entrepreneurial career

Before starting this activity, there are some resources which it will be helpful to look back over and have available from the work you have done in Chapter 2. Table 8.3 lists these.

You can revisit and draw on much of this information in developing your career plan, and you may find that a lot of the thinking is already there, especially in the review exercise. The planning process will help you to think it through, bring it together and decide what you want to do and how to make it a reality.

Table 8.3 Personal development exercises from Chapter 2

Personal enterprise	Entrepreneurial learning model
	Career options exercise
	Your goals and direction
	Mapping your starting point for entrepreneurial learning
	Drawing your entrepreneurial learning map
	How you make life decisions
	Personal orientation to risk and uncertainty
	Developing entrepreneurial awareness & mindset
	Developing entrepreneurial capabilities
	Interpersonal interaction skills
	Leadership and entrepreneurial teamwork
	Networking activity
	Review exercise

The career planning process has five headings, shown in Figure 8.2. Each of these five headings is explored through a set of questions. These are intended to prompt you to think through each aspect and to help you to develop your career plan around it.

Personal value:
– Self esteem
– Value to others as a person
– Value created by applying your abilities
– Know-how
– Reputation, social capital
– Financial value

• What goals do you want to achieve, and why?
• How will you accomplish your goals?
• What is your personal value, how can you increase this?
• What do you need to learn in order to achieve your goals, and how will you gain this learning?
• What networks will be helpful in achieving this?

Figure 8.2 Your career plan

Select the format you prefer for your career plan: this could be a mind-map, a table plan (there is a format in the toolkit) or whatever approach works best for you.

You will find that there are many interconnections between the headings of the plan. The five headings given here are a suggestion, and you can develop your own if you prefer. It could be, for example, that you create financial, learning and venture plans which lock into the career plan. In each of the five sections, start to develop your career plan, based on the work you have already done and on the further thinking which you do in response to the questions posed.

Goals and motivations

Even if you do not have goals and prefer to take life as it comes, it can be helpful to consider what your goals might be. In Chapter 2 we explored personal goals, values and motivations quite deeply.

Activity: Your goals and motivations

Revisit your work in Chapter 2 and reflect on it:
- What do you now consider your motivations to be?
- What values are most important to you?
- Can you describe a personal vision for your future?
- Do you have goals for: (as appropriate)
  - business
  - career
  - personal growth
  - family
  - social life?
- For each of these goals, think about how you will measure or assess when you have achieved it.

Activity: entrepreneurial career planning

Use the next section of the book to develop your thinking about your future.

Work through the questions and activities. These will help you to develop your own career plan to enable you to achieve your goals.

Suggested headings or sections include:
- Your personal goals, values and motivations
- Increasing your personal value
- Roles and ventures: options and strategies for achieving your goals
- Building networks and social capital
- Personal learning plan

Increasing personal value

An important theme of this book is developing both personal and social value to create new opportunities. As an approach to your career, it is about creating and growing your personal value over your lifetime. Your value takes a number of different forms: your self-esteem and value to others as a person, the value created by applying your capabilities, know-how and reputation, your financial value and so on; the list could be much longer. Personal enterprise involves self-reliance and increasing personal assets which provide security, choices and independence. The key point here is to assess your current value, under the headings which are most important to you, and to decide how and to what level you want to increase your value.

- How do you assess your own self-worth?
- What do you consider is your greatest value to other people?
- From the exercises in Chapter 2, think back and consider what you would assess your personal value to be in terms of your:
  - capabilities
  - know-how
  - personality.
- How do you consider you can use these qualities most effectively to develop your career?
- In what ways do you aim to increase or develop these qualities further?
- Now consider the financial aspects, a vital measure for most entrepreneurs.
- What is your total net financial worth? You can work this out by estimating the value of your main assets, such as any property, business equity, investments and savings, pension plan, valuable possessions and ready cash. Then deduct your liabilities: debt, student loan and fee repayments, mortgage and so on.
- Are you satisfied with this value?
- At present day values, to what figure do you aim to increase your net assets, and by when? If you plan to retire at a given age, how much personal wealth do you aim to generate by then? How many times can you aim to multiply your present value? The younger you are, the higher the multiple of your current wealth this can be.
- How much of your personal wealth would you invest in your own business venture, given the risks and potential returns?
- What is your current annual income, after tax and deductions?
- How satisfied are you with this figure, which is the current financial value placed on your work?
- To what figure do you aim to increase this next year? In two years? In ten years? Again, use present day values for this.

Think of these questions as helping you develop your personal business plan, by considering financial targets which quantify your goals.

Roles and ventures

In Chapters 3–5 you developed ideas around possible opportunities, assessed their potential for venturing and as investment propositions and developed a venture plan. Consider how far your successful involvement in entering, growing and exiting a venture has the potential to accomplish your goals and realise your personal value.

Think about your personal expectations in terms of goals, motivations and financial targets, and the optimum route to achieving these.

- If you continue to do what you are currently doing, will this enable you to achieve your aspirations?
- If the answer is 'yes' then possibly you do not need to continue with this exercise. If the answer is 'no', then continue below.
- My aspirations will be best achieved through:
  - a salaried career role in an organisation
  - becoming a manager with an equity share in a business
  - investing in an existing business, with or without a management role
  - creating and growing my own business
  - starting or joining a social enterprise
  - improving the returns from what I do now
  - another option not described above.

The best options will differ at different stages of a career. For example, the first option may not seem very entrepreneurial. However for a younger person at the start of their career it may be the best way of building up experience, capabilities, contacts and financial resources to prepare for an entrepreneurial move after a few years.

Whichever option you have chosen, you need to plan for it. If you are seeking a management role with an equity stake, unless that can be achieved in your current organisation you will need to search for a suitable opportunity. If you are looking to acquire or invest in an existing business, again you need to decide on your investment criteria and to start searching.

If you intend to create your own venture, then researching and preparing a venture plan, which was covered in Chapter 5, is an essential step.

If you aspire to improve the returns from what you do now, this suggests that you want to work in a business which is either your own or you share in the profits in some way. You will need to identify opportunities from which your business can unlock value. Revisit Chapters 3–4 to look at how you can identify and exploit such opportunities. Aim to identify at least one project which is a sound investment proposition, and develop a plan to exploit it.

Personal learning

None of this can be realised without effective learning; applying what you have already learned, as well as learning new capabilities and developing new ideas.

Look at the goals you have set yourself, and the ventures you plan to run which will achieve your goals. Then look at your self-assessment of your entrepreneurial capabilities and review which you completed in Chapter 7.

You should to consider these questions:

- Does your learning up to this point provide you with all the personal capabilities and knowledge you will need to accomplish the opportunity you are planning?
- What further learning, experience and development do you therefore need?
- Looking at your personal goals overall, does your current learning provide you with all the capabilities and knowledge you will need to achieve them?
- What further learning do you think you need in order to achieve your goals?
- List your areas for personal learning and development. For each of them, think about:
- What do you need to learn – to develop your capabilities, knowledge, experience, understanding?
- Why is the learning important, and what could the consequences of 'not learning' be?
- When do you need to learn it by; what are your priorities?
- How can you gain the learning you need?
- Based on these questions, what are your learning goals?

Planning your learning and development

Since learning is such an integral aspect of entrepreneurial achievement, these suggestions are included to help you develop additional ideas and options for developing the learning aspects of your career plan. It includes three types of learning methods, as shown in Figure 8.3:

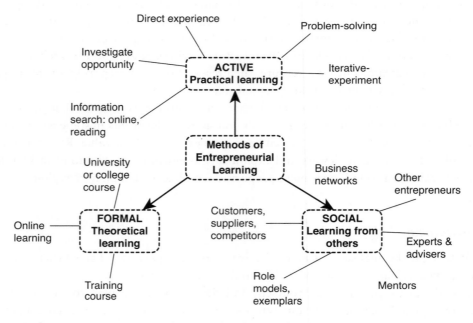

Figure 8.3 Entrepreneurial capability: sources of learning

- *Active*: learning through experience and practice.
- *Social*: learning from others.
- *Formal*: theoretical learning.

Active learning

This is opportunity or problem-based learning. In establishing a new venture, you are faced with a set of novel problems and decisions to which you might not have immediate solutions. Insights can be gained from formal courses and from other people, but even after being guided by these, you must decide and act for yourself. Most learning in starting and growing a venture is active, and the new venture creation process is a powerful source of learning.

The results of your decisions and actions, whether successful or unsuccessful, need to be reviewed and learned from. It is important to try and discover 'what works' for you – remember the 'practical theory' approach in Chapter 7? Iterative trial and error learning is often used where you could have found by investigation that 'expert' or well proven approaches to the problem already exist.

Experimenting and 'playing with ideas', for example, developing a strategy or a new product, generate new insights through discovery learning. This is a powerful process. You can try out, different approaches and combinations to reach a reasonably defined goal, going round the learning loop several times until a workable approach is found. Sometimes there are unexpected outcomes from the discovery process, leading to new possibilities.

Learning from others

Learning is, for most people, a social process, and this transfer of experience can take many different forms. Early in their careers, many future entrepreneurs develop their core capabilities through working in organisations where they are able to gain the training and experience which enables them to form or acquire a venture later in their career. Getting into dynamic businesses where you can learn quickly from exceptional people can be a strong early career move. Finding a growing small business to work in can be a good career start for a graduate, since working for an entrepreneurial manager or director can be a highly formative, inspirational and sometimes frustrating process.

Networks of business contacts, including other entrepreneurs, industry experts, customers, suppliers and competitors, can be valuable sources of ideas and experiences. Gaining access to such sources of expertise can also be a learning process in relationship building. Finding out how suppliers and customers operate, and exploring ways of integrating more closely with them, is a rich source of ideas for adding value, as outlined in Chapter 3.

Expert advisers such as accountants, bankers, lawyers, scientists, academics and business advisers can be highly valuable to the entrepreneur as a way of gaining access to expert-based learning. However you need to judge the relevance of the advice to your own situation, and its likely efficacy. No adviser has all the correct answers and you need to assess whether they really understand the business opportunity and your problem or are simply offering generalised solutions.

Formal learning

Academic and short courses together with books and e-learning mean that there is a tremendous resource of learning media readily available. The complexity faced by businesses and the need to reduce the risks of failure mean that some formal business training is a sensible option for the new entrepreneur.

Rapid developments in e-learning and Internet technology are broadening access to entrepreneurship education, making it easier for people to learn what they need part time whilst working or running a business, and overcoming geographical, time and other barriers. The convergence between entrepreneurship, business education and technology makes it easier for the entrepreneur to combine the active learning they gain from starting and growing their business with formal learning to develop their capability. The use of social media, e-mail and desktop video conferencing make global contact and learning relationships much easier, using technology to access an enriched range of learning with a network of other people.

Finally, information searches to access existing knowledge are becoming ever more important. The ease of access to information through the Internet and related sources such as online libraries, databases and newsgroups makes speedy access to the best available information possible. Books and media features on entrepreneurs and business ventures are also useful sources of knowledge: see the list of reference resources.

Building networks and social capital

In Chapters 2 and 6 you drew a map of your relationships and contacts, and considered how your network could help you in a venture. In planning your career, how could people in your existing network be of help to you, for example, by:

- investing or providing other resources
- buying from you or supplying you
- opening access to people, knowledge, resources
- helping you learn and develop, for example, as a mentor?
- Your network forms an important resource, and like any investment it will be more valuable if well managed. So in addition to thinking about its current uses, think about:
  - How can you sustain your network of contacts to promote their future co-operation? Who could be your future customers and investors? Who are the contacts you wish to develop?
  - How can you grow your network: do you need to develop more contacts in specific domains, such as industry contacts and potential investors?

We have now completed the five headings of the career plan. Take time out to develop your own career plan in your chosen format. You may find that this takes several attempts; it is important that you believe in the plan which you create, and that you are fired up to go out and turn it into reality.

Seven suggestions for managing your career plan

1. Think of your plan as a dynamic agenda which evolves and changes as you learn and progress.
2. Reward yourself for your successes; use each achievement as a motivator to spur you on to greater challenges.
3. Encourage yourself to learn continuously and work at capabilities which you need to develop, engaging less favoured as well as your preferred ways of learning.
4. Find someone who can help you as your mentor, such as an experienced entrepreneur who is prepared to listen and coach you through critical moments.
5. Check regularly how you are progressing against your goals and the plan – review what works for you and what does not, and update your plan and personal theory.
6. Learn from achievements, setbacks and failure: analyse why they happened, what you could have identified earlier and how to act differently in future.
7. Keep moving forward and enjoy your entrepreneurial life; search constantly for opportunities, evaluate them, plan how they can be exploited and act on those you judge to be the best prospects.

Entrepreneurial careers: a survival guide

Finally, this section offers a brief 'survival guide' based on applying the ideas of 'New Era' entrepreneurship to getting started in your own business. In the highly competitive job market faced by young people, new graduates and many others, entrepreneurship has to be considered as an alternative career option to simply competing in an adverse and rapidly changing employment market, which is not creating sufficient jobs to absorb all the entrants to it. In this market, planning and working on your career as your personal enterprise, as distinct from simply looking for jobs, is an example of an entrepreneurial mindset which is increasingly both taught and practised (e.g., QAA, 2012; Rae, 2007). It is evident from the foregoing analysis that we all – as societies, institutions, educators, families and graduates – have to learn to work within the conditions of the New Era. Whilst there are no easy solutions, the adaptability, creativity and resourcefulness of entrepreneurial working can generate opportunities and approaches which people can use to get started. These suggestions are drawn from the 'New Era' entrepreneurship principles on how people can take entrepreneurial steps to initiate their career. They can be self-generating by individuals, but can be more productive if supported, either formally or informally, by universities, agencies and businesses:

1. Use micro-entrepreneurship to experiment, gain basic skills, habits and confidence. eBay trading in surplus items, buying or making and selling small quantities of products, either online or directly and offering valued skills are all low-risk ways of making an income and gaining experience, which can be learned from and scaled-up.
2. Seize the moment – ideas and opportunities have an optimum time, place and person to act on them; if you recognise it, make the decision and do it. Timing is fundamental, with

anticipation and early recognition of opportunities conferring advantages over replicating existing approaches.

3. Connect the local and specific with the global and general. If there is an immediate, specific opportunity in your network, how can you use technology (social media, for example) to connect more widely with related opportunities and resources?

4. Be frugal: look for and use free or low-cost resources. There is no general shortage of money, premises, technology, and know-how, for example, but these resources are often controlled by big organisations and not easily available to graduates and start-ups. Finding ways of applying for and gaining access to these 'latent' resources is a valuable skill.

5. Collaborate and co-operate. This applies on multiple levels:
   - Be prepared to do 'free' work selectively to help others and build social capital ('favours in the goodwill bank')
   - Learning to co-create value with others can make best use of your own skills – you can't do it all, so find others and do what you're best at
   - Social enterprise depends on working socially and co-operatively

6. Feminine ways of working (relational, collaborative, intuitive and emotional) are likely to be as least as effective as masculine (competitive, individualistic, control and analysis). Learn from and adopt both.

7. Practise ethical values and approaches as you'd expect to be treated: green, humane, fairness, sustainable, respect and non-exploitation all make sense.

8. Use iterative innovation – try it out to see if it works. The old rules are gone and the new rules are based on finding new business models and approaches which work for you.

9. Your story is who you are and what you can do, so use every experience to learn and develop your personal narrative. A credible life story is an integral part of your self-presentation and personal branding.

The trend which was explored in Chapter 3, towards 'pop-up' shops and businesses, using low-cost premises or empty spaces to try out new business ideas exemplifies micro, momentary and frugal approaches to entrepreneurship as well as iterative innovation. Pop-ups have been used to test out and develop many business ideas, mainly by young entrepreneurs, which have proved to be either successful or flawed in practice. Possibly the 'pop-up' movement was over-hyped, but it generated a mini-industry of its own and contributed to regenerating some recession-hit high streets.

■ So what are you going to do?

The aim of the book has been to increase your entrepreneurial interest, knowledge, skills, confidence and ambition. The book is the same for everyone, yet every reader will read it in different ways and gain different insights in relation to their unique personal journey. This final activity asks you to reflect on your learning from the book, and to consider how you can use this, and what you are going to do as a result.

■ Critical questions to consider from this chapter

- Take a few minutes to review your overall learning from reading and working through this book.
- What are the main learning points you have gained?
- How have your ideas developed?
- How could you use what you have learned, for example:
  - for academic study and coursework, projects or dissertation?
  - to initiate or develop your career?
  - to identify and act on an opportunity?
  - What action will you take?

Toolkit

Chapter Contents

- Entrepreneurial learning model
- Entrepreneurial and management capabilities
- Career plan

- Opportunity assessment questionnaire
- Business action plan
- Finance planner
- Business model template

■ Entrepreneurial learning model

In Chapter 2, Figure 2.3 introduced an entrepreneurial learning model based on social learning, which connects individuals with their social context (Wenger, 1998). It centres on people's *lifeworlds* as they develop their entrepreneurial identity and capability through social learning (Berger and Luckman, 1967). The model is called 'triadic' because it includes three major themes:

- Personal and social emergence: becoming an entrepreneur
- Contextual learning: using your experience to find and work on opportunities
- Negotiated enterprise: interacting with others to create ventures

Each of the three themes is developed in more detail by sub-themes. There are eleven sub-themes added, which are shown in Figure 2.4. A set of reflective questions is integrated into the model to help you think about your own feelings and experiences, and to use this in developing your personal awareness of entrepreneurial practice.

Personal and social emergence: becoming an entrepreneurial person

'Becoming an entrepreneurial person' and creating an entrepreneurial identity is an outcome of personal and social emergence, including:

- narrative construction of identity – our changing story of who we are
- identity as practice – what we do shapes our identity, how others see us
- the role of the family – how family relationships influence us
- tension between current and future identity – how dissatisfaction can lead to entrepreneurship.

Opportunity recognition arising from contextual learning

Recognising and acting on opportunities is an outcome of learning within our social context, including:

- learning through immersion in an environment such as career or work experience within an industry or community
- opportunity recognition and innovation through participation – developing ideas from experience and practice
- practical theories of entrepreneurial action – finding out 'what works for me'.

Negotiated enterprise

Starting and growing a new venture is an outcome of processes of negotiated enterprise, which include:

- participation and joint enterprise – working with others on the venture
- negotiating meaning, structures and practices – developing shared beliefs about the venture
- engaging in networks of external relationships – building and managing relationships with people around the venture
- changing roles over time – roles which grow with the venture.

Personal learning and entrepreneurial working

You can use each of these three themes of the entrepreneurial learning model in turn to explore your personal understanding of entrepreneurial working. Figure 2.4 is a diagram of the full entrepreneurial learning model, showing the three major themes and eleven sub-themes.

How to use the entrepreneurial learning model

The purpose of this entrepreneurial learning model is to stimulate your personal awareness and prompt you to reflect on your journey of entrepreneurial learning. It is not a simplistic 'Am I an entrepreneur?' questionnaire, but is about understanding what it means to become an enterprising person, in your own way and on your own terms. This section explains the model and provides a set of questions on each of the sub-themes. It aims to help you to reflect on your entrepreneurial development, either individually or in a small group discussion with other people.

Read through each of the three themes and clusters of sub-themes to gain an overall understanding, then return to the first theme, personal and social emergence.

Not every sub-theme will be relevant to your experience at present, unless you have been involved in a venture of some kind. Focus first on those which make sense to you. Those where you have not yet gained experience, for example, in the 'negotiated enterprise' theme, may be where you can aim to do so through the practical activities included in Chapters 3–7 of the book, by working on an opportunity as part of your development.

Start to take notes on paper or a digital device as you go through it. This will help make sense of your own learning. You can do this by using the opportunity mapping approach to map your learning so far and ideas for your development, taking each sub-theme as a branch and making notes of your thoughts on each of the questions as you go along. An example was shown in Figure 2.6 to help you to get started. In this way, you can build up your personal map of your entrepreneurial learning.

Allow several periods of time for this, to reflect on each theme in turn.

Personal and social emergence

We use narratives, or our life story, to express our personal and social emergence. We tell stories about ourselves to explain our biography of who we are and the person we are becoming, as we move through transitional life experiences, being influenced by early life and family experiences, education and career formation, and social relationships. When someone asks, at a job interview or in conversation, about what you do or what interests you, your response will tell them about your identity. Forming an entrepreneurial identity means thinking, becoming and behaving as an entrepreneurial person.

Through personal and social emergence, people develop an identity which expresses their sense of who they are, their self and future aspirations. Becoming an entrepreneurial person often involves people renegotiating and changing personal and social identity which expresses who they are, who they want to be, and how they prefer to be recognised within their social world.

Questions in each of the four sub-themes aim to help you reflect on your personal and social emergence:

- narrative construction of identity
- role of the family
- identity as practice
- tension between current and future identity.

Narrative construction of identity

We relate our lives and identities to other people through the stories we tell about ourselves. Personal and social identity develops over time, shaped by life experiences of change and learning. This identity is negotiated with others through self and social perceptions, and as we renegotiate or 're-invent' ourselves, we can develop an entrepreneurial identity through our life story, as if we are the lead actor within a self-narrated entrepreneurial drama. Think of when you meet someone new at a business networking event: how would you describe being an entrepreneur?

- How would you tell the story of your life? Reflect on your past, your present and how you expect your future to be.
- How do you feature in your story? Think of examples of when you have acted as an enterprising person who seeks out and takes advantage of opportunities, or as an innovator who experiments with new ideas.
- How do you want your identity to change as your life story unfolds?

Role of the family

Families are often significant in shaping people's identities and actions. Families in which parents have started or run businesses often encourage their children's entrepreneurial behaviour as role models. Entrepreneurial stories are constructed with reference to personal relationships with spouses, parents and children. In turn, relationships with family members and expectations are renegotiated through entrepreneurship. This is especially the case within the 'family business' where traditional gender and cultural roles such as husband and wife, father and mother, can play an important part in the construction of identity. These can constrain people's development through an assumption that they will conform to stereotyped roles, for example, the role of women in certain communities, unless they are able to renegotiate their roles by changing social perceptions.

- What are your roles in your family? What does your family expect of you?
- Have any business experiences of family members influenced your aspirations? Has this been helpful or unhelpful to you?
- How do your family's expectations affect your life, career and entrepreneurial aspirations?
- How do you feel about these family expectations?
- Do you wish to change your family's expectations of you? If so, how?

- What consequences for your own relationships and future family could result from your becoming an entrepreneur? How would you manage these?

Identity as practice

People also develop their identity from their activities, practices and roles in social interactions. They discover from experience what they are good at, through education, hobbies or interests, through finding and gaining confidence in natural talents and abilities, and learning how these can be applied and be of value within networks of social relationships and situations. Identity and capabilities developed in education and early employment are often applied in the core activity of a new enterprise.

- What are you good at doing, and what do you enjoy doing?
- How can you best apply your skills, talents and abilities?
- How can you find the situations, opportunities and people where you can make best use of your capabilities?

Tension between current and future identity

There are sometimes significant points in life at which an enterprising person becomes dissatisfied with his or her existing reality and identity and seeks to change this by starting a new venture. For example, employees may feel increasingly at odds with work roles and practices that are defined by others and just 'don't feel right' for them. Or people have experiences where they are dissatisfied and frustrated with the way they are treated and feel something better should be provided. A response may be to seek to change this reality through a new venture, enabling them to work in harmony with their personal values and practices. This may lead to a change in identity by becoming an entrepreneur.

- What do you want to achieve from your life at work or in education?
- Does your existing situation give you the space and opportunity to fulfil your aspirations?
- What might cause you to move on from your current role?
  - Would you start your own business? If so, why?
- Do you have a dream of a 'future reality' you want to create which is different from the present? What could this be?
- Do you believe you can make this happen? How can you start to do this?

The entrepreneurial act is imagining the possibility of 'what could be' and acting to make it happen. Entrepreneurial people create their new reality, taking responsibility for shaping future events. They move from assuming an identity defined by others, through work and family roles, into creating, changing and renegotiating a new identity as the author of an entrepreneurial drama. They will experience emotional uncertainties, and need to draw on resources of personal confidence and self-belief that it 'feels right' and they are able to make it happen.

Self-efficacy is our belief that we can accomplish what is important to us. People demonstrate the ability to change the relationships between themselves and the social world around them through the way they think, speak and act. This is fundamental in entrepreneurial behaviour and performance. Self-efficacy grows and develops through successful experience, social learning from others, positive feedback and reinforcement and personal maturity. People who work in entrepreneurial ways are less likely to accept 'given' conditions, and to act to change things around them in order to get things done. If they decide to do something, they will often set out to accomplish it, 'no matter what'.

These are characteristics which often mark out entrepreneurial people:

- ambition to be successful
- motivation to achieve and accomplish difficult tasks
- pursuit of opportunities
- creative, unconventional thinking
- innovating, experimenting, causing change and pioneering new activities
- resilience in learning from failure and setbacks
- desire to be independent and in control of their lives and businesses
- desire to make a difference, for themselves and frequently for others.

Which of these are your usual behavioural characteristics?

Which ones are unlike you?

Which behaviours do you think it would help you to develop?

Not all entrepreneurs display all of these characteristics, and most of them are displayed by many 'high achieving' people other than entrepreneurs. Athletes, performers and scientists, for example, might well display similar characteristics. So these characteristics might be seen as behaviours practised by achieving people who wish to be successful in their given field. They may be inherent aspects of personality, but equally they may be developed through experience.

Personal and social emergence: review

Creating personal goals involves learning through self-discovery and social emergence. Forming and agreeing goals, and deciding how to assess their success are important processes in considering the wider impact and outcomes we aim to achieve. This exercise on personal and social emergence encourages you to reflect on your intentions. What do you seek to achieve in your life and career, and why do you feel this is important? What are your emotional, social, material and achievement needs? The development of self-belief and social confidence is essential for entrepreneurial attainment.

What do I want and why? Personal values, goals and motivations

- What personal values are most important to you? Values are the enduring beliefs which always guide our direction and decision-making.

- What factors motivate you? What would you say you want out of life?
- What excites, interests and stimulates you?
- What does 'success' mean for you? Think of what success means in each of these life dimensions:
  - business
  - career or employment
  - financial and material terms
  - social success as judged by you and others
  - self-fulfilment
  - emotional success.
- What are your goals? What do you want to achieve, and why?
- What gives you confidence in your ability to achieve these goals?
- Would you describe yourself as a naturally confident person, or is your self-belief affected by what other people say?

Learning in context

Our learning is shaped by the context, the environment or situation within which it takes place. Awareness of the context often provides potential opportunities, such as in the workplace, and through social participation in social, cultural, industry and other networks. Contextual learning is interpersonal and shared, occurring through people relating and comparing their individual experiences, at work and in other arenas. Through these social relationships and contextual experiences, people create shared meaning, learn intuitively and can develop the ability to recognise opportunities and generate the ideas for innovation.

Contextual learning connects people's personal emergence with the negotiated enterprise, as they learn in their social world 'who they can become' and 'how to work with others to achieve their goals' as well as the realism of 'what can and cannot be'. But contextual learning can be limiting and discouraging, for if the social context does not encourage innovative or entrepreneurial activity, or is poor in opportunities, people may learn that they have to change their context by leaving it and moving to a different environment.

Questions to help you reflect on your contextual learning are given in each of these three sub-themes:

- learning through immersion within the industry or community
- opportunity recognition and innovation through participation
- practical theories of entrepreneurial action.

Learning through immersion within the industry

People develop skills, expert knowledge and social contacts from their work, often as employees gaining experience, understanding and know-how in an industry. This learning is gained from discovery and experience, and socially by interpersonal participation. It is often functional, technical and problem solving in nature, finding out how things are done, developing intuitive practices and skills which work in given situations and which people can go on to use in creating their own businesses.

- What useful skills and knowledge or expertise have you developed? In what situations could you apply these?
- What abilities and skills have you developed which are intuitive or tacit – that is, you use without needing to think about them?
- What social, industry and professional relationships, contacts and networks have you formed? Who do you know within these networks?
- How could you use these contacts to your advantage in finding or working on opportunities?

Recognising opportunities and innovating through participation

We find or create opportunities through alertness, learning to recognise them, using knowledge, experience and behaviour. By being active within social and industry networks, paying attention to what people say, noticing what goes on, you can often recognise and imagine future possibilities in that environment. If you identify an opportunity to create a new venture within a familiar context, you can find out how things are done and who to talk to.

Contextual learning also aids innovation: you can use your knowledge of what exists now, and combine this with imagination to create future reality. Thinking prospectively is envisaging the future and imagining how an opportunity can be created, before all the necessary knowledge or circumstances exist. This creative and associative learning brings together ideas, opportunities, technologies and resources in innovative ways. Such resources may include people and their expertise, finance, technology, information and physical resources, and acting ahead of others.

- What needs and problems do you recognise in your everyday life or career? Think of things which could be done better or which frustrate you.
- Which of these could provide possible opportunities for you?
- How can your experience and contacts help you to create new opportunities?
- What ideas can you think of for future creative and business possibilities?
- How could you combine existing knowledge, technology and ideas to create new possibilities or innovations?

Practical theories of entrepreneurial action

People develop rules, routines and ways of working which work for them in getting things done successfully. This is knowledge of 'what works', why, how and with whom, gained from contextual experience, intuition and sensemaking. These are practical theories which enable people to reduce risk through experience because they 'know what they are doing'. The concept of practical theory in business is developed further in Chapter 7.

- What 'works' for you, in developing new ideas and making them happen?
- How do you make this work, and why? Which people does it work with?
- What are your 'practical theories', and how could you apply these in a business venture?

Contextual learning: review

Learning in context can connect your personal goals with finding opportunities. The reasons why people select particular opportunities are various, and not necessarily or exclusively rational. Self-learning about the relationships between personal goals and motivations, shared interests between people and the decision to focus on a specific opportunity is important. Our interests and experiences are likely to be significant in the commitment and ability to act on an opportunity successfully.

- What experiences interests and contacts do you have which could be useful to you in finding and selecting entrepreneurial opportunities?
- How would you relate these opportunities to your personal goals?
- How could you use your contextual learning and life experiences from work and community to select and develop opportunities?
- How do you assess 'risk' and uncertainty? How could you use previous learning and experience to manage or reduce risk in acting on opportunities?

The negotiated enterprise

- The concept of the negotiated enterprise is that a business venture is dependent on negotiated relationships between people and is not enacted by one person alone. As Wenger (1998) noted, 'The enterprise is joint…in that it is communally negotiated'. The ideas and aspirations of individuals are realised through interactive processes of negotiation and exchange with others in and around the enterprise, including customers, investors and co-actors such as employees or partners. The negotiated enterprise includes four sub-themes:
- participation and joint enterprise
- negotiated meaning, structures and practices
- engagement in networks of external relationships
- changing roles over time.

The negotiated enterprise is a process which doesn't happen until you start developing an opportunity or a venture with other people. So some of the questions related to the sub-themes can only be answered from experience of working with others, for example, in a business or organisation. If you are a student, you may not yet have gained this experience. If you work on a business idea as a project with one or more other people as a venture team, this will give you experience of negotiated enterprise. 'Young enterprise' company projects at school or college can also provide useful experience of team venturing.

Participation and joint enterprise

People act collaboratively to create enterprises which they could not achieve individually. Entrepreneurship is often collective, not singular. Even the sole founder of an enterprise is dependent on interactions with others for it to become successful. A vital aspect of the entrepreneurial learning process is the ability to engage and work constructively with others towards the goal of venture creation. It is necessary for the entrepreneur to create shared belief in the potential of the venture to exist and succeed. Participative action is required to create this new reality, and to realise personal dreams and aspirations. Co-participants must be prepared to put the collective identity of the enterprise as a project of shared significance before their individual priorities. This is accompanied by social learning in which people learn to work together. Shared interests or goals, such as wealth creation, economic survival or the desire to enact a particular activity, are necessary for joint enterprise.

- How effectively do you work with others in agreeing to shared goals and working towards them?
- Do you know what your preferred role and strengths would be in a team venture? What are you best at?
- Are you more of an individualist or a team player? How well are you able to put a team's shared interests ahead of your own?
- How do you recognise and employ the abilities of others – even when you disagree with their methods?
- Can you trust people you work closely with, and do they trust you?

Negotiated meaning, structures and practices

In an enterprise, people develop practical theories of 'what works' as individuals and these become a shared repertoire of practices and routines within the business, often described as 'the way we do things round here – what works for us'. This produces a distinctive culture within a business, where what is known and done does not belong to any single person, but rather is shared amongst the members.

An enterprise depends on these negotiated ways of working, which often reflect the founders' style, language, values, ambitions and ways of working, and those of the employees. Tom Kirby, CEO of Games Workshop, asserted that organisations have a 'spiritual life' with which people engage – or not. The lives, interests and aspirations of people within the business must be recognised by the founders who hold formal power and ownership of the business, which is of limited value without the employees' participation. Conflict and disagreement are inevitable from time to time and form an integral aspect of this negotiation.

In many successful enterprises, there is a strong emotional engagement between the people and the business, in which the culture is expressed through the style, language, behaviours and feeling between people. For many people, this is why they enjoy coming to work. The 'buzz', the emotional and spiritual life and energy of the enterprise, comes from people expressing themselves, their identities and their abilities in their work, and in sharing this with their customers.

- What works for you and others within a shared project? How do you share goals, values and ways of working?
- How do you stimulate and sustain the emotional life of the venture: the passion, buzz, excitement and fun?
- How do you turn individual learning into shared learning?
- How can you manage conflict and disagreement to positive effect?

Engagement in networks of external relationships

The enterprise depends on relationships being developed and maintained with many individuals and networks. These may include customers, suppliers, investors, lenders and others such as technology experts, resource holders and opinion formers. This starts as soon as you start to talk to people about a possible venture. Social capital ('who you know') is vital in affording access to resources and expertise. Entrepreneurs are selective in developing social networks, seeking to influence certain groups whilst choosing not to participate in others.

Similarly, customers need to be engaged as active participants who identify culturally with the enterprise, not simply as passive consumers; more than economic value is then generated in the interchange. Relationships and 'rapport' with some customers and suppliers may be more productive than with others.

The cultural identity of the enterprise is formed and enacted through the interactions between it and these external groups. The skills of listening, understanding the other party's position, negotiating and storytelling are essential in maintaining effective relationships. The enterprise depends on its identity, practices and the credibility of its message – its story – being accepted and understood within its chosen networks. The rise of social media such as facebook and twitter makes this ever more important.

- What are the most important external relationships for an enterprise? With whom, and why?
- What would your expectations be of them, and theirs of the business? Are these realistic and can they be met or, if not, renegotiated?
- How can the customer be engaged in the life of the business?
- Are there gaps in the external relationships with key groups and individuals, and what actions are needed to fill these?

Changing roles over time

A venture evolves through ongoing learning and negotiation. If this is successful, the business tends to grow, becoming larger and more complex in operation and structure, and employs more people. This clearly applies to existing businesses, though you may not yet have experienced it. It is a series of transitions from informal to formal roles, relationships and structures. Significant changes in the roles of founders and others are inevitable as the business develops. Growth occurs through changes in human and social behaviour and relationships, and productive interpersonal negotiations around the enterprise. Different capabilities are required to manage the enterprise at different stages of its development, and people who do not grow with the business may be best advised to leave it.

This negotiated change in roles means that self-sustaining capability can be developed gradually, through people other than the founders taking responsibility for managing the business. Developing entrepreneurial and work teams, competent managers and functional experts is integral to the growth process and depends on managing relationships effectively, changing past expectations, sharing practices and resolving interpersonal tension and conflict effectively. As new people are employed by the business, a mark of its cultural effectiveness is how well they learn to integrate and identify with it, adopting its cultural values of participation, behaviour and language.

- Can you accept that your role and others roles will change as an enterprise grows?
- How easily can you 'learn to let go' and entrust important roles to others?
- How well can you integrate new people into a team or business?
- How would you deal with people whom you have worked with from the start but who have not grown with the business, and whose skills no longer fit?

Negotiated enterprise: review

These questions focus on an opportunity and potential new venture you may be considering:

- What skills, capabilities and expertise do you think your opportunity will require, which you do not possess yourself?
- How could you identify people with those characteristics through using networks of contacts?
- What would attract people to support your opportunity? What are the prospective benefits for them, and what input would be required?
- How can your individual interests be balanced with bringing other people into the business?

■ Entrepreneurial and management capabilities

Self-assessment

The aim of this section in the toolkit is to enable you to identify your existing capabilities in the key entrepreneurial and management capabilities listed here and mentioned in Chapters 2 and 7. This section will help you to:

- identify your existing capabilities
- identify the strengths and limitations you bring to a venture and a team
- plan your learning in those capabilities you need to develop.

The first part covers the entrepreneurial capabilities, including personal organisation, which applies to both sets of capabilities. It is suggested that you work through this first. It is connected with Chapter 2.

The second part covers the management capabilities. It is suggested that you work through this in connection with Chapter 7.

Personal enterprise	Leading and managing people
Investigating opportunities	Managing organisations and operations
Applying innovation	Managing finance and resources
Strategic venture planning	Responsible management – social, legal,
Market development	environmental and ethical responsibility

Entrepreneurial and management capabilities: self-assessment

In this section you are asked to assess your own level of entrepreneurial capability. This information will then be useful to you in the following sections, which take you through forming and leading entrepreneurial teams, networking and considering your learning and development needs.

The six clusters of personal, interpersonal and entrepreneurial capabilities are set out in the following table. Read through each cluster in turn and ask yourself:

- Have I ever done this? How experienced am I?
- How capable am I? What example or evidence could I give of my capability?
- How confident am I in my ability?
- Assess your level of capability as follows:
    4: I am highly capable in this, and fully confident of my ability.
    3: I am quite capable with some successful experience which I could develop.
    2: I have quite limited capability and experience and need quite a lot of practice to become competent.

1: I have no experience of this and cannot claim capability, so need to develop – but everyone has to start somewhere!

• Write your score for each statement in the column on the right margin (you can photocopy this or download a worksheet if you prefer not to write on the book).

Entrepreneurial capabilities

Cluster	Entrepreneurial capabilities	Assessment
Personal enterprise	• Set and plan to achieve personal and business goals • Take personal responsibility for the outcomes and consequences of my actions • Plan and use time productively to achieve my goals • Apply energy and dynamism to achieve results effectively • Apply self-awareness of personal strengths and limitations to achieving goals • Seek creative and effective ways of solving problems and meeting needs • Manage stress and conflict which may result from uncertainty and investment of effort **Total score out of 28**	
Interpersonal interaction	• Grow and maintain networks of social and business contacts • Find out what is important to people and understand their perspectives • Influence and persuade people to understand, accept and trust my point of view • Negotiate and conclude agreements with people • Lead individuals and groups to achieve common goals • Coach and provide feedback to people on their behaviour and performance **Total score out of 24**	
Investigating opportunities	• Identify and investigate the potential value of new opportunities • Investigate and develop options for exploiting opportunities • Identify resources which can be used to exploit opportunities • Assess, evaluate and select the opportunities which offer greatest potential **Total score out of 16**	
Applying innovation	• Apply creative thinking to identify new possibilities and initiate new products, services and processes • Access and use social media and web technologies to develop the innovation • Connect needs, resources, knowledge and technologies to develop innovative solutions • Ensure innovations can be produced to solve customer problems and meet actual and potential requirements and expectations **Total score out of 16**	

Cluster	Entrepreneurial capabilities	Assessment
Strategic venture planning	• Propose a strategic vision and strategic plan for the future development and growth of a venture • Prepare a credible business proposal to gain support from and identify the benefits to investors, partners, customers and other stake-holders • Define a realistic business model which will enable a venture to meet customer requirements and create value from the opportunity • Identify and plan the resources needed for the launch and development of a venture: what will be required, when and potential sources? • Identify and assess the strengths and weaknesses of competitors and differentiate the venture in ways customers will value • Identify the critical factors for success of a venture and integrate these into the venture strategy and business model so that they can be achieved **Total score out of 24**	
Market development	• Identify market segments and their characteristics • Find out actual and emerging customer needs, preferences and decision-making criteria • Develop and implement marketing plans to engage and sell to target customers • Contact, meet, negotiate with and sell to customers • Set targets and monitor performance for sales • Review and evaluate the effectiveness of marketing plans **Total score out of 24** **Final score out of 132** **Divide your score by 132 and multiply by 100 to give a percentage**	

Now review your self-assessment.

Please bear in mind that this self-assessment is just that. It is based on your recollection and scoring of your feeling of capability and confidence in these areas. It does not predict future performance but it can help guide your future development.

So if you are a student with limited work experience you may have scored quite strongly in the personal and interpersonal clusters, but much lower in some of the other clusters where you do not yet have practical experience. However by completing the exercises in Chapter 4, you may already be developing capabilities in opportunity investigation and market development. Other capabilities can be developed by completing the practical exercises in Chapters 5 and 6.

A designer, engineer or IT specialist may have scored well under applying innovation, but lower in the clusters which involve more business skills. A manager in a large or public sector organisation may have scored well in the strategic venture planning but lower in opportunity investigation and market development; conversely a marketeer would do well in this area.

Only an experienced entrepreneur and manager is likely to score highly in all clusters!

What to do next?

Rank the clusters by score, from highest to lowest.

Which of the six are your top two?

These capabilities are distinctive strengths, for you to use and to develop further. They are likely to be your important contributions to an entrepreneurial team.

Which of the six are your middle two?

These capabilities are potential strengths, which can and need to be developed further, through practice, study, experience and learning from experts.

Which of the six are your lowest two?

These capabilities are limitations or weaknesses. This may be because of lack of opportunity to practise and gain experience in your career so far. Or it may result from choices you have made about subjects, career options or from feeling your strengths lie in other areas. Some understanding and practical ability will be needed in these areas for you to be effective in entrepreneurial working. However the choice you will need to make is how far you want to develop these capabilities, or alternatively how far you can compensate for them by relying on your strengths by seeking to work with others who have complementary skills to your own. You can consider this in planning your development at the end of this chapter.

Management capabilities

Complete the management capabilities self-assessment in the same way by reflecting on each statement in the table:

- Have I ever done this? How experienced am I?
- How capable am I? What example or evidence could I give of my capability?
- How confident am I in my ability?
- Assess your level of capability as follows:
  - 4: I am highly capable in this, fully confident of my ability.
  - 3: I am quite capable with some successful experience which I could develop.
  - 2: I have quite limited capability and experience and would need quite a lot of practice to become competent.
  - 1: I have no experience of this and cannot claim capability, would need to develop – but everyone has to start somewhere!
    - Write your score for each statement in the column on the right margin.

Management capabilities

Cluster	Management capabilities	Assessment
Leading and managing people	• Develop and communicate a clear mission, direction and values for the organisation which everyone can relate to their work • Ensure effective, clear and regular two-way communications with everyone in the organisation • Develop and implement effective people management practices (e.g., for employment and performance management) which meet organisational and statutory requirement • Ensure everyone in the organisation is aware of his/her responsibilities • Ensure all employees have access to development and training opportunities to meet organisational, personal and statutory requirements **Total score out of 20**	
Managing organisation and operations	• Create an organisation structure able to support achievement of the business goals • Define key responsibilities within the organisation and ensure these are filled • Define and implement the key processes to provide the product or service effectively, efficiently and in line with customer expectations • Define and introduce performance measures to monitor effectiveness, efficiency and quality • Introduce and maintain systems and methods to continuously improve performance, cost and quality **Total score out of 20**	
Managing finance and resources	• Plan the financial requirements of the business to meet its business goals • Plan and monitor financial performance of the business against key targets • Plan to meet investor and lender requirements for their interest in the business • Develop systems to plan and monitor (one score): • break-even, viability and profitability overall and of individual products, services and key accounts or operations • Resource requirements and liabilities of contracts are identified and can be met • Investment and working capital requirements • Plan and monitor cash flow • Monitor debtor and creditor payments • Ensure statutory financial reporting requirements are met, e.g., accounting, taxation and VAT **Total score out of 20**	

Responsible management	• Display sensitivity to stakeholder interests, concerns and expectations of the business • Identify legislative and statutory requirements for the business and monitor evidence of compliance with these • Maintain dialogue with community and media organisations to ensure people in the business are aware of their interests and respond effectively to them • Ensure the business develops and implements appropriate policies and practices in relation to social, environmental and ethical responsibility, equality of opportunity and diversity

Total score out of 16

Final score out of 76

Divide your score by 76 and multiply by 100 to give a percentage

Now review your self-assessment.

Please bear in mind that this self-assessment is just that. It is based on your recollection and scoring of your feeling of capability and confidence in these areas. It does not predict future performance but it can help guide your future development.

Only an experienced and versatile manager is likely to score highly in all clusters!

What to do next?

Rank the clusters by score, from highest to lowest.

Which of the four is your highest?

This capability is a distinctive strength, for you to use and to develop further. It is likely to be your important contribution to a management team.

Which of the four are your middle two?

These capabilities are potential strengths, which can and need to be developed further, through practice, study, experience and learning from experts.

Which of the four is your lowest?

This capability is a limitation or weakness. This may be because of lack of opportunity to practise and gain experience in your career so far. Or it may result from choices you have made about subjects, career options or from a feeling that your strengths lie in other areas. Some understanding and practical ability will be needed in these areas for you to be effective in managerial working. However the choice you will need to make is how far you want to develop this capability, or alternatively how far you can compensate for them by relying on your strengths or by seeking to work with others who have complementary skills to your own. You can consider this in planning your development.

Overall, out of the ten clusters of capabilities, which were your highest three?

Are these primarily entrepreneurial or managerial?

It is important to seek opportunities to use these. These are likely to be the main contributions you can make to a venture team and will help to define your role in the team.

Which clusters show moderate strength, which you think you can develop further?

Plan how you can find ways of achieving this.

Which clusters showed least strengths? These may in part be due to lack of experience, but lack of aptitude is also likely to be a factor. You may need and be able to develop them to some extent, and it would be in your interest to do this. But be aware that you have limitations in these areas and you will need to find and work with people who have greater skill in these areas and whom you trust.

■ Career plan

What do I want to achieve?

Goals and motivations

- My Personal Vision for the future is:
- These are the values which are most important to me:
- These are my Life Goals for:
  - business
  - career
  - personal growth
  - family
  - social life

When do I expect to achieve each goal?
How will I measure the success of each one?

Increasing my personal value

- My value to myself and to others is based on:
- These are the ways in which I aim to build on my personal qualities to develop my career further:

Financial value

By when
- I aim to increase the value of my total net financial assets to:
- I aim to increase my annual financial income to:

How I will achieve my goals

These are my plans for how I will achieve each of my goals:

Personal learning

These are my goals for learning, through which I will be able to achieve my life goals:
  Include in each plan how you will gain the learning, by when and who will help your learning.

Sign:_ _ _ _ _ _ _ _ _ _ _ _ _ _ _ _ _ _ _ Date: _ _ _ _ _ _ _ _ _ _ _ _ _ _ _ _ _ _ _

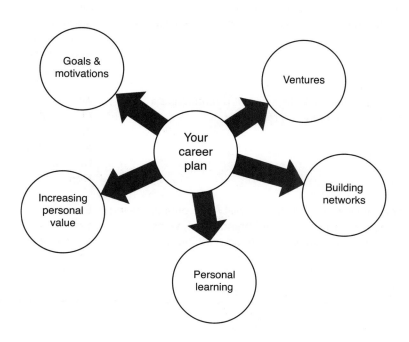

■ Opportunity assessment questionnaire

Use the following questionnaire to assess your opportunity.

- Answer the questions on each dimension.
- Where possible, use factual data to answer the questions.
- Total the scores for each dimension and plot these onto the scoring pentagon at the end of the questionnaire.
- Join the plotting points to show its profile.
- What does the profile suggest about the potential for exploiting this opportunity? (See notes following the questionnaire).

Name or type of venture:_____

1. Investment

How much of the available financial assets does the venture require?	All	5
	Above 75%	4
	Above 50%	3
	Above 25%	2
	Below 25%	1
	None	0
How much of the human capital available does the venture require? (Includes time, commitment, expertise, knowledge, and skills)	All	5
	Above 75%	4
	Above 50%	3
	Above 25%	2
	Below 25%	1
How much external financial investment is required as a percentage of the total funding required?	All	5
	Above 75%	4
	Above 50%	3
	Above 25%	2
	Up to 25%	1
	None	0
How far does the venture rely on credibility or reputation being invested (e.g., through a recognised brand name, website, franchise, partnership, joint venture or accreditation)?	Essential	5
	Significant	4
	Moderate	3
	Low	2
	None	0
Total points		

2. Risk

What proportion of the investment could be realised through sale of tangible assets with resale value?	All	0
	Above 75%	1
	Above 50%	2
	Above 25%	3
	Up to 25%	4
	None	5
Have all the essential elements on which the venture depends been tested and proved to be predictable and reliable (consumer behaviour, marketing, process technology, suppliers, etc.)?	Completely untested	5
	Largely untested	4
	Partly unproven	3
	Significantly proven	2
	Completely predictable	1
How far do the people who will run the venture have proven skills, experience and track record in all its essential elements? (Includes marketing, finance, operations, technology)	Few elements	5
	Some elements	4
	Most elements	3
	All significant elements	2
	All elements	1
Have all the essential elements on which the venture depends been tested and proved to be predictable and reliable (consumer behaviour, marketing, online technology, suppliers, etc.)?	Completely untested	5
	Largely untested	4
	Partly unproven	3
	Significantly proven	2
	Completely predictable	1

3. Return

What is the net profit margin the venture is expected to make?	21+%	5
	16–20%	4
	11–15%	3
	6–10%	2
	Less than 5%	1
What is the anticipated return on investment each year, once the venture is in profit?	21+%	5
	16–20%	4
	11–15%	3
	6–10%	2
	Less than 5%	1
What is the anticipated growth in the value of the investment per year, after the first year (for example, value of equity or assets such as intellectual property or real estate)?	31+%	5
	21–30%	4
	11–20%	3
	6–10%	2
	Less than 5%	1
How quickly will positive cash flow be reached?	Within 3 months	5
	Within 6 months	4
	1 year	3
	18 months	2
	2 years	0
Total points		

4. Impact of change

How far does the venture create or find a new market, identify unmet demand or meet customer requirements in a new way?	Opens a completely new market	5
	Serves an underdeveloped market with little competition	4
	Extends an existing market	3
	Meets customer requirements in a new way	2
	Serves an existing market	1
Does the venture apply innovation to offer customers new benefits to meet their needs more effectively (e.g., by creating a new product or using new processes)?	Highly innovative	5
	Significant innovation	4
	Moderate innovation	3
	Some innovation	2
	Little innovation	1
Does the venture use a new delivery method to communicate with and sell to customers (e.g., Internet, Broadband, digital media)?	Totally new	5
	Significantly changed	4
	Moderately changed	3
	Little changed	2
	Unchanged	1
Will the venture lead to significant change in the structure of the industry (e.g., for competitors and suppliers?)	Radical change	5
	Significant change	4
	Moderate change	3
	Little change	2
	No change	1
Total points		

5. Time

Will the project start:	Significantly in advance of competitors	5
	Slightly in advance of competitors	4
	At same time as competitors	2
	Later than competitors	1
How quickly will the project start to produce a return on the investment?	More than 2 years	5
	1–2 years	4
	6–12 months	3
	3–6 months	2
	Within 3 months	1
For how long will the venture continue to produce a return on the investment?	Indefinitely	5
	5–10 years	4
	2–5 years	3
	1–2 years	2
	Up to 1 year	1
How likely is the project to create additional profitable opportunities during its lifespan (e.g., spin-off business, new products, product extensions, new markets, market extensions)?	A series of high-return opportunities identified	5
	Moderate-return opportunities identified	4
	Strong potential for future opportunities	3
	Future opportunities highly likely	2
	Limited future potential	1

Interpreting the profile

Use the questions that follow to analyse the profile and consider ways in which the venture could be re-configured to improve its prospects.

- Is the profile aggressive: a large profile showing greater risk, higher reward, bigger investment, larger-scale change and medium-to-longer timescales? This will require a high level of entrepreneurial management capability. Do you – or your team – possess this?
- Is the profile defensive: a tightly grouped profile with lower degrees of investment, risk, reward, change and short-to-medium timescales? This may suggest an over-cautious approach which will provide modest rewards. How can its potential be enhanced?

- Can the investment required be reduced, or more of it obtained from other investors?
- Is it an attractive investment, and to what type of investor? Will you invest your own money?
- What factors give rise to the degree of risk, and can any of these be reduced, for example, through an incremental approach to finding 'what works' such as market or product testing, research, planning, finding people with the right experience?
- Is the projected return proportionate to the degree of risk?
- Does the impact of change in the venture increase its risk, and if so can this be reduced without detracting from the venture's competitive advantage?
- Can the venture achieve greater results through applying more innovative approaches?
- Can more value-adding spin-off services be created from the venture to enhance its earnings and lifetime?
- Can the timescales be altered, for example, to bring forward the start of earnings, and to extend the earning lifetime of the venture?
- Can the value of the venture be increased over its lifetime?

■ Business action plan

Business name:

Business leader:
Address & contact details:
E-mail address:
Website:
Completed by: Date:

1. Overview of the business

- Main business activities
- Reasons for competitive advantage
- Purpose of this plan

2. Strategic direction of the business

- Future vision or purpose of the business
- What is the strategic direction?
- What are the business goals?
- What are the most important decisions or issues to be addressed?

3. Opportunities

1. What opportunities are most attractive for the business?
2. Define these:
   - Demand from customers – is it viable?
   - Innovation – what will be different?
   - Feasible – resources and capabilities?
   - Attractiveness – to business, customers, investors?

4. Capabilities and resources

- What capabilities (skills, knowledge, capacity, connections) are available to the business to realise these opportunities?
- What resources are required (financial, technical, capacity, legal)?
- Who are the essential partners, agents and suppliers for the business?

5. Marketing and customer plan

- Who is the ideal customer?

- What are the target customer segments?
- What is the sales target?
- How will this be reached?

6. Financial plan

- Show your business model as attachment
- Include profit and loss projection as attachment
- Expected sales, gross and net profit this year
- Expected sales, gross and net profit next year
- Breakeven as percentage of sales
- Actions necessary to improve:
    - Working capital and cash flow
    - Payment by debtors and bad debts
    - Payment commitments to creditors
    - Other actions

7. Operations plan

- How will the business manage and improve its operations – for example:
    - Customer order process
    - Productivity and efficiency
    - Cost reduction
    - Quality improvement
    - Speed of response
    - Supplier management

8. People plan

- Management structure of the business – show key responsibilities
- Recruitment, staffing and development plan

9. Actions

Business goals

Complete the following for up to three major goals

- Goal – define the future outcome:
- Timescale to achieve:
- Measures of achievement:
- Current state:

- Closing the gap:
  - Options and decisions
  - Actions required
  - Risks and controls
  - Responsibilities
  - Inputs:
    - Finance
    - Management commitment
    - Other resources/capabilities required

■ Finance planner

1. Cash flow projection

The cash flow projection is simply a forecast of when cash payments are expected to be received or paid out from the business. What actually takes place will be recorded in the cash flow statement and compared with the projection.

It is essential to be realistic in your assumptions about timing of cash receipts and payments. New and small businesses live or die on their cash flow, so managing cash flow is critical to business health, as the more positive the cash position is at the end of the month, the less reliant the business is on borrowing or overdraft. A cash flow is different from a profit and loss statement, as it records accounting transactions when they actually occur.

A typical format for a cash flow forecast follows.

2. Profit and loss forecast

A profit and loss (P&L) forecast shows the level of profit (or loss) which the business is expected to produce at the end of each accounting period. A P&L forecast is different from a cash flow as it is drawn up on an accounting rather than cash basis.

On page 271 is an example of a P&L statement for the Pizza Base business from Chapter 5 for a 12-month period broken down by trading periods of a month, week and a single day. This means that assumptions for income and costs data which can be generated by the business model for one of these periods, such as a day or week, can be scaled up to show what this would mean for a full year. The version of the online toolkit includes formulas to calculate this.

Interpreting the figures is important. This takes time and experience, but understanding the P&L as a live accounting tool and using a simple accounting software package will help you to manage the business much more effectively.

Cash Flow Forecast – 12 Months

Month:	Pre-Start	1	2	3	4	5	6	7	8	9	10	11	12	Totals
Receipts														
Cash sales														0.00
Collections from credit sales														0
New equity inflow														0
Loans received														0
Other														0
Total Receipts	0	0	0	0	0	0	0	0	0	0	0	0	0	**0.00**
Payments														
Cash purchases														0.00
Payments to creditors														0.00
Salaries and wages														0
Employee benefits														0
Payroll taxes														0
Rent														0
Utitities														0
Repairs and maintenance														0
Insurance														0
Travel														0
Telephone														0
Postage														0
Office supplies														0
Advertising														0
Marketing/promotion														0
Professional fees														0
Training and development														0
Bank charges														0
Miscellaneous														0
Owner's drawings														0
Loan repayments														0
Tax payments														0
Capital purchases														0
Other														0
Total Payments	0	0	0	0	0	0	0	0	0	0	0	0	0	0.00
Cashflow Surplus/Deficit (–)	0	0	0	0	0	0	0	0	0	0	0	0	0	0.00
Opening Cash Balance	0	0	0	0	0	0	0	0	0	0	0	0	0	
Closing Cash Balance	0	0	0	0	0	0	0	0	0	0	0	0	0	

Business:	Pizza Base			
Customer group:	**Takeaway & delivery pizza & drinks for students**			
Period:	Daily	Weekly	4 weeks	Year 1
Sales target (units)	100	700	2,800	36,400
Average order (£)	8	8	8	8
Sales income:	800	5,600	22,400	291,200
Variable costs:				
Food	160	1,120	4,480	58,240
Drinks	80	560	2,240	29,120
Packs	20	140	560	7,280
Delivery	20	140	560	7,280
Total	280	1,960	7,840	101,920
Gross profit:	520	3,640	14,560	189,280
Fixed costs:				
Wages*	224	1,568	6,272	81,536
Rent	70	490	1,960	25,480
Rates	20	140	560	7,280
HLP	30	210	840	10,920
Insurance	20	140	560	7,280
Marketing	40	280	1,120	14,560
Bank loan	20	140	560	7,280
Other costs	20	140	560	7,280
Total	444	3,108	12,432	161,616
Net profit:	76	532	2,228	27,664
Gross profit margin	65.00	65.00	65.00	65.00
vc per unit	3	3	3	3
Net profit margin	9.50	9.50	9.95	9.50
Breakeven sales value (£)	683	4,782	19,126	248,640
Breakeven volume	85	598	2,391	31,080

3. Balance sheet forecast

A balance sheet for your business will show what the business is owed (debtors) and what it owes (creditors) on a specific day, for example, a forecast at 12 months from the start of trading.

A typical format for a balance sheet forecast:

Balance Sheet Forecast (on 31st December 2014)

Assets   £
1. Fixed assets
   Freehold property
   Leasehold property
   Office equipment
   Vehicles
   Plant/machinery
   Other equipment
   Total fixed assets (A)
2. Current assets
   Cash in hand and at bank
   Stock
   Debtors
   Total current assets (B)
   TOTAL ASSETS (A+B)

Capital and liabilities

3. Capital
   Shareholders'/prop capital
   Profit and loss
   TOTAL CAPITAL (C)
4. Medium-term liabilities
   Loans
5. Current liabilities
   Overdraft
   Tax payable
   Creditors
   TOTAL LIABILITIES (D)
   TOTAL CAPITAL AND LIABILITIES (C+D)

Balance sheet terms

Fixed assets	Permanent assets (e.g., property, plant and equipment)
Current assets	Cash/debtors (money owing to business)/stock
Capital	The shareholders' funds invested in the business
Liabilities	Loans/overdraft/tax payable/creditors owed by the business

4. Key financial ratios for a business with sales of £500,000

Gross margin	Gross profit as a percentage of sales	
Gross margin	Variable costs/sales * 100 = £150,000 / £500,000 * 100	= 30%
Net margin	Net profit as a percentage of sales	
Net margin	Fixed + variable costs/sales * 100 = £50,000 / £500,000 *100 = 10%	
Break-even sales (revenue)	Fixed costs divided by gross margin	
Break-even (SR)	= £100,000 /0.3 (30%) = £333,333	
Break-even sales (volume)	Fixed costs divided by total selling price less variable cost	
Break-even (SV)	= £100,000 / (£10 – £7)	= 33,333 units
Margin of safety	Margin of safety revenue as a percentage of actual sales	
Margin of safety	= £166,667 / £500,000 * 100	= 33%

The importance of break-even analysis (B/E)

- B/E defines minimum sales level required for the business to be viable.
- It is used to assess financial viability of new products/services and to assess customer profitability, and enables more effective business decisions to be taken.
- A break-even calculation on any business can be applied at any point, providing the split between income, fixed and variable costs is known.
- B/E analysis can also be used to work out if a contract or order is worthwhile.
- Knowing the B/E position makes it possible to track the performance of the business daily, weekly or monthly, to ensure it is making money.
- B/E can be used to assess the extra sales needed to employ an additional member of staff, an important decision for a small business. Here are performance ratios for employing people in the business:

$$\frac{\text{Sales turnover}}{\text{No. staff}} = \text{sales per person} \qquad \frac{\text{Net profit}}{\text{No. staff}}$$

$$\frac{500,000}{5} = 100,000 \text{ per person} \qquad \frac{20,000}{5} = 4,000$$

$$\frac{\text{Employment costs}}{\text{Gross margin \%}} \times 100 = \text{sales needed to employ an extra person}$$

$$\frac{20,000 \times 100}{60} = £33,333$$

$$\frac{\text{Sales – input costs}}{\text{No. staff}} = \text{value added / person} \qquad \frac{75,000}{3} = 25,000$$

■ Business model template

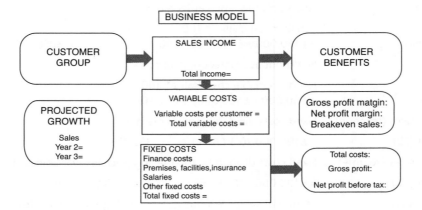

References and Additional Study Resources

Ancona, D. (2005). *Leadership in an Age of Uncertainty*. MIT Leadership Center Research Brief, MIT, Cambridge, MA.

Argyris, C. (1970). *Intervention Theory & Method: A Behavioral Science View*, Addison-Wesley, MA.

Bailey, R.A. (2008). *Design of Comparative Experiments*, Cambridge University Press, Cambridge.

Banks, W. and Isham, E. (2009) 'We Infer Rather Than Perceive the Moment We Decided to Act'. *Psychological Science*, 20(1), 17–21.

Berger, P. and Luckmann, T. (1967). *The Social Construction of Reality*, Allen Lane, London.

Blenker, P., Frederiksen, S., Korsgaard, S. et al. (2012) 'Entrepreneurship as Everyday Practice: Towards a Personalized Pedagogy of Enterprise Education'. In *Industry and Higher Education* 26(6), 417–430.

Branagan, A. (2011). *The Essential Guide to Business for Artists and Designers*, Bloomsbury Publishing, London.

Bridge, S. and Hegarty, C. (2012). 'An Alternative to Business Plan-Based Advice for Start-Ups?'. *Industry & Higher Education*, 26(6), 443–452.

Burgelman, R. (1983). 'Corporate Entrepreneurship and Strategic Management: Insights from a Process Study'. *Management Science*, 29, 1349–1364.

Burns, P. (2013). *Corporate Entrepreneurship*. Palgrave Macmillan, London.

Buzan, T. and B. (2003). *The Mind Map Book*, BBC Books, London.

Casson, M. (2003). *The Entrepreneur: An Economic Theory*, Edward Elgar Publishing, Cheltenham.

The Centre for Retail Research on business failures in 2012. http://www.retailresearch.org.

Coltman, E. (2012). *Refreshingly Simple Finance for Small Business: A Straight-Talking Guide to Finance and Accounting – Business Bitesize*, Brightword Publishing.

Cope, J. (2005). 'Toward a Dynamic Learning Perspective of Entrepreneurship'. *Entrepreneurship: Theory & Practice*, 29(4), 373.

Dew, N. (2009) 'Serendipity in Entrepreneurship'. *Organization Studies*, 30, 735–753.

Dichter, T. and Harper, M. (eds) (2007) *What's Wrong with Microfinance?* Practical Action Publishing, Rugby.

Drucker, P. (1985) *Innovation and Entrepreneurship*, Heinemann, London.

Erdélyi, P. (2010). 'The Matter of Entrepreneurial Learning: A Literature Review'. In International Conference on Organizational Learning, Knowledge and Capabilities (OLKC), 3–6 June. Northeastern University, Boston, MA, USA.

European Commission (2012). *Effects and Impact of Entrepreneurship Programmes in Higher Education*, European Commission, DG Enterprise & Industry, Brussels.

Gartner, W., Carter, C. and Hills, G. (2003). 'The Language of Opportunity'. In C. Steyaert and D. Hjorth (eds), *New Movements in Entrepreneurship*, pp. 103–124. Edward Elgar, Cheltenham.

Global Entrepreneurship Monitor
—— (2013). *Global Report.*

GEM (2012). *Women's Report.*

GEM Youth Business International Report (2013). The State of Global Youth Entrepreneurship.

Gibb, A. (2000). 'Corporate Restructuring and Entrepreneurship: What Can Large Organisations Learn from Small?'. *Enterprise and Innovation Management Studies*. Vol.1. No.1. pp. 19–35.

Gibb, A. (1996). 'Entrepreneurship and Small Business Management: Can We Afford to Neglect Them in the Twenty-First Century Business School'. *British Journal of Management*, 7, 309–321.

Gladwell, M. (2005). *Blink: The Power of Thinking without Thinking*. Penguin Books, London.

Guth, W. and Ginsberg, A. (1990). 'Guest Editor's Introduction to Special Issue on Corporate Entrepreneurship'. *Strategic Management Journal*, 11, 5–15.

Hills, G. and Shrader, R. (1998). *Successful Entrepreneurs' Insights into Opportunity Recognition*. Paper presented at the Babson/Kaufman Entrepreneurship Research Conference, Wellesley, MA.

Hjorth, D. and Steyaert, C. (2004). *Narrative and Discursive Approaches in Entrepreneurship*, Edward Elgar, Cheltenham.

Jack, S. and Anderson, A. (1999). 'Entrepreneurship Education within the Enterprise Culture'. *International Journal of Entrepreneurial Behaviour and Research*, 5(3), 110–125.

Joseph, K.J. (2012). *India's Software Industry in Transition: Lessons for Other Developing Countries and Implications for South-South Cooperation*, Centre for Development Studies, Kerala, India.

Kaletsky, A. (2010). *The Birth of a New Economy*, Bloomsbury, London.

Kanter, R. (1983). *The Change Masters*, Allen & Unwin, London.

Kirzner, I. (1973). *Competition & Entrepreneurship*, University of Chicago Press, Chicago.

—— (1997). 'Entrepreneurial Discovery and the Competitive Market Process: An Austrian Approach'. *Journal of Economic Literature, American Economic Association*, 35(1), 60–85, March.

Kneller, G. (1965). *The Art & Science of Creativity*, Holt Rinehart & Winston, New York.

Koestler, A. (1964). *The Act of Creation*, Hutchinson, London.

Kollmann, T. and Kuckertz, A. (2006). 'Venture Archetypes and the Entrepreneurial Event: Cross-Cultural Empirical Evidence'. *Journal of Enterprising Culture*, 4 (1), 27–48.

Krugman, P. (2008). *The Return of Depression Economics and the Crisis of 2008*, Penguin, London.

Lave, J. and Wenger, E. (1991). *Situated Learning: Legitimate Peripheral Participation*, Cambridge University Press, Cambridge.

Lumpkin, G.T., Hills, G.E. and Shrader, R.C. (2004). 'Opportunity Recognition'. In H.P. Welsch (ed.), *Entrepreneurship: The Way Ahead*, pp. 73–90. Routledge, London.

McMullen, J. Acs, Z. and Plummer, L. (2007). 'What Is an Entrepreneurial Opportunity?' *Small Business Economics*, 28(4), 273–283.

Mitchell, R., Busenitz, L., Bird, B., Marie Gaglio, C., McMullen, J., Morse, and Smith, J. (2007). 'The Central Question in Entrepreneurial Cognition Research 2007'. *Entrepreneurship: Theory & Practice*, 31(1), 1–27.

Mumford, A. (1995). *Effective Learning*, Institute of Personnel & Development, London.

Murray, R., Caulier-Grice, J. and Mulgan, G. (2010). *The Open Book of Social Innovation*, NESTA. http://www.nesta.org.uk/publications/assets/features/the_open_book_of_social_innovation.

Murray, R., Mulgan, G. and Caulier-Grice, J. (2010). *How to Innovate: The Tools for Social Innovation*, NESTA/Young Foundation, London.

Nathan, N., Vandore, E. and Whitehead, R. (2012). *Silicon Roundabout to Tech City*, Demos, London.

ODI (2013). 'Opening Up Big Data in Finance': Show Me the Money. See http://smtm.labs.theodi.org/ODI-P2P-report-16jul13.pdf#page=1&zoom=auto,0,842ing up Big Data in Finance.

Osterwalder, A. and Pigneur, Y. (2010). *Business Model Generation*, Wiley, Hoboken, New Jersey.

Penaluna, A., Coates, J. and Penaluna, K. (2009), *Seeing Outside the Box: Creativity Based Assessment & Neural Understandings*, chapter presented at ISBE conference, October 2009, Liverpool.

Pittaway, L., Robertson, M., Munir, K., Denyer, D. and Neely, A. (2004). 'Networking and Innovation: A Systematic Review of the Evidence'. *International Journal of Management Reviews*, 5(3–4), 137–168.

Quality Assurance Agency. (2012). *Enterprise and Entrepreneurship Education: Guidance for Higher Education Providers in the UK*, QAA, Cheltenham.

Rae, D. (2004) 'Practical Theories from Entrepreneurs' Stories: Discursive Approaches to Entrepreneurial Learning'. *Journal of Small Business and Enterprise Development*, 11(2), 195–202.

—— (2005). 'Entrepreneurial Learning: A Narrative-Based Conceptual Model'. *Journal of Small Business & Enterprise Development*, 12(3), 323–335.

—— (2007). 'Mid-career Entrepreneurship'. In M. Ozbilgin and A. Malach-Pines (eds), *Career Choice in Management and Entrepreneurship: A Research Companion*, Edward Elgar Press.

—— (2010). 'Universities and Enterprise Education: Responding to the Challenges of the New Era'. *Journal of Small Business and Enterprise Development*, 17(4), 591–560.

—— (2012). 'The Contribution of Momentary Perspectives to Entrepreneurial Learning and Creativity'. *Industry & Higher Education*, 27(6).

Rae, D. and Frith, K. (2008), *Innovation and Learning in New Wave Firms*, Paper presented at ISBE conference, Glasgow, November.

Rehn, A. and Taalas, S. (2004). 'Crime and Assumptions in Entrepreneurship'. In D. Hjorth and C. Steyaert (eds), *Narrative and Discursive Approaches in Entrepreneurship*, pp. 144–159. Edward Elgar, Cheltenham.

Revans, R. (1980). *Action Learning: New Techniques for Managers*, Blond & Briggs, London.

Rogers, S. (2014). *Entrepreneurial Finance: Finance and Business Strategies for the Serious Entrepreneur*, Harvard University Press, Cambridge, MA.

Sarasvathy, S. (2001). 'Causation and Effectuation: Toward a Theoretical Shift from Economic Inevitability to Entrepreneurial Contingency'. *Academy of Management. The Academy of Management Review*, 26(2), 243–264.

Schein, E. (1993). *Career Anchors: Discovering Your Real Values*, Pfeiffer, San Francisco, CA.

Schumpeter, J. (1934). *The Theory of Economic Development*, Harvard University Press, MA.

Scott, J.T. (2004). Doing business with the devil: Land, Sovereignty, and Corporate Partnerships in Membertou Inc, Atlantic Institute for Market Studies, Halifax, CA.

Shane, S. (2003). *A General Theory of Entrepreneurship: The Individual–Opportunity Nexus*. Edward Elgar, Cheltenham.

Shepherd, D. and Krueger, N. (2002). 'An Intentions-Based Model of Entrepreneurial Teams' Social Cognition'. *Entrepreneurship Theory & Practice*, 27(2), 167.

Shotter, J. (1995). The Manager as a Practical Author: A Rhetorical-Responsive, Social Constructionist Approach to Social-Organizational Problems. In Hosking, D-M, Dachler, HP & Gergen, KJ, 1995. (eds), *Management and Organisation: Relational Alternatives to Individualism*, Avebury, Aldershot.

Smith, R.L., Smith, J. and Bliss, R.T. (2011). *Entrepreneurial Finance: Strategy, Valuation, and Deal Structure*, John Wiley, New York.

Stevenson, H. and Jarillo, C. (1990). 'A Paradigm of Entrepreneurship: Entrepreneurial Management'. *Strategic Management Journal*, 11, 17–27.

Tucker, R. (2008). *Driving Growth through Innovation*, Berrett-Koehler Publishers, San Francisco, CA.

Tunstall, R. (2011) *Understanding Social Processes in the Development of Internal Corporate Ventures: A Social Constructionist Perspective*, University of Glamorgan, Pontypridd.

UNCTAD (2012). *Entrepreneurship Policy Framework and Implementation Guidance*, United Nations Conference on Trade and Development, Geneva, http://unctad.org/en/Pages/DIAE/Entrepreneurship/UNCTAD_Entrepreneurship_Policy_Framework.aspx.

Wallas, G. (1926), *The Art of Thought* Harcourt Brace, NY.

Weick, K. (1979). *The Social Psychology of Organizing*, Addison-Wesley, MA.

—— (1995). *Sensemaking in Organizations*. Sage, CA.

Wenger, E. (1998). *Communities of Practice: Learning, Meaning and Identity*, Cambridge University Press, Cambridge.

Williams, C. (2008). *The Hidden Enterprise Culture: Entrepreneurship in the Underground Economy*, Edward Elgar, Cheltenham.

World Economic Forum, (2009), *The Global Competitiveness Report 2009–2010*, World Economic Forum, Geneva.

Websites

Entrepreneurship and business start-up

Business Model Generation, http://alexosterwalder.com/
Cobweb: subscription based business information site http://www.cobwebinfo.com/
Effectuation Institute http://www.effectuation.org/learn
Entrepreneur Handbook www.entrepreneurhandbook.co.uk
Entrepreneur magazine http://www.entrepreneur.com/
Inc. online entrepreneur magazine http://www.inc.com/
Intellectual property office www.ipo.gov.uk
Shell Livewire: entrepreneurship support for young people http://www.shell-livewire.org/
Smarta startup site http://www.smarta.com/
Start up donut: resources for new business http://www.startupdonut.co.uk/
UK government site for starting a business https://www.gov.uk/business
UK startups site http://startups.co.uk/

International, social innovation and social entrepreneurship

Ashoka social enterprise network www.ashoka.org
Changemakers community for social innovators www.changemakers.com
Global Entrepreneurship Monitor www.gemconsortium.org
Global Ideas Bank www.globalideasbank.org
Peter Drucker Foundation for Non-profit Management www.drucker.org
Social Enterprise UK http://www.socialenterprise.org.uk/
Social Innovation Exchange www.socialinnovationexchange.org/

Entrepreneurship journals

Academy of Entrepreneurship Journal (Academy of Entrepreneurship)
Enterprise and Innovation Management Studies (Taylor & Francis)
Entrepreneurship and Regional Development (Taylor & Francis)
Entrepreneurship: Theory and Practice (Baylor University) (ABI)
Family Business Review (Family Firm Institute)
Industry & Higher Education (IP Publishing)
International Journal of Entrepreneurial Behaviour & Research (Emerald)
International Journal of Entrepreneurship and Innovation (IP Publishing)
International Journal of Entrepreneurship and Innovation Management (Inderscience)
International Journal of Entrepreneurship and Small Business (Inderscience)
International Small Business Journal (Sage)
Journal of Business and Entrepreneurship (Ass. for Small Business and Entrepreneurship)
Journal of Business Venturing (Elsevier)
Journal of Developmental Entrepreneurship (Norfolk State University and Miami University)
Journal of Enterprising Culture (World Scientific)
Journal of Entrepreneurship (Sage)
Journal of Small Business and Enterprise Development (Emerald)
Journal of Small Business Management (West Virginia University and ICSB)
Journal of Small Business Strategies (Small Business Institute Directors Assoc.)
Journal of Small Business Finance (JAI)
Small Business Economics (Kluwer)
Small Enterprise Development: An International Journal (Intermediate Technology Publications)
Technovation (International Journal of Technical Innovation & Entrepreneurship) (Elsevier)
Venture Capital (Taylor & Francis)

Index

CARDIFF AND VALE COLLEGE